W9-CHL-363

MICHIGAN MOLECULAR INSTITUTE
1910 WEST ST. ANDREWS ROAD
MIDLAND, MICHIGAN 48640

How to Manage Plastics Waste

Polymer Processing Institute Books from Hanser Publishers

Series Editor: Joseph A. Biesenberger*

Xanthos	Reactive Extrusion: Principles and Practice
Bisio/Xanthos	How to Manage Plastics Waste: Technology and Market Opportunities

*Dr. Joseph Biesenberger is Professor of Chemical Engineering at Stevens Institute of Technology and President of the Polymer Processing Institute at Stevens, which he co-founded in 1982 together with Professor L. Pollara, Provost Emeritus of Stevens Institute. Dr. Biesenberger received his B.S. in Chemical Engineering in 1957 from New Jersey Institute of Technology, and M.S.E. and Ph.D. in Polymer Engineering and Chemical Engineering, respectively, from Princeton University. During 1962 he was a Montecatini Fellow with Professor G. Natta at the Milan Polytechnic Institute. He joined Stevens Institute in 1963 and served as Department Head of Chemistry and Chemical Engineering from 1971 to 1978. Dr. Biesenberger's areas of research are polymerization engineering (reaction kinetics, reactor design) and polymer processing (reactive extrusion, devolatilization). He is co-author of *Principles of Polymerization Engineering*, published by Wiley in 1983, and editor of *Devolatilization of Polymers*, published by Hanser in 1983. He is also author or co-author of numerous book chapters and more than 100 research papers.

How to Manage Plastics Waste

Technology and Market Opportunities

Edited by
Attilio L. Bisio and Marino Xanthos

Hanser Publishers, Munich Vienna New York

Hanser/Gardner Publications, Inc., Cincinnati

The Editors:
Attilio L. Bisio and *Dr. Marino Xanthos*, Polymer Processing Institute at Stevens Institute of Technology, Castle Point on the Hudson, Hoboken, NJ 07030, USA

Distributed in the USA and in Canada by
Hanser/Gardner Publications, Inc.
6600 Clough Pike, Cincinnati, Ohio 45244-4090, USA
Fax: (513) 527-8950
Phone: (513) 527-8977 or (800) 950-8977

Distributed in all other countries by
Carl Hanser Verlag
Postfach 86 04 20, 81631 München, Germany
Fax: +49 (89) 98 48 09

The use of general descriptive names, trademarks, etc., in this publication, even if the former are not especially identified, is not to be taken as a sign that such names, as understood by the Trade Marks and Merchandise Marks Act, may accordingly be used freely by anyone.

While the advice and information in this book are believed to be true and accurate at the date of going to press, neither the authors nor the editors nor the publisher can accept any legal responsibility for any errors or omissions that may be made. The publisher makes no warranty, express or implied, with respect to the material contained herein.

Library of Congress Cataloging-in-Publication Data
How to manage plastics waste: technology and market opportunities /
edited by Attilio L. Bisio and Marino Xanthos.
    p.   cm. -- (Polymer Processing Institute)
Includes bibliographical references and index.
ISBN 1-56990-136-8
1. Plastics--Recycling.   I. Bisio, Attilio.   II. Xanthos, Marino.
III. Series: Polymer Processing Institute (Series)
TP1122.H69   1994
668.4--dc20   94-28957

Die Deutsche Bibliothek - CIP-Einheitsaufnahme
How to manage plastics waste : technology and market opportunities / ed. by Attilio L. Bisio and Marino Xanthos. -
Munich ; Vienna ; New York : Hanser ; Cincinnati :
Hanser/Gardner, 1994
    (Polymer Processing Institute books from Hanser)
    ISBN 3-446-17751-5
NE: Bisio, Attilio L. [Hrsg.]

© Carl Hanser Verlag, Munich Vienna New York, 1995
Typeset in Ireland by Datapage International Ltd., Dublin
Printed and bound in Germany by Schoder Druck GmbH & Co KG, Gersthofen

Prologue

This monograph represents the second in a series edited under the auspices of the Polymer Processing Institute (PPI). The topic is *plastic waste recovery and recycling*, rather than *polymer devolatilization*, as speculated in the prologue to the first volume (*Reactive Extrusion: Principles and Practice*), the reason being the recent completion of PPI's report on the former subject, under contract to the U.S. Department of Energy (DOE) and the desire for timely dissemination of the results.

The ground swell, worldwide, related to the recovery of material and energy from manufactured polymers ("plastics") is being driven by several forces. In the U.S. the desire to conserve our natural resources and protect our environment has led to an explosion of legislation to mandate recovery and even to impede further manufacture of certain plastics. The high cost and undesirable environmental consequences associated with disposing of plastic waste, together with the need to reduce the amount of imported oil, constitute strong economic incentives for recovery.

These forces, among many others, confront all segments of our society, and in particular the polymer/plastics industry, with opportunities as well as challenges. The amount of material involved and the potential growth for new business and jobs are enormous. In the U.S. alone over 70 billion lb of plastics (including polymeric matrices in composites) were manufactured in 1992 with over 2.5 million associated jobs nationwide. Current targets to recycle 25% could be revised upwards, which would then require the reuse or reprocessing of more than 25–30 billion lb (excluding textiles) annually.

Plastics recovery efforts in the U.S. to date, while growing rapidly within local communities, in general have been fragmented and non-uniform. Also, industry has been slow to respond, partly because product markets and material requirements for recovered and/or recycled plastics are unclear, and business opportunities are concomitantly uncertain. Offshore industries, especially in Europe and Japan, are aggressively pursuing the development of recovery technologies. The establishment in the U.S. of viable methods for recovery and recycling of plastics most likely will require the development of new technologies, as well as modification of existing ones.

This book identifies and focuses on the major waste streams and presents a critical review of existing recovery/recycling technologies, as well as prioritized research needs and market opportunities. It is based upon the results of a two-year DOE sponsored study by PPI, which was especially well poised to carry out this study in view of its previous experience with research on "green technologies" for the plastics industry. This experience includes product and process R&D for such relevant waste streams as commingled municipal plastic waste, polymer auto shredder scrap, and discarded fish nets, as well as process development of low-density plastic foams from "environmentally friendly" physical blowing agents, such as inert gases.

Future topics planned for the PPI series include polymer mixing, compounding, blending, and devolatilization. It continues to be our hope that these monographs will facilitate the flow of important, timely, technological information among the industrial organizations and universities.

Joseph A. Biesenberger
Series Editor

Preface

Until recently, consumer goods and industrial wastes containing plastics were discarded in landfills and scrap heaps. Today, increasing quantities of discarded objects are collected and processed to recover their plastics content. Broad public support exists for these activities; both the U.S. Federal Government and many state governments are promoting the expansion of current programs and the initiation of new ones.

Numerous potential outlets have been found for the plastics recovered from waste streams. However, only a limited number of products are currently being produced on a commercial basis from the recovered plastics. In part, this is because collection programs until a few years ago were largely limited to bottles and containers. Recently, there has been developing a considerable interest in finding outlets for plastics that can be recovered from waste streams such as autoshredder residues, discarded carpets, and obsolete wire and cable.

The studies summarized in this book were conducted during 1991–1993; they were supported by the U.S. Department of Energy under Contract DE-AC02-91ER30168 to the Polymer Processing Institute. They have utilized the talents of a large number of participants including a significant number of peer reviewers from industrial companies, government agencies, and research institutes.

The views and opinions expressed in this book do not necessarily state or reflect those of the U.S. government or its agencies.

A common vision of a "road map" as to how the recycling of plastics can be increased has been developed in the following four parts:

- An overview of critical waste streams and relevant recovery/recycling technologies;
- An assessment of the technologies used for the recovery of plastics from waste streams;
- An assessment of the technologies used for the recycling of the recovered polymers;
- A summary of research needs and business/market opportunities.

Each part can be read independently.

The first part, "An Overview of Critical Waste Streams and Recovery/Recycling Technologies" consists of three chapters. Chapter 1 provides an overview of the different approaches that can be used to reduce the quantities of wastes containing plastics going to landfills, scrap heaps, and incinerators. Recovery/recycling of plastics from waste streams is only one approach in a hierarchy of alternatives. In the second chapter and the related Appendix, what is known about the nature and quantity of waste streams that contain plastics is reviewed. Four streams that are readily collectable but not recovered/recycled today (except only in a few developmental studies) are identified. Chapter 3 presents an overview of the technologies that are utilized for the recovery/recycling of plastics. Since there exists a variety of technologies, a life cycle energy flow analysis is used to rank them in a priority order.

The second part, "Status, Development, and Assessment of Recovery Technologies" consists of four chapters. Sortation, wash/float separation, micro-sortation, and solvent separation technologies are each assessed in separate chapters. Particular emphasis is placed in identifying their applicability to the critical waste streams identified in Chapter 2.

The third part, "Status, Development, and Assessment of Recycling Technologies" consists of six chapters. Separate chapters are devoted to the melt reprocessing of generic thermoplastics, generic thermosets, and commingled polymers. Other chapters consider solvolysis, pyrolytic processes, and polymer modification/compatibilization. Each of the chapters, after an assessment of the relevant literature, reviews the applicability of the technologies to the plastics recovered from the critical waste streams identified in Chapter 2. Extensive references to the literature are provided in the Bibliography for each of the technologies that are reviewed.

The fourth part, "Research Needs/Market and Business Opportunities" consists of two chapters. In Chapter 14, the major research issues and findings identified in this study are summarized. Ten research areas have been identified and ranked in order of priority. Two to four research needs are discussed in some detail for each research area. Our studies identified 26 research needs; only the ten of highest priority are discussed in this chapter. In Chapter 15, potential business and market opportunities are reviewed. Some specific examples of markets and businesses are presented along with a discussion of critical economic issues. Finally, the Appendix contains detailed statistics on production values and recycling rates of eight commodity thermoplastics in 1990 as well as a summary of projections for the next 15 years.

It is perhaps useful to suggest to a reader a "road map" for using the book. One possible itinerary is, of course, going from the first to the last page without skipping anything. However, most industrial practitioners would benefit from reading Chapters 2 and 3 before proceeding to the reprocessing or chemical conversion chapters of greatest interest. Careful attention should also be given to the extensive references that are an integral part of Chapters 8 to 13.

Some readers will be tempted to immediately start with Chapters 14 and 15. We recommend that this not be done; it is absolutely critical to read Chapters 2 and 3 before Chapters 14 and 15.

This volume should be regarded only as a first attempt to identify polymer recovery/recycling approaches that are both workable and commercially viable without significant government support or subsidies. Much work remains to be done; hopefully, this book will assist those in industry, universities, and government who are already undertaking some of the needed tasks.

Hoboken, New Jersey

Attilio Bisio
Marino Xanthos
Volume Editors

Contents

Part II
Status, Developments and Assessment of Recovery Technologies

Part III
Status, Development and Assessment of Recycling Technologies

Part IV
Research Needs and Market Opportunities

Contributors

This volume is derived from a report titled "Waste Plastics Recycling — A Research Needs Assessment" prepared by the Polymer Processing Institute and submitted to the U.S. Department of Energy (DOE) under Contract DE-AC02-91ER30168. Chapters of this book were authored and/or edited by: *A.L. Bisio*, *M. Xanthos*, *S.L. Wythe*, and *S.H. Patel*.

This volume became a reality thanks to the word processing skills of Ms. Maribel Gonzalez and Ms. Ana Garcia of the Polymer Processing Institute.

The following individuals collaborated in the studies summarized in the present volume and the report submitted to DOE:

Polymer Processing Institute at Stevens Institute of Technology, Castle Point on the Hudson, Hoboken, NJ 07030, U.S.A.

—Staff

Joseph A. Biesenberger	Overall assessment
Subhash H. Patel	chapters 8, 11, 13, Bibliography
Harry Papadopoulos	Bibliography
Chang J. You	chapter 13
Marino Xanthos	chapters 8, 9, 10, 11, 12, 13

—Associated Consultants

Attilio L. Bisio	chapters 1, 2, 3, 12, 15, Appendix
David B. Todd	chapter 7
Stephen L. Wythe	chapters 2, 14, 15

Center for Plastics Recycling Research, Rutgers University, Piscataway, NJ 08855, U.S.A.

Neale C. Merriam	chapters 2, 3, 10, Appendix
Edward M. Phillips	chapter 4
Sidney Rankin	chapters 2, 5, 6, Appendix

—Consultants

Peter Canterino (Towaco, NJ)	chapter 13
Philip N. Eisner (Summit, NJ)	chapter 2, Appendix
Reuel Shinnar (CUNY, NY)	chapter 12
Salvatore S. Stivala	chapter 8
(Stevens Inst. of Tech., Hoboken, NJ)	

The Peer Review Panel, which both assessed the studies and assisted in the prioritization of the research needs in the DOE report included:

Charles Beatty	University of Florida
J. Frank Bernheisel	Gershman, Bricker & Bratton, Inc.
F. Peter Boettcher	Du Pont Polymers
Kim Carr	Environmental Protection Agency
T. Randall Curlee	Dept. of Energy—Oak Ridge
Jerry L. Dickerson	Monsanto
Ken Domeshek	Hoechst Celanese
Marty Forman	Poly-Anna Plastics Products
Edward Fox	Proctor and Gamble
Peter Juliano	General Electric Co.
Thomas Izod	Allied Signal Inc.
Ron Kowalski	Exxon Chemical (retired)
Sandy Labana	Ford Motor Co.
Robert Leaversuch	Modern Plastics
Richard Leitman	Mobil Chemical Company
Robert Lundberg	Exxon Research and Engineering Co.
George Mackey	Dow, USA
M. Allen Maten	American Plastics Council
Mark Mesczaros	Amoco Chemical Company
Terrence Mohoruk	B. F. Goodrich
Wayne Pearson	Plastics Recycling Foundation
Jackie Prince	Environmental Defense Fund
James C. Randall	Exxon Research and Engineering Co.
Raffaele Sabia	AT&T Nassau Metals
Jan Schut	Plastics Technology
Dan Sliva	General Electric Co.
Ed Sommer	National Recovery Technologies
Carroll Turner	Carpet and Rug Institute

Robert Rosenthal of the U.S. Department of Energy, Office of Energy Research, was the Technical Monitor for the DOE Study. Inputs were also received from the following individuals associated with the Department:

George Jordy and *Walter Warnick*	Office of Energy Research
Stuart Natof	Office of Energy Efficiency

Part I

An Overview of Critical Waste Streams and Recovery/Recycling Technologies

Chapter 1

Waste Management Opportunities

1.1   General

Only a small portion (roughly 1% in 1990) of the plastics in numerous waste streams are being recovered and recycled. Opportunities for rapid growth exist; companies are continuously being formed, modified, merged, and dissolved.

Many of the companies involved in the recovery and recycling of plastics are young and small. Often they have developed their own proprietary process. Frequently, the technology that is practiced is not covered by patents. These companies are subject to failure, merger, and takeover, as continually reported in the trade press.

Major producers of virgin polymers, e.g. petrochemical and chemical companies are just beginning to offer grades that contain recycled plastics. Undoubtedly, in future years these producers will increase their activities in recovery of plastics from waste and in marketing recycled polymers. However, the extent and timing of their participation will be both uncertain and highly variable.

The activities involved in the recovery and recycling of plastics can be divided, as shown in Fig. 1-1. Among the participants are:

- Collectors of waste plastics through curbside recycling programs, recycling centers, reverse-vending machines in stores, and private purchases from factories;
- Material recycling facilities (MRFs) that process waste streams (both municipal and private) into saleable fractions, e.g. metals, plastic, glass, and paper, which are then further processed;
- Processors who clean and separate the plastics into saleable material as a flake or pellet.

Mixtures of plastics (after having been cleaned to some degree) have often been manufactured into either low-valued goods or specific items that have displaced comparable wood products.

1.2   Environmental Management of Plastics and Composites

Given the commercial availability of a significant number of resins and chemicals to be used in the manufacture of plastic and composite parts, three activities are involved in achieving proper environmental management:

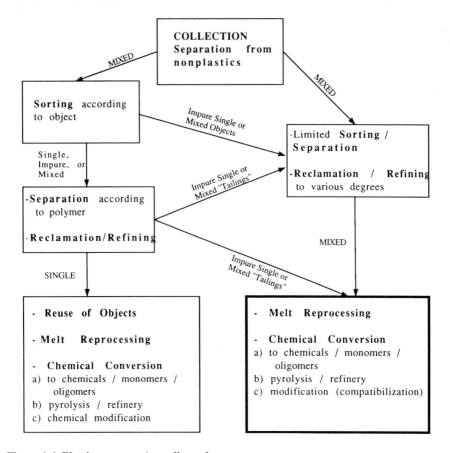

Figure 1-1 Plastics recovery/recycling scheme.

– *Waste prevention* through use of proper part/product design techniques and manufacturing processes.
– *Reuse* of plastic and composite parts/products.
– *Waste management* through recovery/recycling (reprocessing), chemical/fuel conversion, waste-to-energy combustion units, and landfilling.

The focus of this study is on waste management alternatives and their impact on energy consumption.

Once a system containing plastic parts or plastic objects is discarded, the waste management alternatives (shown in Fig. 1-1) must be carefully considered. In the U.S., about 75 billion lb of plastics (including fibers, and polymeric matrices in composites) were fabricated into parts and objects in 1992. The energy consumption to produce these parts and objects was about 3 trillion BTUs (3×10^{15}) or roughly 3.5% of the total energy consumption in the U.S. In 1990, roughly 1% of the plastic resins produced in the U.S. were recovered and recycled. The bulk of the plastic parts and objects discarded that year were landfilled. Therefore, improvements in plastic recovery and recycling have the potential for a significant reduction of the energy devoted to the manufacture of plastic parts and objects.

The proper goal of environmental management should be minimization of the quantity of wastes generated. *Waste prevention, reuse,* and *waste management* should be viewed as a hierarchy that systematically addresses resource conservation, energy efficiency, pollution prevention, and economic constraints.

Waste prevention reduces pollution by minimizing the factors that can lead to it. For example, one can reduce waste generation significantly by standardizing containers to facilitate *reuse* after proper washing. Initially, however, an additional quantity of plastic over that in single use containers may be used to construct them (as is the case with PET bottles in Latin America and the Pacific Rim) to make them suitable for washing and reuse.

Similarly, one should consider designing a complex system of parts in such a manner that the parts can be readily separated when the system is discarded. This involves consideration of design alternatives that may be more expensive than current practices. For example, screws might be used for assembly, rather than fusion welding, and if cements and adhesives are used for bonding, they should preferably be water soluble to facilitate debonding. Marking of parts to identify the specific resins used not only facilitates reuse but also recovery/reprocessing. Identification is the key to materials segregation for reprocessing or the selection of mixtures of resins that can be reprocessed successfully.

Obviously, the most desirable strategy would be to use less material in manufacturing a part, while still meeting performance specifications. This requires both the use of advanced design techniques based upon fracture mechanics and access to the *proper* physical property data for the polymers being used. Often, critical data, such as fracture toughness, fatigue life, fatigue/crack growth rate, and creep and stress rupture data, are not readily available to a designer. As a result, a designer compensates for this lack of needed information by over-engineering through either the use of more material or selection of a material whose recovery and recycling after use may be less efficient.

Reductions in the use of thermoplastics by a minimum of 10% should be possible for over 80% of the plastic and composite parts currently being produced in the U.S. However, this will require the use of complex design and material selection procedures. At the design stage, this requires consideration of the interplay between the product design, the range of candidate polymers, and the manufacturing and waste management processes that could be used. For example, studies of the Design and Manufacturing Institute at Stevens Institute of Technology have shown that, in many applications, injection-molded fiber-reinforced thermoplastic composite parts match the performance of fiber-reinforced thermoset parts (which are much more difficult to recycle).

Having made "optimum" choices during design and manufacturing, one should consider whether it is possible to reuse the plastic and composite parts and systems after they have been removed from service. Reuse has been practiced on a limited scale in many industries; however, reuse on a broad basis is a relatively new concept. The Xerox Corporation has shown that it is possible to significantly reuse plastic parts in copiers both as replacement components and in new equipment.

Similarly, reuse of composite parts in automobiles and trucks is increasing. However, reuse of parts for which historical data on extended performance are not available requires the development of methods to predict service-life performance.

To date, the recovery and recycling of polymers (plastics) has been a low technology business. However, lack of technology has not been a significant obstacle to expanding the business. Rather, issues such as the price of recycled plastics relative to virgin and the availability of certain reclaimed polymers (PET and HDPE) have been critical constraints to the growth of recycling.

While plastics recovery/recycling efforts in the U.S. have grown rapidly during the past years, the industry is both fragmented and highly nonuniform. Moreover, the industry has been slow to respond to possible opportunities since both the market for the products and the nature of the available wastes are often unclear.

The recovery of materials and energy from plastics and composites will require the development of new technologies, as well as modification of existing ones. These technologies will impact all phases of production for plastics, including: product design; materials development, testing, specification, and standardization; optimization of manufacturing processes; and development of processes for both the separation of generic plastics and the compatibilization of inseparable mixtures.

Chapter 2

Polymer Streams Available for Recovery/Recycling

2.1 General

Discarded polymers in residential, commercial, and industrial waste streams that are not incinerated have been disposed of in landfills as shown in Table 2-1 for a number of commodity plastics; these landfills have been operated primarily by local government agencies. Increasingly, polymer-containing objects are being source separated by residents and commercial businesses or being recovered from municipal solid waste (MSW) streams. However, there are significant waste streams containing large quantities of polymers that could be diverted from incinerators and landfills for recovery of their polymer content.

Table 2-1 Disposition of Eight Commodity Polymers in 1990[a]

	Millions of pounds					
	Total[b] production	Fabrication[c] losses	Additions to[d] inventory	Recycled[e]	Incinerated	Landfilled[f]
LDPE film	6,507	65	0	19	963	5,459
LDPE non-film	4,289	43	920	1	499	2,826
PVC	8,136	81	6,091	5	294	1,665
HDPE	7,793	78	1,014	134	985	5,582
Polypropylene	6,592	66	1,173	67	793	4,493
Polystyrene	4,941	49	607	13	641	3,631
Polyurethane	3,265	33	1,565	6	249	1,413
Thermoplastic polyester	2,069	21	113	233	255	1,448
ABS	1,014	10	370	4	94	535
Totals	44,606	446	11,853	482	4,773	27,052

[a]The development of this table is documented in Volume 2, Appendix I of the DOE Report.
[b]From January 1992 issue of Modern Plastics, a McGraw-Hill publication.
[c]The disposition of fabrication losses is uncertain; however, they are often sold to a reprocessor.
[d]A significant fraction of the plastics produced in 1990 were used in applications that have a life greater than 1 year (see Table 2-4) or have been abandoned in place; often the final disposition of these objects is not clear. Unfortunately, all errors in the numbers are cumulated in this column.
[e]Plastics actually returned to the market as products made from recycled resins.
[f]Plastics are landfilled in both municipal and industrial (private) landfills.

This analysis focuses on polymer streams available for recycle that are not in commercial recycling programs currently under way such as PET and HDPE containers and PP battery cases.

Four streams that are readily collectable or already assembled at a limited number of specific locations have been identified:

- Automobile, light truck, and large appliance-shredded residues (ASRs);
- Carpets;
- Wire and cable coverings;
- "Tailings" from plastic-containing streams recoverable from MSWs.

Containers, some films, and a number of other polymer-containing objects are increasingly being source separated [Table 2-2, MSW Fraction (1)]. Hand sorting and mechanical sorting of MSW are increasing; these sorting activities will eventually produce mixed (commingled) polymers of many types rather than the PET and HDPE containers that presently dominate MSW Fraction (1). This additional quantity of polymer (that can be recovered using straightforward extensions of known technology) is identified as Fraction (2) in Table 2-2. Some portion of MSW Fraction (3) (the balance of the plastics contained in MSW) contains many contaminants and is currently being incinerated; this may not be an acceptable future option.

Reclamation of plastics from MSW Fraction (1) and Fraction (2) will generate a discard stream (often referred to as "tailings") of mixed (commingled) and often dirty plastics. Estimates of the quantities of tailings that could be generated by processing MSW Fraction (1) and Fraction (2) are highly uncertain; in our judgment the quantity of tailings could range from 20 to more than 40% of the total

Table 2-2 Estimates of Plastics in Municipal Solid Waste[a]

	1990	1995	2000	2010
		(Billions of pounds)		
MSW (Total)	33	38	45	60
Fraction (1)[c]	0.7[b]	2	5	12
Fraction (2)[d]	19	22	27	33
Fraction (3)[e]	13.5	13	13	15
"Tailings" from reprocessing (1) and (2)[f]	0.2[b]	5–10	6–12	8–16

[a]All numbers have been rounded off; the complete methodology used to develop these estimates is given in Volume 2, Appendix I of the DOE Report.
[b]The quantity of plastics actually returned to market as products made from recycled plastics was approximately 0.5 billion lb; 0.2 billion lb were "tailings".
[c]Plastics recoverable by source separation and hand-sorting as practiced today.
[d]Additional plastic potentially recoverable by a combination of known technology, mostly source separation and hand/mechanical sorting of MSW. This represents a significant but attainable advance over today's practices. Therefore, the 1990 number represents a lost opportunity.
[e]The remainder of the plastics in MSW.
[f]Included in the numbers for MSW Fractions (1) and (2).

Table 2-3 Polymer Streams Available for Recovery/Recycling[a]

	1990	1995	2000	2010
	(Billions of pounds)			
ASRs	1.8	2.1	2.3	3.0
Carpets	2.1	2.3	2.5	3.0
Wire and cable covers	0.4	0.5	0.6	0.8
Tailings from MSW[b]	0.2	5.0	6.0	8.0
Total	4.5	9.9	11.4	14.8

[a]Does not include plastics recovered/recycled in current (1993) Recycle Programs; by the year 2010, these plastics are projected to be an additional 11 billion lb.
[b]Conservative estimate from data in Table 2-2. This stream is the largest and most dispersed; its use has the most demanding technical and economic challenges.

of Fractions (1) and (2). In Table 2-2, our best estimate of the quantity of tailings is given; unless the tailings are reprocessed into useful materials, they will have to be landfilled or incinerated.

The total amount of plastic available for recovery and recycle from the four identified streams is shown in Table 2-3. The estimates given are the result of considering factors controlling the generation of each stream, trends in present polymer recovery programs, and plans for expansion of polymer recovery activities/programs by numerous industrial groups and governmental units. Estimates of the average period of use (life span) of plastic products (Table 2-4) are critical in the development of Table 2-3.

2.2   Energy-Saving Opportunities

Our studies show that the quantity of plastics available for recovery/recycling will grow from 4.5 billion lb in 1990 to about 15 billion lb in 2010. What does this mean with respect to the opportunity for energy savings?

Table 2-4   Average Period of Use for Plastic Products

Product category	Years
Packaging	<1
Adhesives and others	4
Consumer and institutional	5
Furniture and fixtures	10
Transportation	11
Electrical and electronics	15
Industrial machinery	15
Building and construction	25

Table 2-5 Maximum Energy Opportunity through Recycling Above Heat of Combustion[a]

| | 10^{13} BTUs[b] | | | |
	1990	1995	2000	2010
ASRs	4	4	5	6
Carpets	16	18	22	29
Wire and cable coverings	0.7	1	1	1
"Tailings" from MSW[c]	0.4	10	12	16
Total	21	33	40	52

[a]Does not include items collected in today's recycle programs. By the year 2010, about 11 billion lb of these items will be collected (equivalent to about 20×10^{13} BTUs/yr).
[b]The maximum energy opportunity is a "gross" energy; the energy requirements to recover/recycle the contained plastics would have to be deducted to obtain the "net" energy that could be recovered.
[c]See Table 2-2; the energy opportunity estimates have been based on the minimum of the quantity range shown.

Since the heat of combustion of plastic can be recovered as usable energy (to a maximum of about 80%), the energy savings that can be obtained through recycling over (i.e. in addition to) those obtained if the waste polymers were incinerated are shown in Table 2-5. The energy opportunity over incineration will be about 50×10^{13} BTU in 2010. However, one must keep in mind that:

- In Table 2-5 the potential gross energy savings are shown; from these savings the energy required to recover/recycle the plastics would have to be deducted.
- The replacement energies used to develop the potential gross energy savings in Table 2-5 need critical analysis and updating. For example, the energy opportunity shown for carpets is highly dependent on the high values of the replacement energy for nylon 6 and 66.
- The energy savings in Table 2-5 do not include the savings that will result from an expansion of current recycling programs for beverage bottles, battery cases, and some containers. We estimate that these activities could add another 20×10^{13} BTU annually to the total shown for 2010.

50×10^{13} BTUs/yr (0.5 quads) in absolute terms is a large quantity of energy; it is the energy content of about 225,000 barrels per calendar day of crude oil. However, in 1988, according to Franklin Associates (1990), of the 80 quads of energy consumed in the U.S., 3% or 2.4 quads were utilized for the manufacture of 14 commodity plastics. Therefore, the maximum potential for recovery/recycling was about 20% (0.5/2.4) in 1990. Not all of this potential can be achieved.

2.3   Automobile Shredder Residues (ASRs)

Retired automobiles and light trucks have reusable or valuable parts such as radiators, catalytic converters, bumpers, batteries and fuel tanks. What remains of the automobile after these are removed is then sent to a shredder. Large appliances (white goods) are also sent to automobile shredders; small appliances are mostly discarded in MSW.

The shredder separates the metals from everything else; the non-metal fraction called "fluff" or automobile shredder residue (ASR) is presently being landfilled. ASRs are composed of plastics (roughly 15–30%), rubber, glass, cloth, leather, papers, tar, lead, dirt and oily fluids.

In the future, polymer-containing parts will increasingly be removed from discarded automobiles. Removal will be facilitated by design changes that facilitate dismantling and labeling of the polymer content during parts manufacture.

An infrastructure to collect plastic containing parts does not exist today to a significant degree. However, one could be readily developed. To the extent that plastic containing parts are collected and recycled by dismantlers, the polymer content for ASRs given in Table 2-3 will be reduced.

In 1992 the average retired automobile contained 180 lb of plastic; those retired in 2010 will contain over 350 lb. There can be 700 different grades of plastic resins in an automobile. The major plastic types in ASRs are polyurethane foam, ABS, PP, LDPE, HDPE, PVC and glass reinforced polyesters.

2.4   Carpets

Discarded carpets are found today primarily in MSW. Some are left at the curb for municipal collectors; however, others are picked up by the new carpet installers and commercial collectors.

The fibers in carpets are primarily nylon 6 and nylon 66 (70%). However, polypropylene (16%), polyester (9%) and small amounts of acrylics and other polymers are also used. Carpets also contain about 30–40% of filler materials and adhesives in their backing.

Only limited quantities of the polymers in discarded carpets are being recovered. However, technologies to recycle the polymers in carpets either as fibers or monomers are being developed for nylon 6 and nylon 66 by fiber producers and by several firms specialized in carpet recycling.

2.5   Wire and Cable Coverings and Insulation

Scrap wire and cable coverings are the by-products of metal recovery by specialized reclaimers. The coverings are about 70% plastic, the remainder is fiber, paper, cotton, cellulose, dirt, and some metals (primarily copper and aluminum). The metal content is typically 1–2%; however, advanced metal removal techniques will reduce the metal content to less than 0.5%.

A huge inventory of wire and cable is in place in America's infrastructure. Contemplated upgrading of communication systems and particularly the installation of fiber optic cables will significantly increase the quantities of coverings from scrapped wire within the next few years.

2.6   MSW Plastic-Containing Streams

The total U.S. MSW (Municipal Solid Waste) stream has been estimated to be about 180–190 million tons by Franklin Associates (1990); about 13% of this was recycled or composted. The total amount of MSW generated nationwide continues to increase steadily, as does the per capita generation which is now about 4 lb of MSW per person per day.

The plastic content of MSW is about 8–9% or roughly 30 billion lb. This is less than 50% of the fibers and plastic resins currently being produced each year because:

- Significant quantities of the polymers utilized in producing objects and parts have a long life span (Table 2-4).
- Present discard rates are related to the level of plastic production in past years, i.e. plastic and fibers production has continued to grow at a significant rate.
- Some discards (particularly industrial waste and construction debris) are not sent to municipal landfills.

Table 2-6 Recent Recycling History[a]

	Plastics Recycled Million Pounds		
	1990[a]	1991[b]	1992[c]
Packaging			
PET	227	293	402
HDPE	137	275	416
PVC	2	8	10
LDPE, LLDPE	43	47	53
PP	—	3	15
PS	13	24	32
Other	—	—	19
Subtotal	422	650	928
Non-Packaging	60	262	338
Total	482	912	1,285

[a]Plastics actually returned to the market as products made from recycled plastics, i.e. net of "tailings" (MSW Fraction).
[b]As reported in Modern Plastics (a McGraw-Hill Publication, Dec. 1992).
[c]1993 estimates of the Society of Plastics Industry.

However, in recent years there has been a significant expansion of both post-consumer and industrial plastics recycling, as shown in Table 2-6. Source separation of containers by households and films and other plastic by commercial and institutional establishments is expected to grow. Estimates of the disposition for nine major resins in 1990 are given in Table 2-1.

MSW Fraction (1) in Table 2-2 reflects current trends in source separation. The basic assumption driving the estimate of MSW Fraction (1) is that source separation will significantly increase both geographically and in the numbers of plastic containing objects that are collected.

Combined mechanical and hand sorting in trial runs at the Pembroke, Florida Material Recovery Facility suggest that 80% of the plastic in MSW could be recovered. The estimates for MSW Fraction (2) are based upon an assumption that up to 70% of plastic might be recoverable by 2010.

These estimates should be viewed as being the maximum amount of plastic that could be recovered from MSW with attainable advances in technology. However, the infrastructure to accomplish this does not yet exist. In 1990, only about 1% of the polymers in MSW were recycled compared to the potential of 60% in Table 2-1.

Recovery of plastics currently in MSW Fractions (1) and (2) by a combination of source separation and sorting produces a residual "tailings" plastics stream. Currently, these "tailings" are being landfilled. However, they do represent a potential source of plastic that has already been collected. In 2010, "tailings" from reclamation of the polymers in MSW Fractions (1) and (2) could be over 10 billion lb. MSW Fraction (3) is the remainder of the plastics contained in MSWs; this material cannot be recovered in our judgment.

Chapter 3

Technologies for Polymer Recovery/Recycling and Potential for Energy Savings

Polymer recovery/recycling (Fig. 1-1) involves a variety of technologies; each of the technologies has technical, economic and institutional components. A decision to recover/recycle a polymer involves decisions on technologies for:

- Collection of discarded objects and parts.
- Polymer(s) separation
  - Sortation of the plastic object(s) and parts(s) containing the desired polymer.
  - Reclamation of the objects into polymer(s) streams for recycling and discard streams "tailings" for landfilling.
- Polymer processing
  - Reprocessing into objects, or
  - Chemical conversion into monomers, chemicals or fuels.

The decisions will be highly influenced by such factors as the quantity of the discard objects and parts in the waste streams, their composition and the availability of markets for products (objects) containing recycled polymers.

Recycling in this study refers only to polymers recovered from objects and parts in waste/discard streams. Scrap materials that are recovered and reused during manufacturing processes, e.g. extrusion and injection molding are excluded. "Prompt industrial scrap," i.e. scrap generated in production processes that is returned to the polymer resin manufacturing facility is not a significant stream for the polymers considered in this study.

3.1 Polymer Recovery Technologies

3.1.1 Collection

There are numerous alternative methods of collection for discarded plastic objects: drop-offs, deposit returns, curbside collection, trash sortation and reverse distribution. Curbside collection of source separated plastic objects, e.g. bottles and containers, is a growing trend. Reverse distribution is significant only for bottles (deposit returns) and wet cell automobile batteries. However, reverse distribution is being tested in pilot programs for computer housings, and copier parts; it is expected to be used for automotive parts in the future.

With the exception of trash sortation, all the collection alternatives require some degree of specialized equipment or service, e.g. collection bins and scheduled collection days. Obviously, the most convenient approach is collection as part of the municipal solid waste (MSW) or some portion of a MSW stream, e.g. "wet" and "dry" trash.

All collection programs except total trash collection will fail to capture 100% of plastic objects for a variety of reasons. Therefore, there is a growing interest in centralized materials recovery facilities (MRFs) where polymers are recovered from MSW by hand sorting and mechanical methods.

The current U.S. polymer recovery/recycling infrastructure handles only a small number of the plastic objects that are present in various commercial, institutional and municipal waste streams. Additional plastic objects can be source separated by both households and commercial/institutional groups. For example, an expansion of PET and HDPE bottle recycling programs ongoing in many municipalities to all rigid plastic containers, flexible packaging, extrusion coated paper, e.g. milk cartons and some small durable items, would increase the collectable plastic stream by a factor of two to three. However, technology to reclaim the polymers from these items is not yet economic.

3.1.2   Sortation

Sortation, the separation of plastic objects in waste streams into groupings by generic resin type and colors has traditionally been the first step in recovering the polymer content of the object. Currently, the technologies used for collection, sortation and reclamation are highly interdependent; they were all developed to meet the goals of specific recovery/recycling programs.

Sortation can be practiced within a household, commercial firm or institution (source separation); at pickup during the collection of waste streams and at facilities that separate and prepare bulk shipments of "segregated" plastic objects for reclamation. Hand sorting has been used to date almost exclusively for separation of plastic objects from waste streams. Mechanical sorting devices, e.g. gates and air streams, have been used to a limited degree. Automated sorting equipment triggered by detectors is under development and in use in prototype lines.

Plastic objects can be sorted only if they are recognizable to a sensor, human or mechanical/electronic. While collection of automobiles, large appliances, and carpets is straightforward, sorting of the polymers contained in them requires both the development of marking/recognition systems and disassembly techniques. The current disassembly procedures are highly labor intensive.

3.1.3   Reclamation

Reclamation processes are designed to produce high purity polymer resins from the plastic objects generated during sortation. Aqueous detergent wash-wastes flotation processes can produce resins acceptable for reprocessing from dirty post-consumer plastic objects such as bottles and film. However, the performance of wash-float is limited by how the feedstock (objects to be reclaimed) have been collected and sorted. Contamination from inadequate separations of the polymers in the feed-stocks, e.g. PVC or PET, and residual contamination by papers, adhesives, metals, glass, and odor bodies can be critical in establishing what applications the recovered polymers can be used, i.e. for manufacture of new plastic objects.

Wash-float processes are not suitable for polymers from feedstocks that are:

- Complex fabrications of different polymers;
- Highly contaminated with debris, dirt and oils;
- Composed of coatings/layers that cannot be removed by washing;
- Composites of incompatible polymers not efficiently separated by density differences.

A variety of separation techniques such as micro-sortation and solvent processes are under development to address the relevant issues involved.

Micro-sortation processes utilize one or more of the following polymer properties to affect separation of ground or flake resins:

- Density differences in float media other than water, e.g. salt solutions and supercritical fluids;
- Surface energy/wetting differences in froth flotation processes similar to those used for the separation of minerals;
- Electrostatic charging, i.e. differences in the electron affinity of polymers; PVC > PET > PP > LDPE > PS > Polyamides;
- Softening point.

Differences in dielectric and optical properties are being utilized for the development of sensitive sensors.

A number of developmental programs and prototype reclamation lines utilitize the approaches listed above. However, only froth flotation is being used in a commercial installation for the separation of trace PVC contamination from PET.

The feedstocks for micro-sortation reclamation processes will almost always have been first processed in some washing/separation technology. Solvent processing by either selectively dissolving individual polymers or dissolving mixed polymers and then selectively precipitating them offers the prospect of handling complex contaminated polymer mixtures that are not suitable for washing/separation processes, e.g. automobile shredder waste (ASRs) and certain MSW streams.

There are no commercial facilities utilizing solution processes; however, pilot facilities are under construction at the Argonne National Laboratories and Rensselaer Polytechnic Institute. In a number of studies, emphasis is being placed on finding solvents that are highly selective for specific polymers; these would allow selective dissolution of individual polymers from commingled mixtures.

3.2   Polymer Recycling Technologies

3.2.1   Melt Reprocessing

Reprocessing of generic *thermoplastics* recovered by sortation/reclamation from post-consumer discard streams and industrial scrap regrind is done in conventional polymer processing equipment. The reclaimed resins are formulated in limited quantities with virgin resins and additives to obtain the desired properties in the plastic object being produced. These practices are different from those used in processing commingled polymer wastes into "plastic lumber" applications.

The present recycling rates for generic thermoplastics are quite low. Bennett's (1991) data for 1989 suggest that the recycling of PET was less than 10% while that for commodity thermoplastics was less than 2% of the 1989 polymer production. With the development of new markets for products containing reclaimed resins the recycling of generic resins could increase to 30% for PET but would not exceed 12% for most other thermoplastics (Table 3-1).

Estimates of market penetration will depend on many factors in addition to cost; the nature of the market, desired properties for the plastic objects and the characteristics of the reclaimed resin will determine the permissible ratio of virgin/reclaimed resins, i.e. the recycle ratio. Of critical importance in determining the characteristics of the reclaimed resin is the extent to which degradation of the plastics has occurred during cycles of use and reclamation. However, studies by Throne [43] suggest that products incorporating reclaimed polymers that have undergone significant reduction of physical properties in each recycle, may still retain an acceptable fraction of the virgin resin property(ies) level(s). The retention is a result of the incorporation of virgin resin in each recycle and the loss (bleed off) of old polymer into fractions, e.g. "tailings", that are not reclaimed. However, the extent to which reclaimed polymers can be reprocessed is an open issue requiring extensive further research.

Table 3-1 Potential Market Penetration for Generic Recovered Thermoplastics

Polymer	Market segments with penetration > 10%
PET	bottles, film, sheeting, strapping, textile
HDPE	bottles, pails, pipe, crates
LDPE	bags, wraps, films, sheets
PP	bottles, appliances, toys, batteries, furniture
PVC	flooring, sheets, pipe, window profiles, hoses
PS	appliances, toys, packaging building

Source: Adapted from Ref. [799].

The reprocessing of *thermosets* is not well advanced compared to thermoplastics. Reprocessing has been limited to the incorporation of reclaimed/reground resins into new polymer formulations with a minimum of flow or additional deformation occurring during processing. While few products are produced from reclaimed thermosets from waste streams, several commercial plants in Europe and Japan have been using SMC plant scrap as filler, i.e. replacement of calcium carbonate. Similarly, plant scrap has been blended into PUR foams.

Development studies are focusing on maximizing the quantity of thermoset regrind that can be incorporated in phenolics, epoxies, PUR, BMC, SMC, and thermoplastics with acceptable properties and surface appearance. In principle, thermosets after being cured can be usable repeatedly since the degradation upon repeated recycles should be minimal. Synthesis of new "thermally processable" resins combining the flow characteristic of thermoplastics with the physical properties of thermosets would open up new recycling approaches.

Processing of mixed thermoplastics to produce marketable products is essential for the expansion of plastics recycling. Separation of many commingled polymers into generic resins cannot be done in a cost effective manner at this time. The processes currently available for fabrication of products from commingled plastics are limited to bulky products that can displace wood in some application areas. Compatibilization technologies will expand significantly the range of application areas.

3.2.2   Chemical Conversion

Step growth polymers such as polyester, polyamides and polyurethanes can be converted to their monomers or to oligomers/chemicals by *solvolytic* processes, e.g. glycolysis, hydrolysis and methanolysis. Utilizing modification of current technologies it should be possible to recover in relatively high purity monomers from the PET, PUR, nylon 6 and nylon 66 polymers contained in the waste streams identified in Chapter 2.

The commercial success of methanolysis and glycolysis processes for source separated PET beverage bottles reflects the importance and technical feasibility of these processes for step-growth polymers. Of course, this implies that the waste feedstocks can meet certain specifications with respect to contamination levels. The technical feasibility of applying solvolytic processes such as hydrolysis and glycolysis has already been demonstrated in small scale experiments for such complex mixtures as PUR foam/nylon fibers/PET fibers and PET/nylon 6 which are among the prime recoverable candidate polymers from the feedstocks identified in Chapter 2. In addition to processing PET, PUR, and the nylons, solvolytic processes could be extended to feedstocks containing other step-growth polymers such as polycarbonates (PC), and polyureas and cured unsaturated polyesters.

Pyrolytic processes involve the heating of plastics to produce gases, liquids and solid residues, chars and inorganic fillers. However, in pyrolytic processes the decomposition of the plastic occurs at elevated temperatures during which oxygen is largely excluded. Consequently, it is not combustion that occurs, but rather a complex set of reactions that depends both on the plastics involved and the precise nature of the pyrolytic process used. Among the possible reaction pathways are:

- Decomposition into monomers, e.g. PMMA and PTFE;
- Fragmentation of the principal chains into organic moieties of variable size, e.g. PE and PP;
- Simultaneous decompositions and fragmentation, e.g. PS and IB;
- Elimination of simple inorganic moieties leaving charred residues, e.g. PVC;
- Elimination of side chains, followed by crosslinking.

In addition, the course of the pathways can be modified by addition of controlled quantities of hydrogen or oxygen or the presence of contaminants (catalysts).

Pyrolysis, therefore, can be utilized to recover materials (monomers and other organic chemicals), fuels (liquids and gases) or both materials and fuels. Many pyrolytic processes to convert wastes to monomers, chemicals and liquid and gaseous fuel products have been studied and practiced on a limited commercial scale over the past 50 years.

In pyrolytic processes plastic wastes are only feedstocks. Their attractiveness compared to other feedstocks (for a given process technology) will depend on both the relative selectivity to the desired products and the cost structure. The embodied energy content of the plastic waste is *not* relevant, only the heat of combustion is. In most cases the recovery of embodied energy in a pyrolytic process will not be significantly higher than combustion, i.e. waste-to-energy. The only exceptions are pyrolytic processes involving polymers with high selectivity to monomers, e.g. pyrolysis of nylon 6 carpets to caprolactam, that cannot be produced in one-step petrochemical processes.

All published studies and our approximate calculations indicate that the maximum value of plastic wastes in most fuel and petrochemical processes will be in the range of 5–10¢/lb; this is equivalent to a crude oil price range of \$15–30/barrel. Moreover, it is reasonable to believe that value of plastics wastes (of a purity acceptable as a feedstock for pyrolytic processes) will fluctuate with the price of crude corrected for any difference in the heat of combustion. Therefore, it is highly unlikely that plastic wastes will be economical for many pyrolytic processes unless their use is subsidized or legislatively mandated.

Polymers may be chemically modified in order to meet specific cost/performance/processability characteristics. Due to the limitations of unmodified resins, chemically modified products have found commercial applications in end-uses which could have been otherwise unattainable.

Modification may involve single polymers or mixtures of two or more polymers. Reactive *modification* of single polymers may be accomplished with a variety of reagents or through radiation. Modification of polymer blends is usually accomplished through agents commonly known as *compatibilizers* that may be added separately, or formed *in situ* during mixing/compounding. In general, reactions are carried out in polymer solutions, in bulk, e.g. in the melt, or on the surface of the plastic part or pellets; the reactions may be promoted or retarded by a variety of foreign substances.

Recent advances in the technology and economics of modification reactions for single polymers and polymer blends (particularly in the absence of solvents, as in reactive extrusion) suggest that this route of chemical conversion should be applicable to polymer wastes. However, all polymer wastes contain polymeric and other contaminants; the specific modification reactions may be affected to different degrees by these contaminants.

Chemical modification of single and mixed plastics is highly relevant to all waste streams identified in Chapter 2. Reclaimed single resins recovered mostly from MSW and textile waste streams may also be upgraded through increases in their molecular weight. For these waste streams, the development of compatibilization technologies combined with the identification of suitable end-uses and applications will present viable alternatives to pyrolysis or incineration.

3.3   Potential for Energy Savings from Recycling

3.3.1   General

There is increasing recognition that the impact on the environment of plastic and composite products, such as PET bottles, composite films for food packaging, and Noryl™ computer housings, cannot be considered in isolation from how these products were designed, manufactured, used, and discarded. Since plastic products can and do affect the environment at many points in their lifetime, there is a growing interest on the part of both government agencies and industry in life cycle assessments, or, as they are often abbreviated, LCAs. The interactions involved in developing an LCA are shown in Fig. 3-1.

LCA is a rapidly evolving procedure for evaluating ("from cradle to grave") the natural resource requirements and environmental releases to air, water, and land

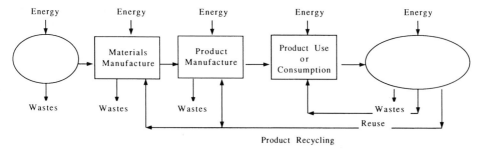

Figure 3-1 General flow for life cycle analysis of a product distribution system.

associated with both manufacturing processes and resulting products. Unfortunately, performing LCAs requires the acquisition and analysis of a significant amount of complex data, some private or proprietary, and some significantly uncertain. The U.S. Environmental Protection Agency (EPA) and industry and professional societies, such as the Society of Environmental Toxicology and Chemistry (SETAC), are striving to enhance both the quality of the data and the resulting analyses.

We are, at least, a decade away from being able to incorporate a formal LCA methodology into the initial design of plastic and composite products or even the selection of the "best" or "most environmentally efficient" plastic and composite materials to produce a part. However, in the interim, we possess the tools to significantly improve the environmental management of plastics and composites, through a combination of conceptual LCA studies and an in-depth knowledge of design, manufacturing, and waste management techniques.

3.3.2   Life Cycle Energy Analysis: Energy Flows

An analysis of the flows of energy involved in the production of any product is only one aspect of life cycle assessment. The focus of the energy flow analysis is the determination of the total (both direct and indirect) energy required for the production of the product of interest.

Energy flow analyses such as those done for the plastics industry by Franklin Associates (1990) consider three broad categories of energy: feedstock, process, and transportation, as being associated with the production of a product. The energy consumption (flow) at each stage of production is determined "beginning at the point of raw material extraction from the earth through processing, materials manufacturing, product fabrication and transportation to market" (Fig. 3-1).

The feedstocks used for the manufacture of resins, the precursors to the plastics, are gas and petroleum; coal is used only to an almost insignificant degree. Since the principal use of these feedstocks is as fuels, the heat of combustion of the consumed feedstock must be considered as is part of the total energy required to manufacture a plastic product.

Total energy consumption values developed by Franklin Associates (1990) used in our studies are given in Table 3-2. Unfortunately, these energy consumption values have been termed in the literature, embodied energy. This is a misnomer that leaves the impression that a value of energy consumption is a thermodynamic quantity; *it is not*!

Embodied energy for plastic products reflect both historic manufacturing practices and markets. At best embodied energy values should be considered as biased approximations (perhaps as much as 20% high) to the energy consumption (replacement energy) required for the production of new plastic products.

Table 3-2 The Embodied Energy of Plastic Products

"Parts" (Products)	BTUs/lb
ABS	47,700
HDPE	42,200
LDPE	44,400
Melamine	48,500
Nylon 6,6	63,500
Polycarbonate	68,200
Polyethylene terephthalate	45,800
Phenolic	38,400
Polypropylene	41,000
Polystyrene	50,400
Polyurethane	31,700
Polyvinyl Chloride	34,000
Polyester (25% Glass)	37,200
Urea-formaldehyde	33,600

Franklin Associates, 1990 "A Comparison of Energy Consumption by the Plastics Industry to Total Energy Consumption in the United States". A study for the Society of Plastics Industry.

3.3.3   Applicability of Life Cycle Analysis to Recycling

The savings in energy that might be achieved by the reprocessing of plastics recovered from waste streams, e.g. ASRs, carpets, wire and cable, and MSW streams, are not inherently obvious. Stauffer [885] has suggested that the energy savings from using recycled HPDE and PET could be in the range of 88–97% of the embodied energy of the virgin resins. Morris and Canzoneri [886] calculate that the energy conserved in manufacturing HPDE and PET products from recycled plastics could amount to 6,232 and 7,203 kWh/ton of plastic, respectively. However, neither study accounts explicitly for the energy required to reprocess plastics recovered from waste streams into new finished articles.

Life cycle analysis can be applied to the recovery and reprocessing of discarded plastics from waste streams to establish an approximate hierarchy of energy savings. Discarded plastic objects and parts currently present in the waste streams of interest identified in this study can be:

- Landfilled;
- Combusted in waste-to-energy units;
- Reused;
- Reclaimed and reprocessed into new finished products;
- Chemically modified to facilitate reprocessing;
- Converted, e.g. by pyrolysis or hydrolysis processes, into liquid/gaseous fuels, monomers, or chemicals.

When the discarded plastic objects and parts are landfilled or combusted in a waste-to-energy unit, separation of the plastic items from the waste streams is not a requirement. However, if other options are to be utilized then some degree of separation and processing as shown in Table 3-3 will be required.

Reuse and reprocessing of plastic objects and parts (regardless of the specific set of technologies used) will never be absolute, i.e. not all of the discarded plastics in a waste stream can be recovered or reused. Therefore, if the identical quantity of plastic objects or parts, e.g. one (1) pound, is to be produced, as has been discarded, some fraction will have to be made from virgin resins. Ideally, one would want to know the minimum quantity of energy required to produce the needed objects or parts, i.e. the replacement energy.

Unfortunately, estimates of replacement energy are not available, nor can they be calculated from available published information. Therefore, Franklin Associates (1990) estimates of embodied energy (Table 3-2) have been used as a surrogate for the replacement energy.

3.3.4   Energy Flows and Calculations in Plastics Recycling

To describe the energy requirements for the performance of a system, such as, for example, reuse of plastic parts (Table 3-3) requires that the overall system be divided into a series of subsystems linked to each other by balanced flows of materials and energy. Each system of interest has been broken down to a level where each subsystem corresponds to a set of physical operations for which the energy requirements are approximately known. In our judgment, the data used in this analysis have an uncertainty of $+25\%$, -10%.

To carry out a life cycle analysis requires that the boundaries of the global system, e.g. a set of subsystems, must be defined precisely. The energy requirements shown as a figure of merit for the hierarchy of alternatives given in Table 3-4 are based upon the following global boundaries:

Input
One (1) pound of discarded objects and parts in a waste stream that can be either source separated, sorted, landfilled or combusted. Additional energy will be required for each option considered[1].

Output
One (1) pound of identical finished plastic parts or objects and 18,000 BTUs of energy.

Producing a fixed amount of energy (that produced from combustion of one (1) pound of plastic in a waste-to-energy combustion unit) and an identical quantity of finished products places all the alternatives considered on a comparable basis.

---

[1]Some of the energy is consumed in the production of finished plastic parts and objects from virgin resins so that one pound of output is produced.

Table 3-3 Waste Management of Discarded Plastic Objects and Parts

Landfill	Waste-to-energy	Reuse	Reclamation/ reprocess	Reclaim/ compatibilize	Pyrolysis to fuels	Pyrolysis/ hydrolysis to monomers
Collect	Collect	Source Separate	Collect	Collect	Collect	Collect
↓	↓	↓	↓	↓	↓	↓
Handle	Handle	Collect	Sort	Sort	Sort	Sort
↓	↓	↓	↓	↓	↓	↓
Bury	Combust (Recover Energy)	Inspect (Accept/Reject)	Transport	Transport	Transport	Transport
		↓	↓	↓	↓	↓
		Wash/Repair	Reclaim (Flake/Pellet)	Reclaim (Flake/Pellet)	Pyrolyze	Reclaim
		↓	↓	↓	↓	↓
		Inspect (Accept/Repair)	Fabricate Products	Transport	Fuels	Pyrolyze/ Hydrolyze
		↓	↓	↓		↓
		Package	Package	Compatibilize/ Modify		Purify Monomer
		↓	↓	↓		↓
		Transport to User	Transport to User	Fabricate Products		Transport
				↓		↓
				Package		Polymerize
				↓		↓
				Transport to User		Fabricate Products
						↓
						Package
						↓
						Transport to User

Table 3-4 Life Cycle Energy Flow[a]

Disposal/recycling alternative	Fraction of plastic content of waste stream recovered	Energy flow index of merit[b]
Landfill	1.0	138
Pyrolysis to fuel products	1.0	102
Waste to energy	1.0	100
Pyrolysis to	0.6	91–96[c]
Monomers	0.9	69–78[c]
Reprocess/	0.6	90
Modification	0.9	62
Reuse of product	0.6	84
or object	0.9	54

[a] 1 pound plastics in waste streams converted to 1 pound plastic products and 18,000 BTUs of energy.
[b] The index of merit has been developed relative to waste-to-energy incineration; the lower the merit number, the lower the energy consumption.
[c] Range reflects differences in selectivity to monomers.

The point of view in this analysis is not one of the participants in the recovery/recycling of plastics but the economy as a whole. The participants are concerned only with the productivity of their specific facilities. Replacement of the discarded objects with new objects (made from a combination of virgin and recycled plastics) is not directly of concern to them.

The value of 18,000 BTUs of energy was selected as a typical value for the heat of combustion of many plastics, e.g. polystyrene. In an efficient waste-to-energy-unit integrated with power generation this would be equivalent to about 1.2 kWh of electric power.

For systems that do not produce energy in one of the subsystems, e.g. landfilling, some fuel will have to be burned to produce the required 18,000 BTUs of energy. Since it is not possible (except for landfilling and combustion) to recover all (100%) of the plastics in a waste stream in a usable form some fraction of the object and parts will have to be produced from virgin resins. The replacement energy for these has been taken to be that of polystyrene, 47,250 BTUs/lb. The calculation of the energy requirements for a system, e.g. landfilling are straightforward once the boundary conditions (input/output) have been established and the energy requirements for each of the subsystems in Table 3-3 have been estimated. The procedures and data used in our calculations can be found in the report to DOE, Volume 2.

3.3.4.1 Landfilling

Collection of discarded polymer parts and objects can be done separately, e.g. carpets and ASRs, or with other wastes. If done separately, fuel is consumed for their collection. However, it is reasonable to assume that the average transportation distance to a landfill is about the same; once at the landfill, the handling of the waste should be similar. We have assumed that all plastics are handled as part of a total waste stream and that only limited quantities of additional fuel are required for their handling. However, sufficient fuel needs to be burned to provide 18,000 BTUs of energy per pound of plastic in the waste stream. Moreover, the discarded parts and objects need to be replaced with those made from virgin resins. Since the replacement energy for one pound of the parts and objects is 47,250 BTUs, landfilling one pound of discarded polymer objects results in the consumption of 65,250 BTUs of energy.

3.3.4.2   Waste-to-Energy

Combustion of one pound of plastic parts and objects (as part of a total waste stream) generates 18,000 BTUs/lb of contained plastic. However, the plastic parts and objects would have to be replaced with those made from virgin resin; the total energy consumption, therefore, is 47,250 BTUs.

3.3.4.3   Reuse of Plastic Objects and Parts

Some plastic objects and parts, e.g. gasoline tanks, can be reused. However, the part must be sorted (perhaps, source separated), cleaned, inspected and returned to the user. The limited available information suggests that the energy consumption for these activities is 2,500–3,500 BTUs/lb plastic processed. However, these estimates do not include the personal energy requirements for the workers involved in the activities.

Not all of the recovered parts and objects will be acceptable for reuse after inspection; a fraction will always be unacceptable and, therefore, discarded. Those that cannot be reused will have to be replaced with parts and objects made from virgin resins; in addition, fuel must be burned to provide 18,000 BTUs of energy. Therefore, the energy consumption for reuse will depend on the fraction of the parts and objects found to be acceptable for reuse. Significant changes in the energy consumption for the subsystems involved (+ 100%) will not significantly change the total energy consumption. No credit has been taken for the polymer objects and parts that are discarded, i.e. they are landfilled.

3.3.4.4   Reclamation/Reprocessing of Plastic Content of Wastes

Today, HDPE and PET resins after being collected and sorted are reclaimed into flakes or pellets that can be fabricated into new plastic objects and parts. The energy consumption needed to produce clean flakes and pellets is estimated to be about 4,000–5,000 BTUs/lb of processed plastic. In addition, about 1,750 BTUs/lb of reclaimed plastic will be required to fabricated parts and objects from the reclaimed resin.

Reclamation and reprocessing of plastics do not generate energy; therefore fuel will have to be burned to supply 18,000 BTUs/lb of finished parts and objects.

Again, reclamation of the plastics objects and parts is not complete, i.e. plastics containing materials are discarded during sorting and reclamation; therefore, additional parts and objects have to be produced from virgin resins. In our judgment, the energy consumption shown for sortation/reclamation is reasonable but probably at the "low end" of the current commercial practice. Therefore, we would expect the total energy consumption to be higher particularly when the fraction recovered is below 0.7.

3.3.4.5   Melt Reprocessing/Modification

Mixtures of polymers after sortation and reclamation may have to be chemically modified if the mixture is to be successfully reprocessed into finished parts and objects. Two possible modification schemes might involve:

- Addition of a compatibilizing agent, e.g. styrene-butadiene block copolymers, at a level of 1–5% for mixtures of polystyrene and polyethylene.
- Reaction, e.g. maleation to a maximum of, say, 5% for mixtures of PET and polyethylene.

Case 1: Compatibilizing Agent   The compatibilizing agent will have to be blended into the reclaimed polymer. While it may under some circumstances be feasible to blend it while preparing the new parts and objects more typically the blending will be done in an additional step. Blending will require mixing energy which is judged to be about 1,000–1,500 BTUs/lb of polymer. Compatibilization must also be debited by the energy required to produce the agent that is used. Many compatibilizing agents are polymeric in nature with embodied energies of 40,000 BTUs/lb, others are not. Reasonable values for the embodied energy of many compatibilizers appear to 20,000–40,000 BTUs/lb. There are small differences in the energy consumption associated with fabrication and replacement compared to those for reprocessing; these differences are a direct result of the addition of the compatibilizers at a 2% level.

Case 2: Reaction   There are large numbers of possible chemical reactions that could be considered for compatibilization of a polymer mixture. For the purposes of this analysis, we only considered maleation at a 5% level on reclaimed polymer. Higher levels of chemical reactant at fractions recovered greater than 0.8–0.9 will result in more than one pound of polymer being produced.

Rudd [887] indicates that the net energy consumption for the production of maleic anhydride by the air oxidation of butane is about 7,000 BTUs/lb; the heat of combustion of butane is 19,943 BTUs/lb. About 1.2 lb of butane are consumed to produce one pound of maleic anhydride. Therefore, the embodied energy of maleic anhydride is about 31,500 BTUs/lb.

Maleation can be carried out in a properly designed extruder; the mixing energy should be about the same as that for compatibilization. The differences in total energy between compatibilization and maleation are small, perhaps no more than a few hundred BTUs/lb. However, chemical modification may permit high valued products to be made from mixtures of plastics, e.g. tailings from MSW that would otherwise have to be landfilled or combusted.

3.3.4.6 Pyrolysis

The main advantage of pyrolysis over combustion in a waste-to-energy unit is a five to twenty (5–20) fold reduction in the volume of product gases. This leads to a significant reduction in the complexity of the exhaust gas purification system.

Case 1: Liquid and Gaseous Fuels   If pyrolysis is to be used to produce liquid and gaseous fuels, mixtures of plastics would have to be separated from the other components in a waste stream. The energy requirement for the separation should be lower than when plastics are reclaimed as generics (1,000 BTUs/lb); 500 BTUs/lb appears to be a reasonable estimate. If the plastics were not separated from organic components in the waste streams additional upgrading of both the liquid and gaseous fuels would be required.

Pyrolysis is an endothermic process; 900 BTUs/lb of plastic (three times the heat of polymerization of polystyrene) appears reasonable based upon the available data in the literature.

Pyrolysis to fuel would generate fuels that could be combusted to produce net energy of 16,600 BTUs/lb of plastic, i.e. $18,000 - (900 + 500)$. Fuel would have to be burned to increase the level of energy generation to 18,000 BTUs/lb of plastic. In addition, the relevant plastic objects and articles would have to be made from virgin resin. Therefore, the total energy consumption would be about 48,650 BTUs/lb of plastic, which is higher than that for the combustion of a plastic containing waste stream in a waste-to-energy combustion unit.

Case 2: Monomers   Pyrolysis of plastics to monomers requires that:

• The polymers be sorted and reclaimed to a reasonable level of purity;
• The product gases (the monomers) be purified to an acceptable level;
• The monomers be polymerized to resin suitable for fabrication.

Most importantly not all polymers produce monomers at high selectivity when they are pyrolyzed.

At a low selectivity to styrene monomers, i.e. at selectivity below 0.8, the pyrolysis process produces both net energy and monomer. This is a result of an assumption that the coproducts have only a fuel value; this may not be correct in a specific case, i.e. the coproducts from the pyrolysis may be useful in their own right. Moreover, our pyrolysis energy balance assumes that the char is primarily inorganic and does not have any heating value.

For simplicity, we have assumed that 95% of the styrene produced in pyrolysis is purified; the discarded impure styrene from purification is burned. Polymerization of the recovered styrene into resin and fabrication into finished products (including all of the required transportation) consumes 6,100 BTUs/lb of styrene. Therefore, the total energy required to produce one pound of finished products from one pound of reclaimed polymers is significantly dependent on the selectivity to styrene obtained in the pyrolysis unit. Unfortunately, to produce one pound of reclaimed polymer may require the processing of significantly more than one pound of discarded polymer objects and parts. As a result the total energy consumption, including the generation of 18,000 BTUs of energy, is dependent upon both selectivity and the fraction of the polymer reclaimed from the waste stream.

3.3.5   A Perspective on Energy Flows

Our estimates of the energy flows (consumption), associated with alternatives for the disposal or recovery/recycling of plastics in waste streams, are summarized in Table 3-4. For convenience in analysis, the estimates of energy flows have been converted to a figure of merit. (Estimates of the energy flows, from which the figures of merit have been derived, and the calculation procedures/data are given in detail in the original report to DOE, Volume 2, Chapter 3.)

The figures of merit have been keyed to waste-to-energy incineration, which is given a value of 100. Values higher than 100 are less efficient (from an energy consumption point of view) than waste-to-energy incineration. Those alternatives with a figure of merit less than 100 are more efficient.

All the figures of merit (and our energy consumption estimates) are based upon the conversion of one pound of plastics in a waste stream to one pound of finished (new) plastic products and 18,000 lb of energy. In all the alternatives, some fraction of the new plastic products will have to be made from virgin resin since not all the plastics in the waste streams can be recovered or recycled.

Landfilling has the highest figure of merit (highest consumption of energy) and reuse of a product or object the lowest (the lowest consumption of energy). This is not surprising since:

- If the plastics are landfilled, virgin resin will have to be used to make new products. This will require the consumption of the replacement energy of the new products and 18,000 BTUs of energy.
- If the plastic objects that have been discarded can be reused, the energy consumption is lowest. However, the reduction is highly dependent upon the fraction of the discarded objects that can be reused. All the objects that cannot be reused must be replaced; this requires consumption of their replacement energy.

Regardless of the analytical scheme that is used, i.e. whether or not 18,000 BTUs of energy are generated in addition to the new finished plastic products, the rank order of the alternatives would not change. However, the numerical value of the figures of merit would be different.

3.3.6   Energy Recovery Potential

The data in Table 3-4 and the calculations of energy flow strongly suggest that reclamation and subsequent reprocessing of the recovered polymers/monomers can result in a consumption of energy that is 10,000–20,000 BTUs/lb of polymer lower than that associated with the combustion of the polymer containing wastes in waste-to-energy units and producing new parts and objects from virgin resins. Therefore, reprocessing/recycling should have a 25–50% advantage over combustion depending on the mix of recovery/recycling alternatives used.

The plastic content of ASRs, carpets and wire and cable was about 4.3 billion lb in 1990. Our studies indicate that the plastic content of these streams will grow to 6.8 billion lb by 2010 (Table 2-3). If these wastes (which today are almost exclusively landfilled) were combusted in waste-to-energy units, about 0.2 trillion BTUs/calendar day (CD) would have been generated in 1990, this will grow to about 0.3 trillion BTUs/CD by 2010. (These quantities of energy are roughly equal to 30,000–50,000 equivalent barrels of oil/CD, respectively.)

Our studies of the potential for recovery/recycling of the polymers contained in ASRs, carpets and wire and cable suggest that a number of feasible alternative approaches exist. Some of the alternatives are being developed, e.g. pyrolysis of carpets to monomers; others that could be acceptable from a cost and recovery point of view could be developed. Therefore, the controlling factor is what fraction of these wastes would be processed through alternative recovery schemes.

Table 2-5 projects that the maximum energy opportunity through recycling of ASRs, carpets and wire and cable above the heat of combustion in 2010 is about 1 trillion BTUs/CD (roughly 160,000 equivalent barrels of oil/CD). However, from this estimate there must be deducted the energy required to recover/recycle the plastic content. Therefore, the realizable potential after these deductions is 0.2–0.4 trillion BTUs/CD or about 30,000–60,000 barrels of oil/CD.

Tailings from MSW (Tables 2-2 and 2-3) will grow to 8 billion lb by 2010; the maximum energy opportunity through recycling above the heat of combustion is 0.4 trillion BTUs/CD. The alternative that can be envisioned for recovery/recycling will involve either reprocessing with compatibilizers or reprocessing and modification. The yield of acceptable plastics is likely to be rather low (as a fraction of the potential feed available). Therefore, the realizable potential is about 0.05–0.1 trillion BTUs/CD (8,000–16,000 barrels/CD).

In summary, the maximum realizable potential above the heat of combustion in 2010 is about 40,000–80,000 barrels/CD. In our judgment, it should be possible (considering the multitude of activities that are required) to achieve 25–50% of the potential by 2010. This would result in a total saving of 60,000–130,000 barrels of oil equivalent/calendar day in 2010 including the heat of combustion.

Part II

Status, Developments and Assessment of Recovery Technologies

Chapter 4

Sortation

4.1 Status

Sortation is critical to the success of all recycling programs since discarded plastic objects must be separated by both generic resin type and/or color. Sortation technology is the first step in isolating waste plastic articles into streams amenable to further reclamation.

Currently practiced sortation technology has evolved from the technical and economic requirements of many recycling programs. The current technologies for collection, sortation, and reclamation are strongly interdependent to satisfy the goals of a specific program.

Sortation is practiced: within the homesite, commercial location or institution (source separation); at pick-up during collection of recyclables; at recycling centers or material recovery facilities (MRF) that separate and prepare bulk shipments for reclamation processing; at mixed waste processing facilities (MWPF) that sort and prepare a variety of materials for shipment to reclaimers.

Hand sorting is used almost exclusively for the separation of plastic items from other discards. While mechanical devices such as grates or air streams can separate a plastic bottle fraction from a commingled container stream, hand sorting is required to isolate specific individual items. Automatic plastic bottle sorting equipment is in the developmental stage; several commercial demonstrations are undergoing extensive evaluation.

There are specific differing degrees of difficulty in sorting plastic waste streams. For example, plastic items can be sorted out from municipal solid waste (MSW) if they are commonly recognizable objects. However, some would be rejected during separation due to the lack of recognition, being "dirty," at a low occurrence level or of insignificant size.

Mixed waste sorting can isolate into a mixed pile 50% or more of the plastic articles in the MSW. Therefore, there is a need to develop automated mechanical devices to sort the rigid plastic containers to the level of purity needed to feed conventional reclamation plants.

While there is no problem in collecting automobiles and white goods (large appliances) for metal recycling, the complexity of removing the plastic parts is so great that practical sorting requires the development of a marking/recognition system along with disassembly operations.

Carpeting can be easily sorted from the MSW but sorting of generic polymers from the carpet structure itself has not been demonstrated on a commercial scale.

4.2   Developments

4.2.1   General

Sortation, or sorting technologies, must identify and separate (or segregate) specific waste plastic objects; whether performed manually or by mechanical means, sortation isolates and separates a particular plastic item into a relatively uncontaminated stream. In some situations, the plastic may be separated by both type and color as well. In general, sorting produces a segregated polymer stream whose purity and quality is suitable for reclamation.

Technologies for sortation of waste plastics, as well as for other recyclable materials, have evolved from a variety of driving forces to accommodate the materials produced in voluntary drop-off centers, buy-back programs in deposit states and various forms of curbside recycling. Owing to the myriads of recycling programs one finds that the technologies for collection, sortation, and reclamation have become strongly interdependent.

Sorting of waste plastics may be performed to different levels at several locations [788, 825, 826]:

- At the point of discard or generation (home, business, institution).
- At the collection pick-up point.
- At a centralized location for mixed recyclables.
- At a total solid waste disposal operation.
- At a plastics reclamation processing facility.

Curbside recycling of plastic beverage containers requires homeowners to source separate soft drink, milk and juice containers.

"Similar" containers can be collected in a separate section of a truck or a commingled container stream can be taken to a MRF for sorting into specific types in adequate quantities for shipment to reclaimers. MRFs generally ship mixed bales of plastic bottles which are generically sorted into PET and HDPE fractions at the reclamation site.

Institutions which maintain food service operations source separate plastic plates, cups, clamshells and plastic tableware from the waste stream. These materials are compacted and shipped to a polystyrene recovery facility.

Commercial business such as the garment companies in New York City generate both large amounts of corrugated boxes and polyethylene bags. The solid waste collector sorts these items at a central transfer station for recycling.

Product distribution warehouses have large amounts of polyethylene pallet wrap which is source separated and collected along with the corrugated board. If the levels of contamination are low, the film can be extruded directly by passing standard wash reclamamation.

4.2.2   Materials Recovery Facilities

A MRF accepts collected recyclables and separates these materials into different types. Bulk quantities of the segregated materials are then prepared for transportation to markets. Typical saleable products from MRFs are baled plastics, baled paper, crushed glass and crushed aluminum.

MRFs processing 100 to 200 tons/day of recyclables are generally used to service communities with population exceeding 200,000 people. A substantial number of MRFs in this size range exist either in or near major population centers in the U.S. These MRFs can utilize capital investment in mechanical devices to separate or recover a given object or to facilitate the separation of two different types of items. With a greater proportion of the sorting and separation done mechanically there can be a substantial reduction of labor based efforts.

Some of the equipment found in intermediate sized MRFs include:

- Electromagnet for steel can sorting and removal.
- Eddy current induction system for aluminum can removal.
- Air blowing system for plastic/glass separation.
- Mechanical/gravity device for plastic/glass separation.
- Glass crusher.
- Baler for large load preparation.
- Conveyor(s) for manual sortation of materials.

The layout of a typical MRF is given in Fig. 4-1.

Facilities like those in Fig. 4-1 can recycle aluminum and steel cans, three colors of glass containers, and plastic containers, such as clear and green PET, unpigmented and pigmented HDPE.

Mixed recyclables are placed on the receiving conveyor belt, where an electromagnet is used to remove steel cans. The recovered steel cans are compacted and baled. The steel free recyclables pass through an eddy current separator where the aluminum cans are removed. The removed aluminum cans are also densified for large load shipment. The stream of recyclables, now free of metal cans, passes through an air blower or screening device that produces glass-rich and plastics-rich streams.

The glass-rich stream is manually sorted into clear, green and amber glass; each of the color sorted glass streams are crushed for densification and placed in roll-off bins for shipment. The plastics rich stream is manually sorted to produce high purity clear PET, green PET and unpigmented HDPE streams. Each of these streams are baled and the bales accumulated for shipment to reclamation facilities.

Large Sized MRFs. MRFs that process 500 to 1000 tons/day of recyclables are intended to service communities with population exceeding 1,000,000 people. MRFs of this size are currently under construction. Their large size and large revenue

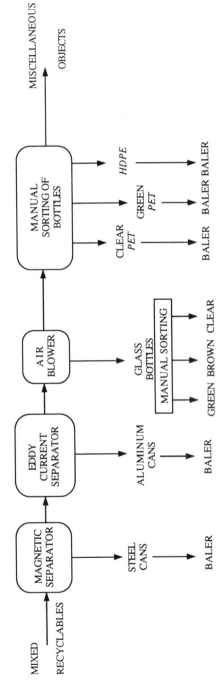

Figure 4-1 Schematic drawing of a typical MRF operation.

generation capability can justify maximum investments in mechanical equipment for sorting and separating specific materials into high purity streams from mixed streams.

Most of these facilities will initially use some level of manual sortation for color sorting of glass and separation of plastics by material type and color. However, significant emphasis will be placed on introducing emerging automated sortation technologies that should facilitate improvements in both product quality and maximum throughput. Improvements in product quality are critical since plastics reclaimers are avoiding acceptance of mixed plastic bales requiring sorting and are placing critical specifications on the bales.

Economic modeling studies on different size MRFs [827] considered both the fixed costs for land, building, and equipment, and the variable cost for utilities, maintenance, and labor as a function of plant size. For a small size MRF of 20 tons/day the total operating cost is about $80/ton while at a plant capacity of 500 tons/day the costs drop to a level of about $25/ton. This shows the economies of scale that are possible.

4.2.3 Mixed Waste Processing Facilities

Thirty-five Mixed Waste Processing Facilities (MWPF)s are in operation, under construction or in final planning stages [823]. In MWPFs the total trash stream is collected from residents and tipped at a central location for sorting. Items to be recycled are sorted by a series of mechanical devices as well as by hand.

Use of MWPFs eliminate source separation by the public as well as separate collection costs. Participation by the public is almost 100% (the same as solid waste collection); the plastic capture rate depends on how deep one wishes to dig into the pile. Trash sorting plants are necessarily large and have the solids handling equipment which has the economy of scale. A MWPF can be coupled with landfilling and waste to energy, production of refuse derived fuel, or composting.

Today's MWPFs are sorting out about the same quantity of recyclables that is obtained in curbside systems. The quantities of recyclables obtained in a composting facility are high since "all" plastic, glass and metal must be removed to insure compost quality. However, reclamation of the recovered plastics presents some difficulties because of the variety of objects and the high level of contamination. A 600 ton/day trash composting facility has been operating in Pembroke Pines, FL, for about a year.

4.2.4 Automatic Sortation

Sorting rates of 500 to 600 lb/hr of plastic containers per sorting person are typically obtained [831]. Separating two types of readily identifiable containers from a stream that has only a small percentage of contaminants is relatively straightforward. However, when the stream to be sorted contains a variety of containers of different sizes, shapes, colors and different resin types both the rate of manual sorting and the purity of the sorted materials decline significantly. This has led to the development of automated high speed technology.

In 1989/1990, H. Frankel of Rutgers University pioneered the development of the first automated sortation line for plastic containers [403]. His system consisted of a specialized container feeding system connected to a long conveyor belt. The special feed system accepted uncrushed whole containers, oriented the containers so that they were horizontal, and singulated the containers so that only one container at a time entered the conveyor with appropriate spacing in between them. Along the length of the conveyor at three locations, detectors were affixed to the line; air jet stations downstream of each detector displaced passing containers from the line into collection bins.

Working in collaboration with Asoma Instruments, Inc., a modified X-ray fluorescent (XRF) emitter instrument was placed at the first detection station on the line. The detector emits low level X-rays that cause secondary fluorescence of chlorine atoms in PVC. When the presence of chlorine is detected, an electronic signal from a receptor activates a downstream air jet which displaces the passing PVC container from the conveyor line. The detection system can operate as fast as 1/125 of a second.

In a similar manner, light emitting diodes (LED) were placed at the next two detector stations on the line and a photocell receptor placed opposite each LED. Emitted light striking a clear PET bottle results in only a minor reduction in light intensity. However, emitted light striking a translucent unpigmented HDPE container produced a substantial reduction in light intensity as measured by an opposing photocell. In both cases, requisite electronic signals from the receptor photocells are used to activate downstream air jets that displace the requisite containers. Performance testing of a pilot automated system showed that up to 150 containers a minute can be sorted with high accuracy.

Engineering analysis of the pilot line performance data indicated that some equipment modifications would be required to separate the mixed container into high purity product streams with contamination levels less than 1%. Three improvements were identified: (1) a need for greater volumes of resin identification data coupled with data redundancy to improve identification accuracy; (2) a container position tracking system which facilitates container diversion at any line speed; and (3) improvements in the bottle feeding (singulation) and container diversion system. This analysis led to development of a second generation single station multi-sensor-array sortation line.

The concept behind the second generation sorting line is quite simple. Two separate hierarchical levels of sensors are used for resin identification and color determination. A universal product code (UPC) scanner is used in concert with a high speed computer to simply "look-up" the resin type and material color in the computer's memory. If the bar code label is absent from the container, an XRF and LED system is used to discriminate resin type and material color. By placing several sensor systems in a single array configuration in one location at the beginning of the line, significant identification data can be generated and averaged to improve the accuracy of these determinations. In addition, the container's position and speed can be monitored and the transit time of a container to the desired diversion location can be calculated.

The feasibility of a second generation system has been demonstrated. A multi-camera and laser based UPC reading system was retrofitted onto the existing line and coupled with the high speed computer system. Improvements were made to the container feeding system to reduce jams and improve reliability. Computer software has been developed and implemented to increase control of the conveyor system, monitor container position on the line and improve container diversion. The new system shows promise for high purity container separation; it opens the possibility to separate other types of waste plastic materials automatically at high speeds.

Subsequent to the joint development work performed at Rutgers University, Asoma Instruments, Inc., upgraded its prototype X-ray fluorescence detection and sorting system to a commercial system termed the VS-2 system [830]. The VS-2 system consists of a high performance, high speed sensor head and an electronic controller/data processing module. The head senses signals from the bottles being sorted and the controller determines whether PVC is present or not. The controller will generate a signal to actuate a pneumatic ejector to deflect a PVC containing bottle.

Magnetic Separation Systems (MSS) of Nashville, TN has developed a prototype commercial system that accepts bales of mixed plastic containers and separates them into the four common plastic packaging resins: PET, PVC, HDPE, and PP [404, 831]. An MSS system is in the early phase of operation at an Eaglebrook Plastics, Inc. facility in Chicago, IL. The system is designed to process 5,000 lb/hr of mixed plastic bottles in four separate parallel lines that are fed by a single bale breaker and singulator system. On the processing line(s), infra-red optical and X-ray scanning coupled to a microcomputer are used to identify containers by polymer type, and a machine vision system coupled to a microcomputer is used for container color identification.

The MSS system has been designed in a modular fashion such that some of the three primary streams produced are acceptable feedstocks for some plastic container reclaiming operations. Alternatively, additional detection and separation modules can be added, as necessary, to any of the above-cited primary streams to recover individual components present in these three streams. Four optional detection and separation modules are available:

- PVC Module: Separates PVC from PET containers.
- PET Module: Separates green and amber PET from clear PET.
- PP Module: Separates unpigmented PP from unpigmented HDPE.
- Color Module: Separates mixed color opaque HDPE containers into seven individual color streams.

The early separation test results from Eaglebrook are encouraging as shown below:

Output	Primary stream	Purity	Recovery
HDPE	1	96.9	92.2
Clear PET	2	97.9	90.4
PVC		N/A	99.7 (removal)
Mixed color HDPE	3	98.2	97.9

Either crushed or uncrushed containers can be processed.

Automation Industrial Control (AIC) of Baltimore, MD, is developing a proto-type system that will accept bales of mixed plastic containers and separate these materials into six common plastic packaging resins: PET, HDPE, LDPE, PVC, PP, and PS [831]. The AIC system uses a pair of sensors at a single station to determine resin type and container color. Resin type is determined by optical sensing using an infra-red detector coupled to a microcomputer; container color is sensed with a color camera. A microcomputer tracks each container's position so that a container of a given resin type and specific color, for example clear PET, is ejected into the appropriate collection bin. The prototype line is designed to handle 1,500 lb/hr of plastic containers, either crushed or uncrushed. A singulator developed by Cham-berlain MRC of Hunt Valley, MD is used for feedstock bottle orientation and spacing prior to the measuring station. The system is now in the start-up phase of operation.

National Recovery Technologies, Inc. (NRT) of Nashville, TN has developed its VinylCycle technology with the assistance of the U.S. Environmental Protection Agency, the Vinyl Institute, and other industry sources. The NRT technology separates PVC bottles from a mixed stream of whole or crushed bottles of HDPE, PET and PVC. This is done on a mass sort basis as opposed to a singulated or object-oriented stream approach.

A screening process enables the NRT system to sense the presence of chlorine atoms within vinyl resins. This in turn triggers a computer-timed air burst that separates vinyl containers from the mixed plastic stream. The operations monitor-ing system guarantees that the maximum PVC contamination in the end product will not exceed 50 parts per million.

NRT's commercial application of its technology has produced three models capable of continuous high speed unattended duty. The largest has a processing capacity of up to 10 bottles per second, or approximately 4,500 lb/hr, and the two smaller units have throughput rates of 2,500 and 1,500 lb/hr, respectively[1].

4.2.5   Marker Systems

Continental Container Corporation has developed a technique to mark containers with an easily detectable invisible ink that allows this separation by resin type, resin grade, and container color [831]. While the system is appealing because of its simplicity, its use would require every product packaging line to have a marking system installed on it. Moreover, the cooperation of all product producers would have to be obtained.

The Eastman Chemical Company and Bayer have developed techniques that incorporate a readily detectable molecular marker in any plastic during the resin

---

[1]J. Sommer Jr., National Recovery Technologies, Inc., Nashville, TN, personal communication.

manufacturing operation [832]. The marker would allow subsequent identification of post-consumer plastic material by resin type, resin grade, and other product/packaging parameters. Eastman and Bayer have both suggested that the cost of adding chemical markers to a resin would be low. The use of this marking technique for sorting post-consumer plastics would require the close cooperation of all resin producers. Furthermore, while some have visualized that a very large number of plastics could be marked, there may be a practical limit of five to ten markers for each plastic due to intermixing of base resins in virgin compounds as well as commingling during recycling.

4.3   Assessment and Relevance to Critical Waste Streams

4.3.1   Municipal Solid Waste

The opportunities for recovery of plastics from municipal solid waste are numerous. Existing recycling programs can capture more material if participation is increased. However, this requires motivating individuals to source separate. Efficient automatic sorting of collected material would also result in the recovery of additional plastic items for recycle.

Existing plastics collection and generic sorting systems generate a by-product pile of mixed plastic items. While the quantity of this stream, currently 20–30% by weight of plastics in MSW, could be reduced further with automatic sorting, processes to recycle the stream as a blend or alloy of several generic polymers need to be developed.

Additional plastic articles can be source separated by the public from MSW. The public will source separate plastic objects such as toys, housewares, clothes hangers and plastic appliances. The existing sorting system is only one of many factors limiting the expansion of the scope of plastics recycling beyond bottles. Only a small portion of the available plastic film discards are collected because of the variety of components in the mix and the additional cost of washing film.

Every existing collection program fails to capture 100% of any item. Even dedicated recyclers sometimes fail to separate all items due to the inconvenience of the moment. Many plastic items are not source separated due to excessive food contamination. Pilot curbside projects have determined that only 20–25% of the residential plastic discards arrive at the curb in the recycle bucket.

The technique with the highest capture potential is total trash sortation. Developers of total trash sortation coupled with composting, estimate that 80% of the plastic discards could be segregated by mechanical devices and hand sorting. The driving force to remove all the plastics is improvement in the quality of the compost product.

There are no collection barriers to total trash handling except some problems associated with compaction in the collection vehicle. Broken glass, cross-contamination and interlocking of several materials at high compaction will reduce the efficiency of sortation. Major technical innovations of automatic sorting equipment will be required to dig deeper into the trash pile for recyclables.

4.3.2   Automobiles

The collection infrastructure for discarded automobiles exists; however, recovery of the metal content produces waste containing plastics that is not amenable to conventional sortation or reclamation. A variety of options and new technologies are currently studied by the U.S. car manufacturers.

In Germany, a series of recycling laws have been passed that require the recovery of all materials in automobiles. The parts are to be returned to the manufacturer for reclamation or reuse. The necessary infrastructure is being established.

4.3.3   Carpets

Residential and commercial carpeting can be sorted from MSW or collected from carpet installers. Sortation of generic polymers such as nylon, polyester or polypropylene is difficult since all carpeting is a composite of more than one material.

Since nylon, polyester and polypropylene predominate as the face fiber in carpets, sorting techniques are under development. At Du Pont and Hoechst Celanese processes under development produce short fibers. Hoechst Celanese is developing polyester carpets that eliminate the latex adhesive and polypropylene woven backing (approximately 50% of the carpet by weight). These new carpets could be recycled completely through methanolysis or solvolysis.

4.3.4   Wire and Cable

Significant quantities of discarded wire and cable are processed to recover the copper and aluminum content. Plastic insulation is removed by mechanical means and is landfilled. The commodity plastic insulation is polyethylene and PVC; however, there is a large number of formulations including some that contain significant quantities of carbon black and plasticizers. Generally, wire and cable constructions are reclaimed in large batches at a few locations.

In large telephone communication cable the 2 to 3″ diameter polyethylene jacket can be slit and stripped from the communication singles bundle. Sortation on the metal recycling line would greatly reduce the complexity of any reclamation process.

Chapter 5

Wash/Float Separation

5.1 Summary

Plastics wastes derived from rigid plastic containers are cleaned and separated into generic plastics using wash/float separation technology in the U.S., and in other parts of the world. The American Plastics Council estimated that as of August 1992, approximately 140–150 companies in the U.S. were engaged in commercial wash reclamation processing of post-consumer waste plastics to yield purified washed flake or repelletized resin products.

Commercial waste plastics recycling in the U.S. primarily involves processing carefully sorted post-consumer rigid HDPE and PET plastic bottles. These are commonly available, relatively easy to recognize and sort, and straightforward to reclaim. A small number of commercial facilities are also equipped to process contaminated post-consumer polyethylene film wastes.

The reclamation approaches used in these facilities can also be applied to plastic wastes other than HDPE and PET bottles when the feedstocks become available. For example, rigid PVC bottles and containers are only sometimes reclaimed by wash technology in the U.S., but in Europe where PVC bottles are more common, reclamation of PVC is widespread [788]. Wash technology is also used in the U.S. for the reclamation of contaminated post-consumer foam polystyrene packaging and food service wastes.

Reclamation is generally carried out by some variations of well established and effective washing/separation technology. Some, but by no means all, of the existing reclamation operations are capable of producing reclaimed generic resins with a sufficient degree of cleanliness and purity that they can be used in some of the same applications segments which currently use virgin resins.

Like all technologies, plastics reclamation has its own specific problems and idiosyncrasies. It is a rapidly growing technology, relatively new, and not yet fully formed. Variations in product quality obtained from the many commercial reclamation operations may be a result of the rapidly changing targets for reclaimed product quality. Products which met quality targets six months or a year ago may no longer be good enough for current end-user requirements. It should be recognized that targets have been always "equivalent to virgin" and reclaimed material will probably never meet that goal because of degradation, contamination and presence of additives.

While there is considerable published information on the business aspects of plastics reclamation, the technology is generally considered by its users to be proprietary. As a result there are few detailed publications on reclamation technology for processes other than those developed by the Center for Plastics Recycling Research at Rutgers University. The information in this chapter was derived from the center's publications, unpublished research, industrial contacts and plant visits.

5.2 Developments

5.2.1 General

In order to reclaim discarded plastic products sorted from the municipal solid waste stream as generic reclaimed plastic resins, four steps are generally involved:

- The plastic objects (products) must be recognized and separated from the waste stream, or separately collected.
- Since collected waste plastics products are often mixed together with other dissimilar products, the mixture must be sorted into processable groups to create suitable feedstocks for reclamation. This is particularly important for post-consumer plastics wastes from the municipal solid waste. Plastics wastes from commercial and industrial sources are often of known plastic type, and available as collected in sufficient quantities and purity that further sorting is not required.
- Waste plastics are processed at a reclamation facility into new reclaimed resin materials or new fabricated products.

Reclamation processes vary according to the nature and quality of the material being processed. For post-consumer plastics, this depends to a great degree on the methods used to sort collected plastics wastes into processable reclamation feedstocks.

Currently collectable household plastics wastes are composed mainly of discarded single-use packaging of one type or another. In general, when household plastics wastes are collected, they are a mixture of both *object* types and *resin* types. That is, the wastes may be a mixture of objects, such as plastic containers (bottles, tubs, cups, etc.), plastics films (such as plastic bags), plastic housewares, plastic toys, etc.; these objects, in turn, are composed of a variety of resin types (or composites thereof).

The most common resin types found in current recycling collections include both HDPE and LDPE, PET, PP, PS, and PVC. HDPE is the most common resin type, followed by PET. In order to be processed into higher value reclaimed resin for reuse, these collected objects usually must be sorted into single resin types or classes.

Waste plastics sortation methods have a strong impact on the quality of the feedstocks for reclamation, and, in turn, on the quality of the reclaimed generic resins. Large scale reclamation units must obtain feedstocks from a growing infrastructure of multi-material recycling programs. The feedstocks are often not well sorted; additional sorting prior to reclamation is usually required.

5.2.2   Current Technology

There are two major reclamation processing technologies currently being used commercially in the U.S. for post-consumer plastics wastes—generic and commingled. Each technology can handle different feedstocks and produce plastics for a variety of end-uses.

Generic reclamation. Multi-million pound quantities of a single contaminated plastic resin are processed, normally by a variant of a washing/separation process, to yield a clean reclaimed resin product for multiple conventional uses.

Commingled processing. Mixed contaminated waste plastics are granulated, and processed into molded products, usually some form of "plastic lumber" [853].

Under development is a hybrid process in which contaminated commingled plastics wastes are cleaned and separated to the maximum extent possible. The cleaned plastics are then repelletized for use in molding applications. Other resins, fillers, reinforcements and additives are often added to the reclaimed plastics.

Generic reclamation produces a clean, single-type plastic resin in either flake or pellet form that can be used in conventional plastics conversion processes as a full or partial substitute for virgin resins.

The nature of the processes used by commercial firms to reclaim resin products from available feedstocks is often proprietary. However, all use some variation of the wash/float process at CPRR Rutgers University [788, Chapter 4]. This process for post-consumer plastic bottles, involves the following steps:

1. Collection of waste plastics.
2. Pre-sortation of collected waste plastics into "uniform" feedstock types, followed by baling for transportation to the reclamation facility.
3. Resorting after the bales are broken at the reclamation facility.
4. Chopping of the resorted feedstocks into flakes of about 3/8″ size; these are air classified to remove loose light contaminants, rocks, glass, etc., and conveyed to a wash operation.
5. Dirty flakes are often pre-washed in cold water and then in a hot aqueous detergent solution.
6. Washed flakes are then separated from the wash solution in a suitable dewatering device. The wash solutions are filtered and reused many times. The filtrate ("dirty" water) should be sent to a treatment plant for the removal of oils, greases, etc., before discharged into the sewer.
7. Wet washed chips are reslurried in rinse water and pumped through a set of hydrocyclones or float sink tanks to separate the "light" components (e.g. polyethylene base cups and polypropylene caps and labels) from the "heavy" components (e.g. PET and aluminum bottle tops). Float separation step also provides a rinsing of contaminated wash solution from the washed flakes. The

rinse/float water is filtered and reused to some extent. The comment made about the "dirty" water on step 6 above applies also here.

8. Light and heavy components are individually dewatered and dried. The light component stream, a complex mixture of low molecular weight HDPE base cup resins, high molecular weight PP label materials and injection molding grade PP bottle top resins, is suitable for sale after drying. It should be recognized that PP and PE are incompatible and this limits the allowable maximum PP contents to about 5%.

9. The heavy component flotation stream from a soft drink bottle reclamation process is PET; it includes aluminum flakes from bottle tops. This stream is sent to one of several available processes for separating PET and aluminum.

10. Drying and packaging of the clean separated plastic flakes is the final step in all wash/reclamation processes. Reclaimed PET is usually sold in flake form. Reclaimed HDPE is usually extruded and repelletized.

The products of this reclamation process are:

- Clean (99.9 + % Pure) PET flake;
- Clean, mixed polyolefin flakes;
- Aluminum flakes.

Bottles other than soda bottles, such as polyethylene milk/water jugs, polyethylene laundry product bottles, mixtures of PET and PE containers, polystyrene containers, and PVC bottles can also be processed in a similar manner. Indeed, a PET soft drink bottle wash/float process, if designed properly, can be used to reclaim almost any type of available post-consumer rigid container feedstock.

The reclamation process generates the following waste and by-product streams:

- Sortation trash and fluff from air classifier;
- Wet sludge (mainly paper fibers);
- Dirty rinse water ("dishwater");
- Dirty wash solution (concentrated "dishwater").

These are typically not hazardous; indeed the waste water may not be appreciably different than dirty "dishwater" from, say a large cafeteria. However, in some cases, waste waters may need further treatment.

5.2.3   Alternative Wash Technologies

The process developed by Graham Engineering (York, PA) is a variation of wash/float separation; however, a distinct separate wash step is not used. The use of wet grinding claims that the intense agitation in the wet grinder eliminates the need for a separate wash step. No systematic data are available that compare the cleanliness of this process with the more conventional hot detergent wash processes.

Reclamation of post-consumer polystyrene foam products is a special case of a typical wash/reclamation process. In the reclamation system originally used by the National Polystyrene Recycling Co. in its three plants, collected post-consumer PS foam waste products are unloaded onto a feed conveyor where preliminary manual inspection and sorting out of undesired materials is carried out [90]. The feed is then simultaneously ground and washed, using hot water without added detergents. The washed PS particles after dewatering are dried in a hot air fluidized bed dryer to produce a clean fluff. The fluff is extruded and pelletized. Foam PS building insulation or package cushioning scrap may not require washing. If so, the foam is densified usually by heating to the softening point, and then extruding and repelletizing.

The Reco process [369] marketed by Johnson Controls in the U.S. reclaims resins from PET soft drink bottles that do not use metal caps. The bottle components are separated before the granulation and washing steps as summarized below:

1. Sortation of dirty baled bottles without metal caps.
2. The stretch oriented PET bottle shrinks in a hot water bath (70–100°C) liberating the base cups and plastic labels and many of the PP caps.
3. Vibrating screens separate labels and bottle caps and then base cups from the bottle.
4. Bottles and base cups are granulated separately.
5. Plastic flakes are separately washed and rinsed.
6. Residual light materials are separated from the PET by a hydrocyclone float separation step.
7. Flakes are dewatered and dried.
8. PET flakes are passed through a metal detector before packaging.

The Pure-Tech process[1] differs from the other processes in that the dirty bottles are washed, whole, before sortation/separation and granulation. Crushed whole bottles, preferably cap-free, are first thoroughly washed in a hot solution containing a proprietary noncaustic cleaning agent. The wash and rinse cycle, which takes 30 minutes, processes 500 pounds per batch. The labels and base cups come loose from the bottles; they are largely removed from the wash drum, when the solution is drained. Base cups are removed mechanically, or by hand sortation. The washed PET bottles and the HDPE base cups are separately granulated into flakes. There was no further processing in the original process. In a more recent version, the PET flakes are subjected to a further conventional wash and rinse step before drying.

5.2.4   Film Reclamation

Reclamation of post-consumer plastic films is basically generic in nature. Used films are collected, washed, converted into pellets, and processed into new film type products.

---

[1]Pure-Tech, Springfield, MA, Plant Open House, 1989.

This technology, while practiced in Europe for many years, is just beginning to be considered in the U.S. [67, 236]. In April 1992, the Union Carbide Corporation opened a plant to reclaim post-consumer PE films as well as PET and PE bottles[1]. To accomplish this, they purchased a turn-key plant built by the Italian firm Sorema that utilizes wash/float separation technology but with added equipment to cut/granulate baled films, and other equipment designed to handle film flakes as well as the heavier bottle flakes.

Although the appropriate technology for film reclamation is available and turn-key processing plants can be readily purchased the supply of collected household waste plastic films is currently almost non-existent in the U.S. Plastic film reclamation is a major challenge for the U.S. recycling collection/sortation infrastructure.

5.2.5   Commercial and Industrial Wastes

For industrial and commercial plastics wastes, reclamation is often relatively straightforward. Since the composition of the wastes is usually of a single resin of low contamination, reclamation of industrial wastes may involve only granulation of the waste objects, and perhaps, repelletizing. Where removal of some contaminants is required, the wash steps used may be either simplified versions of the process described for the beverage bottles or more elaborate such as in the case of PP batteries where neutralization of the water is required.

5.3   Assessment

The basic technology for generic resin reclamation is reasonably well developed. Commercial plants designed to produce high quality products are being offered for sale by a number of vendors[2]. Whether the plants operate in an economically viable manner depends on the type of feedstock, the presence of deposit laws and the existence of markets for the finished resin. While continuing engineering improvement of this technology will occur, there is no real need or effort required for the development of new technologies.

While wash/float reclamation technology of post-consumer plastics wastes is well established, there are problems that need to be addressed.

Contamination from inadequate separations of polymer and residual contamination by paper, adhesives, metals, glass, and odor bodies is often critical in determining what application area the reclaimed polymers can be used.

---

[1]Union Carbide Corporation, Bound Brook, NJ, Plant Open House, April 23, 1992.
[2]Graham Engineering wet grinding process, York, PA, Plant Open House, September 26, 1990.

There are only a few definitive product quality tests, and no industry standard tests. Purchase specifications for reclaimed resins often list zero or very low levels of contaminants such as adhesive, paper fibers, metals, other plastic resins, and odors without indicating how to measure these contaminants. For example, particulate contamination in a reclaimed flake product cannot easily be measured. There is only limited information available on the relationship between impurity levels and behavior of the materials in actual use. Careful use of established wash reclamation processes that incorporate adequate washing and rinsing reduces contamination levels to a point where they are not likely to cause difficulties in some end-use applications.

Studies are needed to develop industry standard procedures for quality in reclaimed PET, HDPE and other resins. Most importantly, measured quality parameters must be correlated with performance in selected end-use applications.

PVC contamination is a significant limitation in PET reclamation since PVC decomposes at PET melt processing temperatures releasing corrosive hydrochloride vapors. Since PVC and PET have essentially the same specific gravity, they cannot be separated by conventional density based flotation techniques. Careful hand sorting of bottles can approach the desired degree of feedstock purity, although it is subject to error arising from human fatigue. Alternately, improvements in feedstock purity can be addressed by using an automatic sorting system. Hopefully, equipment now under development will provide moderate cost automatic PVC detection and removal. Presently, there is no acceptable approach to reduce PVC contamination from "invisible" sources such as cap liners.

Residual odors in reclaimed plastic products are difficult to measure and to control. Studies are needed to adequately measure and define odors. Industry sources have few complaints about odor in reclaimed PET, but there are frequent complaints in reclaimed HDPE. Reclaimed milk jugs can have odor from butyric acid contamination derived from rancid milk residues. However, this is a result of poor washing; the contamination can be removed in well designed and operated wash facilities. Residual odors may also be a problem in the reclamation of household detergent and chemical bottles; the cost effectiveness of their recycling still has to be determined, particularly at the present low cost of virgin resins.

5.4   Relevance to Critical Waste Streams

Generic resin reclamation technology was developed around wash/water float cleaning of single polymer type packaging products, primarily post-consumer plastic bottles. The process removes surface contamination by utilizing a hot detergent solution wash. This can handle contamination such as surface dirt, food wastes, labels, and adhesives. The wash/float separation step will separate plastics with a lower specific gravity than water, generally the polyolefins; from plastics with a specific gravity higher than water, generally everything else.

Wash/float technology can be used for any waste plastic feedstock that has the characteristics of post-consumer plastics bottles, i.e. single polymer type and detergent removable contamination. Other plastic waste streams that can be sorted into other generic feedstocks in large quantities should also be reclaimable using some form of wash/float technology. For example, generic polymer type automotive components, or outdated vinyl siding from buildings could be reclaimed by some variant of wash/float. To do so will require adaptation of existing processes to fit the specific properties of the feedstock.

Conventional generic reclamation technology is not suited for the reclamation of polymer wastes that are:

- Complex fabrications of different materials;
- Highly contaminated;
- Composed of significant quantity of coatings that cannot be removed by washing;
- Composites of incompatible polymers not readily separated by float separation.

Other reclamation techniques such as flake separations and solvent processing may be appropriate for such wastes.

Chapter 6

Micro-Sortation

6.1 Status

Conventional generic resin reclamation processing using aqueous detergent wash-water flotation techniques can produce clean, high purity reclaimed resins from dirty post-consumer waste plastic feedstocks. However, use of wash/float depends on the availability of well sorted, single resin or object feedstocks: whole parts or objects have been sorted, prior to granulation. The limitations inherent to wash/float are the result of how collection and object sorting have been carried out.

Alternative mechanical technologies to sort ground or flaked resin by types or color are under development. These separation processes termed "micro-sorting" would eliminate pre-sorting of the whole object/part feedstocks. They also may permit the reclamation of feedstocks containing composite objects or parts, made up of several different resins.

There is no doubt that the micro-sorting technologies under development are technically feasible [860]. Micro-sorting would eliminate manpower intensive operations, since the process would be highly mechanized and continuous. However, there is doubt at this time as to whether micro-sorting processes will compete both economically and with the level of product quality attainable with the simpler pre-sorted feed wash/float approach. Reclamation processes are feedstock limited; it has been difficult in the past to accumulate the quantities necessary to make mechanically complex technologies economically attractive.

Where resins can be separated from one another as whole objects, the separation of parts is several orders of magnitude less complex than the separation on a flake level. However, if part complexity or difficulty of resin identification makes resin sorting at the part or object level impractical, micro-sortation on a flake level would be needed. Several micro-sorting processes are under study. These processes are generally proprietary and only limited information is available about these technologies. Electrostatic, froth flotation, multi-density flotation, softening point difference, and color difference are being developed for separation of flakes. All these approaches are viable. However, none of these processes have commercially achieved the high degree of separation required for removal of PVC from PET to a residual level of under 50 ppm, except possibly for froth flotation[1].

---

[1] John Meczko, Abstract on "Commercial Application of Froth Flotation", 14th PRF Meeting, Rutgers University, 1992.

6.2   Developments

Advanced micro-sorting processes under development can be separated into four categories depending on the parameter being used to make the separation:

- Density;
- Froth flotation;
- Electrical;
- Optical.

6.2.1   Density Separations

Separation of flakes of different resin types by their density difference is basic to wash/float processes. For example, relatively dense PET flakes can be separated from the relatively light polyolefin flakes using water as the float separation medium. The separation is relatively easy, since there is a wide density difference between the two resin groups and between each resin group and water. The separations can be carried out in float-sink tanks or with hydrocyclones. The latter are more efficient and hydrocyclones are becoming the equipment of choice for wash reclamation facilities[1] [788, p. 51–55].

Wash/float separations can be used for resin pairs or groups with specific gravities all above or below that of water, by using properly chosen float media, e.g. solvent mixtures, alcohol-water mixtures, or salt solutions. Indeed, such mixtures have been suggested and promoted by many. For example, concentrated calcium nitrate solutions have been commercially offered for float separation of aluminum bottle cap flakes from PET flakes.

In most float processes, the water used in the float step rinses residual wash solution off of the mixed flakes and accomplishes the desired separation. Water remaining on the flakes is removed by hot air drying; the vapors are discharged to the atmosphere. The liquid water which is drained off of the flakes is recycled after being treated for the removal of contaminants.

The use of volatile solvents or water solvent mixtures in float separations requires some significant process changes. The float media diluted by the water from the washing step will be on the mixed flakes. Recycling of the float solution will require removal of this water to a specified level.

The solvent vapors from drying of the separated flakes thus generated often cannot be discharged to the atmosphere. Residual solvent in the finished flake product may also have to be reduced to low levels.

---

[1]John Brown Machinery, Providence, RI, Company Sales Literature, 1990.

While solvent mixture flotation separations are often mentioned in the literature [788, p. 56], we have not uncovered any indication that they are commercially used on a significant scale or being considered for future use.

Salt solution float separation requires that salt concentration be maintained within narrow limits [861]. Moreover residual salts on the separated flakes must be thoroughly rinsed off. This is easy to accomplish on a pilot scale but costly to do in production equipment. Normally, multi-stage water rinses are required, followed by water treatment. Water rinses from the process are dilute salt solutions; they cannot be reused for flotation. Concentration by evaporation or other methods is possible, but may not be economical. Lastly, discharge of dilute salt solutions containing suspended matter to the sewer is often not permitted and results in a significant daily loss of salts.

Float separations of multiple resin mixtures can only separate pairs of resin types in one stage and as a result requires a multi-stage process. Mostly as a result of these issues, polymer flake separation by salt solution float separations is not practiced extensively on a commercial scale. The only known commercial process is for the separation of ABS from screws and metal inserts used in telephone hand sets[1].

6.2.2   Supercritical Flotation

Beckman and coworkers [116, 379, 856] are working on a novel float separation process that will separate a complex mixture of plastic flakes into separate polymer types, and remove metals and other contaminants. A fluid near its critical point is used to allow separations by density at mild temperatures and pressures. The work has been done using mixtures of carbon dioxide and sulfur hexafluoride, which by varying pressures allow a density variation between 0.7 and 1.7 g/cc at room temperature.

By varying both pressure and composition, density could be adjusted to within 0.001 g/cc of the desired point. This permits float separation of HDPE from LDPE and PP, which is not possible in water float processes. Natural milk bottle grade HDPE can be separated from dark color HDPE bottle materials and again from light color HDPE bottles. These separations result from the different densities of the pigments used in the bottles. Separations have also been made between polystyrene, PVC and PET; intermediate separations by color have also been possible in some cases. Although this technology has been demonstrated as being applicable to a wide range of separations, significant process and engineering issues remain to be resolved before it can be used on a commercial scale.

---

[1]R. Sabia, AT&T Nassau Metals, Personal Communication, March 1993.

6.2.3   Froth Flotation

Froth flotation is a technology widely used in the mining industry for ore benefici-
ation and coal cleaning. It is being investigated as a technique for separating plastic
wastes at a ground or flake level [858, 860]. Some of this work has advanced
significantly although detailed information is not yet available in the open literature.

Currently a simple froth flotation approach is used for the separation of
aluminum from reclaimed PET flakes derived from soft drink bottles. There are
several large commercial facilities where the PET flakes (after washing and float
separation of polyolefins) are treated in a strong caustic bath. The caustic attacks
aluminum, generating hydrogen gas. Bubbles of hydrogen then cause the aluminum
to float, separating it from the PET [858].

Froth flotation when applied to separations of polymers makes use of the
different surface energy that results in differing wetting characteristics. The surface
energy of plastics can also be changed by the use of additive treatments which
change one resin in a given mixture more than the others present. When both the
surface energies of the resins and the surface tension of the froth bath, into which
the mixture is placed, have been adjusted properly, air dispersed into the resulting
suspension will cause bubbles to selectively adhere to one component of the
mixture. This material is then skimmed off.

Froth flotation is being studied by Yarar [855]. He reports that, when properly
applied to given pairs of plastics, froth flotation techniques can separate polymer
resins that are difficult to separate by other means. However, separation of
multi-resin polymer mixtures would require multi-stage froth flotation systems.

Since quantitative information is not available, the efficiency of froth flotation
separations for plastic mixtures cannot be judged. However, the main application of
froth flotation being considered by several companies is the removal of PVC
contamination from reclaimed PET flake.

Hoechst Celanese has claimed that its froth flotation process provides a PVC
removal efficiency from PET flake down to a residual PVC level in the tens of parts
per million [858]. A commercial PET reclamation plant using this approach for
PVC removal is in start-up. Its level of performance is not yet known. However, if
successful, this approach may be a cost-effective way of ensuring PVC free PET and
preferable to automatic bottle sorting processes under development at this time.

6.2.4   Electrostatic Separations

Electrostatic separation of polymer resin flakes utilize both active and passive
technologies. The active methods involve producing an electrical charge on a
mixture of particles that causes them to fall between a pair of oppositely charged
electrodes. For appropriately selected resin pairs, one polymer type may be attracted to the positive electrode, while the other is attracted to the negatively
charged electrode. Several research groups and commercial firms are developing

technology and hardware systems to accomplish such separations. The primary interest is directed to removal of PVC contamination from reclaimed PET flakes.

A research group at the University of Western Ontario has demonstrated that binary mixtures of PVC and PET can be separated into high purity streams by using a dry electrostatic separation process [854].

A mixture of PVC and PET flakes is agitated in a lean fluidized bed where impacting particles build-up surface charges. The charged particles are then carried in an air stream to an electrostatic separation tower containing plate electrodes of opposite electrical charge. PVC particles migrate towards the negatively charged electrode while the PET flakes migrate to the positively charged electrodes. The flakes are collected in separate bins at the bottom of the chamber. A series of tests on a one-stage separation process indicate that a 50/50 mixture of PET and PVC flakes can be separated into a PET-rich stream having a PET purity greater than 99% at 93% yield, or better. Similarly, a PVC-rich stream is also collected.

Devtech Laboratories of Amherst, NH has developed a dry electrostatic process for separating mixtures of PET and PVC into high purity streams [405, 831]. The process does not require the use of any wet or dry chemical pretreatment to facilitate the separation in the electrostatic chamber. Devtech has granted an exclusive license for its technology to the Carpco Corporation of Jacksonville, FL. A prototype pilot scale machine that processes 200 lb/hr of a PET/PVC flake mixture has been built. The initial test shows that the system is capable of producing high purity PET and PVC streams independent of the feedstock PET/PVC ratio or flake particle size. Carpco is building a large electrostatic separation machine that can process 2,000 lb/hr for commercial applications.

In a more elaborate program, "Kali and Salz AG" (Kassel, Germany) has adapted its electrostatic salt-beneficiation process, Esta Process, to separate plastics wastes in a 100 kg/h pilot plant [378]. The process can separate all types of plastics, including those with similar density, such as LDPE and PP, or PVC and PET. Hydrocyclones and gravity floaters, which use density differences, cannot do this. Mixed plastic waste is ground to less than 6 mm. Surface active agents are added to enhance the friction-charging properties, and the plastics are then rubbed together to electrostatically charge them. Since PVC has the largest electron affinity—followed by PET, PP, PE, PS and polyamide—it always becomes negatively charged. The differently charged plastics are separated as they fall between plates having potential differences of up to 120,000 V. The separation process depends on the feedstock being dry and relatively free of tramp contaminants. Most likely, post-consumer materials would have to be put through a wash reclamation process prior to electrostatic separation. The cost effectiveness of this process has not yet been demonstrated.

Gregory and coworkers [856] have been investigating measurement of the dielectric properties of PET and PVC flakes in electrostatic fields. They have developed sensors that measure the dielectric properties of various polymers, and hence can distinguish between polymers. While the original work focused on whole container sensing, it is now planned to build a system with an array of sensors that can detect and separate a mixture of plastic flakes at about 1,000 lb/hr. The signal can be used, in principle, to operate flake sorting equipment which is not yet available commercially. However, mechanical sorting equipment for (crushed bottles) is being introduced into commercial operation. Dielectric identification of polymer resin may be a useful control element for such equipment, and may prove to be more useful than other polymer identification systems under development.

6.2.5   Softening Point Separations

The separation of different plastics, particularly PVC and PET by utilizing their different softening or tacking temperatures, has been pursued for a number of years. A recent article [331] illustrates the concept.

The selective tacking process is based on the concept that different thermoplastic materials have different threshold temperatures, at which they will start adhering to a heated surface. This may be used in a process, described below, for separating different plastic materials.

1. A surface is heated to a temperature at which the material having the lowest tacking temperature will adhere.
2. The waste plastic mixture is flowed over this surface.
3. The portion of the mixture that does not adhere drops off.
4. The portion of the mixture that does adhere is then removed by scraping.
5. The steps are repeated for the higher softening components of the mixture.

This process was studied in a continuous test apparatus fitted with a heated moving belt. Separation of a PVC/PET mixture depends upon the temperature employed and the contact time allowed. PVC contents of 0.5% have been obtained.

6.2.6   Optical Sorting

Optical sorting processes scan flakes for color and transparency; the resulting signals operate sorting devices. While such technology appears to be relatively straightforward, it is not clear how economically attractive it will be. It is worth noting that problems with these processes may lie in staging and indexing since flakes are not uniform in size and shape.

Use of optical scanning to characterize whole objects, such as bottles, seem to be more practical. This approach has already been developed for large scale use, although its economic viability has not been reported.

6.3   Assessment and Relevance to Critical Waste Streams

Micro-sorting technology shows considerable promise for the enhanced reclamation of resins from a variety of waste streams. However, significant additional development and engineering studies are required before selections can be made among the alternative approaches and economics are justified.

Froth flotation techniques appear likely to be useful in the separation of the complex material mixtures that result from the recycling of wire and cable wastes, carpet wastes, or the complex polymer mixtures resulting from the disassembly of scrap vehicles and possibly appliances.

Wire and cable insulation wastes already exist in granulated form. To some extent, these wastes are being separated and reclaimed resins produced, using water flotation techniques. Froth flotation techniques should permit more effective separations, thus providing the potential for resulting in increased resin recovery from this large waste stream.

However, carpets are complex composite products, made of many different materials and polymer types. Textile industry machinery that can rip such carpet wastes into shreds exists; its use would facilitate the washing out of the adhesive backings and dirt. Froth flotation may be able to separate the resulting fiber mass into separate polymer types. However, fiber entanglement may seriously hamper such efforts. Therefore, other approaches, such as solution reclamation, may be more appropriate.

If disassembled automotive or appliance parts can be sorted into single resin groupings, conventional reclamation processing may be able to be used for reclamation of these resins. However, for composite parts, micro-sorting or solvent processing may be a necessary part of resin reclamation efforts.

Chapter 7

Solvent Separation

Solution processing of polymer waste streams either to selectively dissolve individual polymers or to dissolve the polymer content and then precipitate them in a way to separate them into individual polymer fractions that can be reused is a subject of considerable interest to a number of researchers. Particular emphasis has been placed on finding solvents that are highly selective for specific polymers since this would permit the selective dissolution of the individual polymers from a commingled mixture.

7.1   Present Status

There are no commercial plants utilizing solution processes to separate polymers. However, research and development is being funded because the approach may offer specific advantages under some circumstances.

Individual polymers can be selectively removed from commingled ground mixtures of plastics either by sequential dissolution at controlled temperature or sequential treatment with solvents that differ in their ability to leach or dissolve individual polymers from the mixture. In both cases the quantity of solvent used typically results in the production of solutions containing 5–15% polymer. Solutions containing higher concentrations of polymer are not easily processed.

Once prepared, the solution can be readily filtered for the removal of some of the solid contaminants. In addition, additives such as stabilizers, which may enhance the properties of the plastic when subsequently recovered, can be added.

Dissolved polymers are recovered from solution by one of the following techniques:

- Devolatilization in the flash chamber to about 85% polymer solids;
- Precipitation of the polymer from solution by cooling;
- Precipitation of the polymer by the use of a countersolvent (non-solvent).

Use of a countersolvent complicates significantly the recycle system used to recover the solvents since the countersolvent and the solvent will have to be separated. For all routes, a staged devolatilizing extruder would be required to reduce the solvent content of the polymer to acceptable levels before it is packaged.

7.2   Developments

Anecdotal information prevalent in the industry suggests that reclamation of plastics by solution processes has been considered by a number of companies. However, only two active development programs have been identified in the U.S.:

- Selective dissolution of ground commingled scrap is being studied by Nauman and Lynch at Rensselaer Polytechnic Institute (RPI) [533].
- A selective dissolution process for the recovery of plastics from auto shredder waste is under study at the Argonne National Laboratories (ANL) by a team consisting of Daniels, Jody, and Bonsignore [93, 568, 806].
- A dual solvent process for the recovery of PVC from scrap has been described in foreign patents. However, there is no indication that this process has been carried to a substantial developmental stage [803].

7.2.1   RPI Process

The following steps have been demonstrated on a small pilot scale at RPI[1] [530].

- Crude shredding of the commingled polymer;
- Removal of metals by conventional techniques;
- Water wash with minimum use of detergents;
- Charging of partially dry shredded plastics to a leaching vessel;
- Successive leaching with xylene solvent at staged temperature increases to remove: (i) polystyrene at 25°C; (ii) low-density polyethylene at 75°C; (iii) HDPE at 105°C; and (iv) polypropylene at 120°C.
- Solutions containing approximately 5–10% polymer are heated and then flashed in a vessel held at about 2 atmospheres pressure to approximately 85% plastic solids. This technique allows recovery of 98% of the solvent without vacuum equipment.
- The plastic is further devolatilized in a three-stage, single screw extruder and pelletized. The solids remaining in the leaching vessel are leached with an unidentified solvent to separate PVC and PET in a similar manner.

A preliminary engineering and economic analysis of the RPI process has been made by the M.W. Kellogg Company[2]. Their studies projected a processing cost of $0.24/lb for a plant that handles 70 million lb/yr of commingled scrap. The processing cost includes a 10% depreciation charge and a 20% return on a fixed investment of $40 million. The M.W. Kellogg study must be considered highly

---

[1]J.C. Lynch and E.B. Nauman, "Recycling Commingled Plastics via Selective Dissolution", Proceedings of the 10th International Coextrusion Conference (1989), p. 99.
[2]K.E. Battle, A.P. Moore, J.C. Lynch, and E.B. Nauman, "Plastic Recycling by Selective Dissolution", DeWitt Conference, March 1992, p. 25.

preliminary in nature, since all of the studies at RPI have been done on a small scale. It would not be surprising if the processing costs were found to increase substantially over those estimated upon scale-up of the process. Particularly uncertain is how to handle the residue in the leach tank and the impact of contaminants arising from the polymer feed.

Some limited studies indicate that this selective dissolution process can also be applied to:

- Recovery of polyvinylchloride and polyethylene from wire and cable shredder residue;
- Segregation of components from multilayer extrusions;
- Recovery of nylon and polypropylene from carpets.

However, no analysis has been made of the attractiveness of the process when applied to these feedstocks. Also, information on the purity of the material obtained from such feedstocks is quite limited. In particular, the fate of the plasticizers and other fillers in solution processing of PVC remains a problem.

Generally, the purity of the individual plastics recovered by application of the RPI technology is greater than 98%, the remainder being primarily other polymers that can be left in the base resin without detriment, since they are microdispersed, and remain dispersed even through downstream processing steps such as injection molding [531, 533, 534, 895].

With the polymer in solution, there is an opportunity to conduct additional treatments that may enhance the value of the recovered plastics. For example:

- The polymer solution can be passed through a far finer mesh screen than can be used with the very viscous melts to remove trace contaminants. However, this requires that the polymer solution has a low concentration of solids; otherwise, flow through the screen would be significantly restricted.
- Adsorption treatment of low-viscosity polymer solutions with activated carbon or clay for the removal of trace additives, such as antioxidants and pigments, is also possible. If successful the solvent process may, thus, be the only route to recovery of essentially virgin polymer.
- Modification of the polymer is facilitated, since additional components could be incorporated in the dissolved plastic. For example, elastomers could be added to the recovered polystyrene solution to produce an impact grade, or ultra-high molecular weight polyethylene could be added to a recovered polyethylene fraction to improve its blow molding properties [531, 534].

All of these additional treatments are feasible only at low polymer solution viscosities, that is, at low concentration of polymer solids.

7.2.2 ANL Process

The Argonne National Laboratory (ANL) has concentrated its studies on the treatment of auto shredder residue (ASR) to recover the polymer content and to also reduce landfill requirements [93, 568, 806].

ANL envisions that the ASR currently produced would be screened and elutriated to separate out the shredded polyurethane foam settling out a heavy solid fines fraction. The polyurethane foam would then be washed in hexane or acetone to remove any oil contamination. Current studies suggest that the cleaned foam could conceivably be incorporated into low-cost rug paddings. The heavy fines would be separated into an iron-rich magnetic fraction that could be recycled to a steel plant. The remaining solids would go to a landfill.

After removal of the polyurethane foam and the solids fines, the mixed plastics would again be rinsed with hexane or acetone to remove the soluble oils. A sequence of solvents would then be used to separate cuts of ABS, PVC, and mixed polyethylene polymers. In the laboratory, the separation has been accomplished by refluxing each solvent in turn over a solid bed of the ASR. The insoluble portion that could not be dissolved is largely cross-linked or thermoset polymers; this portion would be sent to a waste-to-energy unit.

All of the work to date has been at a bench-scale level directed at demonstrating process feasibility. Design of a five-ton-per-day pilot unit utilizing commercially available equipment is underway. To date, little work has been done on isolation of polymers from their respective solutions

Other Solution Processes

A patent issued to E.A. Haffner [803], an entrepreneur, claims recovery of PVC from scrap by dissolution in methylisobutylketone (MIBK) followed by precipitation of the PVC from the MIBK solution with methanol. Anecdotal information suggests that Haffner has been working on the process for several years on a small scale. However, there is no evidence that the process has been commercialized.

Tingyu et al. [449] have patented a solution process to recover PVC from wire/cables. Thus, PVC-covered copper wires were chopped, left 40 min in xylene at 95°C, mixed with CCl_4, and stirred to separate PVC and copper with 83.9% and 99.8% recovery, respectively.

7.3   Assessment and Relevance to Critical Waste Streams

Selective dissolution processes are, in principle, suitable for handling commingled post-consumer plastic scrap after the metal, glass, and other insoluble solids have been removed. Undoubtedly, the process could be adapted to recover plastics from the fluff generated during wire and cable stripping operations directed at metal recovery. In addition, the process may also be attractive for carpets as well as for recovering thermoplastics from auto shredder residue.

The advantages of selective dissolution are clear:

• A number of different polymers can be recovered in relatively pure ($\geq 98\%$) form from commingled scrap with minor segregation.

- Individual polymeric components can be recovered from co-extruded materials, polyblends or alloys.
- Contaminants can be filtered out.
- Modifiers that may produce recovered polymers with properties approaching virgin polymers can be uniformly incorporated, also while in the solution stage.
- In principle, the solution could be processed to remove additives, fillers, and pigments present in the polymers; removal would produce a truly recycled pure polymer. Thus, lead compounds and other contaminants from wire/cable scrap could be removed, provided economics become favorable. The recovered pure polymer could be reutilized with addition of suitable additives package.
- The process has a significant tolerance for wet feeds. However, the presence of moisture might complicate the solvent recovery process. Undoubtedly, the first waste polymer stream to consider for selective dissolution is the commingled scrap residue that is regenerated after the reclamation of HDPE and PET bottles.

Unfortunately, the use of selective dissolution requires extensive solvent handling. To limit solvent losses to acceptable limits mandated by federal and state regulations requires using modern petrochemical design and operating practices. Moreover, a large plant of roughly 50–100 million lb/yr in capacity may be required for the process to be economically justified.

Selective dissolution, in principle, provides a technique for recovery of most polymers from post-consumer waste. It may also be possible to target it to recover higher valued products left over as being currently unrecoverable by other techniques.

Some of the potential limitations of the RPI and similar processes with reference to wire/cable scrap could be:

(a) A mixed plasticizer stream is obtained (20–40% of the composition). The mixed plasticizer may have little commercial value and not cover the recovery costs.

(b) The mixed additives stream obtained will contain $CaCO_3$, Al_2O_3, Sb_2O_3, PbO, and other heavy metals. The presence of PbO will cancel any potential commercial value. However, at least there would be a smaller quantity of material to go to landfill.

Part III

Status, Development and Assessment of Recycling Technologies

Chapter 8

Melt Reprocessing of Generic Thermoplastics

8.1 Present Status

General

At the present time, recycling of generic thermoplastics in the U.S. involves mostly "reprocessing" of reclaimed post-consumer material and industrial scrap/regrind by remelting/reforming in standard polymer processing equipment. The reclaimed plastics are often reformulated with virgin resin and/or additives for improved properties.

Plastics recycling in the U.S. during the last few years has focused mainly on packaging. Some of the reasons are: waste plastics packaging has high visibility; it is a significant component of the municipal solid waste stream (about 8% by vol.); it has a short life cycle and shows continuous growth in post-consumer and other applications.

Six commodity thermoplastics (PET, HDPE, LDPE, PP, PVC, PS) constitute 97% of all plastics packaging found in the MSW stream. Commodity and engineering thermoplastics in the form of durable items may also be found in the MSW, but mostly in other feedstocks such as industrial scrap, building and construction waste, automotive waste, etc. Over the past few years significant advances have been made towards the development of processing equipment and auxiliary machinery for recycled plastics. A number of references in the bibliography describe recent activities on granulators, feeders, agglomerators, extruders, etc. General information on markets for recycled thermoplastics can be found in Refs. [125, 193, 218, 229]. The following sections summarize the present status of recycling by "reprocessing" of the major thermoplastics, and include examples of current markets and applications of recycled products.

PET

Feedstocks for recycled PET are mostly soft drink bottles and films/fibers. The total 1990 U.S. market for recycled bottle PET was 165 million lb [788, p. 60] with only 10 million lb recycled by chemical conversion to polyols. The remaining 155 million lb were recycled by reprocessing as follows: Fiber (fiberfill, staple, carpeting), 129; extruded strapping, 12; alloys and compounds (e.g. PC/PET blends, glass-reinforced PET), 11; extruded sheeting, 2; bottles and containers, 1.

A description of commercial and developmental activities related to PET bottle recycling, flake characterization, solid-stating and products and applications can be found in Refs. [14, 69, 71–73, 76, 77, 80, 154, 170, 172, 249, 443].

Polyolefins

Feedstocks for recycled polyolefins are rigid containers, films, foams, wire and cable jacketing, PP battery cases, etc. There exist now in the U.S. at least five resin suppliers producing PCR (post-consumer resin) PE flakes, reclaimed mostly from containers; PCR is reprocessed by extrusion, blow molding, or in injection molding equipment. Dow Chemical is producing molding compounds containing mixtures of virgin and PCR at various combinations. It is to be noted that virgin HDPE is presently (1992) less expensive than recycled ($.25/lb vs. $0.31/lb for the lowest PCR)[1]. Typical applications for the recycled plastics include: soap and detergent bottles, drainage pipes, fencing, merchandise bags, trash containers, new battery cases, drums, barrels, tapes and fabrics, etc. In most cases, reclaimed material is used in combination with virgin; for monolayer or coextruded containers, targeted reclaimed incorporation levels are 25% by weight.

A description of commercial and developmental activities related to recycling of HDPE containers can be found in Refs. [46, 77, 107, 408]; PE scrap film in Refs. [58, 67]; PP tapes, fibers in Ref. [395]; agricultural film in Refs. [31, 33].

Polystyrene

Feedstocks for recycled PS originate mostly from food contact applications and cushion packaging. Dow Chemical is marketing PS molding compounds containing various amounts of PCR for injection molding applications. End uses of recycled PS include miscellaneous densified (cassettes, flower pots, etc.) and non-densified (void fill, thermal insulation, etc.) applications. A description of commercial and developmental activities related to PS and EPS post-consumer end-uses can be found in Refs. [90, 162, 451].

PVC

Feedstocks for recycled PVC include bottles, calendered sheet, building products, automotive waste, wire and cable, plastisol products, agricultural and packaging films. Very little PVC exists in MSW as packaging; most of it is in non-MSW streams since PVC is heavily used in other applications (mostly construction-related). PVC recycling is in its infancy in most post-consumer applications although reuse of post-industrial scrap is time-honored. Active commercial programs in the U.S. to recover and reprocess vinyl bottles, wire and cable insulation,

---

[1]"Plastics Recycling Issues", A monthly briefing, March 1992, Phillip Townsend Associates.

rigid films are described in Ref. [405]. A description of commercial and developmental activities on recycling of PVC bottles to new PVC compounds can be found in Refs. [88, 89]; PVC Film and Sheet, industrial scrap, and others in Refs. [28, 32, 63].

Engineering Thermoplastics

Feedstocks for engineering thermoplastics include mostly industrial scrap, automotive scrap and some durables, since very small amounts appear in the MSW. Recycling is in its infancy with the exception of PET as discussed above; in general, no economic incentives exist at this time for the recycling of engineering resins. Examples of some commercial and developmental activities for durable applications include PET in new alloys and compounds, PC as single resin or in blends, PPE from computer housings for roofing applications, nylon gillnets into bicycle seats [798]; it is not clear if ABS from scrapped telephones is still recycled by certain telephone companies [788].

Acrylics

Feedstocks for acrylics include mostly pre-consumer industrial and automotive scrap. Current recycling technologies involve depolymerization and to a lesser extent regrinding/reprocessing. Regrinds may be used in dry paint stripping as the blasting medium since they leave the primer layer undamaged; they may be redissolved in acrylic syrup, or repelletized and molded into reflectors.

8.2 Developments

General

Developmental or experimental work in the general area of thermoplastics recycling by reprocessing addresses the following major concerns:

- Identification of new markets and new product applications [799, 3, 48], including non-plastics such as asphalt modification;
- Design and improvement of processing and auxiliary equipment to accommodate not only the various forms (e.g. films, fibers, foam), but also the variable purity of the reclaimed material (see, for example, Ref. [47]);
- The incorporation of the recyclability concept in the designing of plastics products [36];
- The effects of repeated reprocessing on properties; the prediction of properties after nth recycling [43, 791, 334, 781, 236]; the role of contaminants and stabilizers [25, 56, 121, 381, 393].

Developments related to specific thermoplastics are summarized below.

PET

Advanced reclamation technologies exist, or, are under development to minimize bottle contaminants, e.g. metals and adhesives, that may catalyze PET hydrolysis during processing (alkaline compounds, acidic components, components of hot melt adhesives) or affect color; also, technologies for the removal of silver and PVDC from films. New uses for recycled PET are under investigation [157].

Polyolefins

To minimize the effects of contaminants on certain properties of recycled containers, high ESCR virgin HDPE is mixed with 25% PCR or PCR is sandwiched between two layers of virgin polymers; similarly, new automotive fuel tanks are made from recycled/virgin HDPE [329]. More information on the role of contaminants can be found in Ref. [29] (contaminated fertilizer PE bags), Ref. [783] (HDPE regrind cleanliness for ESCR), Ref. [399] (removal of paint from PP bumpers for recycling), and in Ref. [788 (pp. 93–96)]. The effects of virgin content, fillers and additives on recycled PP scrap are discussed in Refs. [165, 166, and 788 (p. 96)]. The adverse effect of PVC contamination at 5% level on the processability, thermooxidative stability and properties of LDPE films is discussed in Ref. [25].

PVC

Most efforts in PVC recycling are focusing on the separation from PET or other polymers in mixed plastics streams; this is critical, since PVC degrades at PET processing temperatures, whereas PET does not melt at the PVC processing temperatures. To minimize contamination from PET and other polymers, commercial programs are considering techniques such as melt filtration below the melting point of PET, proprietary dry separation processes, and froth flotation. Automatic sorting devices which uniquely identify vinyl plastic containers through technologies based on X-ray fluorescence and electromagnetic radiation absorption are under evaluation (Ref. [405]). The current thinking of an automotive producer (Ford Germany) is to eliminate PVC from future applications where it is in intimate contact with other solid plastics. For waste streams containing fully formulated flexible PVC, major efforts on the part of PVC producers focus on resin purification (e.g. lead stabilizer removal, plasticizer removal). The production of relatively pure resin would facilitate the identification of new markets and applications for new compounds.

Reprocessing for traffic cones from recycled W/C PVC is described in Ref. [795]; (it is thought that, since injection molded items have smaller area/mass than the ground fluff and cones would be painted, only minute amounts of lead stabilizer could leach out). The use of PVC bottles and W/C waste for new compounds is described in Refs. [88, 89, 366, 381]. The removal of plasticizer from PVC followed by crushing and reuse is discussed in Ref. [203].

Engineering Thermoplastics

Concern has been expressed that billions of pounds of engineering thermoplastics are incinerated or landfilled since there are no programs that result in economic incentives for the recycling of durables [788, p. 166]. Some potential applications for nylon fibers extracted mechanically from carpets are their reuse in non-woven applications and felts, or as compounding ingredients for polymer blends [332]. Cleaning and removal of contaminants from PC compact disks, and melt filtering of PPE discarded computer housings are described in Refs. [539, 332], respectively. The effects of repeated processing on the properties of glass reinforced nylon 66 are described in Ref. [19], and for PC industrial scrap in Refs. [22, 26]. The properties of weathered nylon and polyolefin fibrous fishing gear as related to their recyclability are discussed in Ref. [808].

8.3   Assessment

8.3.1   Markets and Applications

At the present time recycling rates of generic thermoplastics vs. virgin sales are very low. According to Bennett's 1989 data [799] actual recovery was about 10% only for PET; for other commodity thermoplastics, recoveries did not exceed 2% of the total sales. Projections for 1996 are presented in Table 8-1. With the development

Table 8-1 1996 Markets for Recycled Commodity Polymers

Polymer	Millions of pounds		% of virgin resin sales	Major markets[c] for recycled resins
	Virgin resin sales[a]	Recycled resin sales[b]		
PET[d]	2,274	646	(28)	bottles, film, sheeting, strapping, textile
HDPE	10,155	562	(5.5)	bottles, pails, pipe, crates
LDPE	19,590	2,316	(12)	bags, wraps, films, sheets
PP	9,710	1,023	(11)	bottles, appliances, toys, batteries, furniture
PVC	9,287	563	(6)	flooring, sheets, pipe, window profiles, hoses
PS	6,640	578	(9)	appliances, toys, packaging, building

Source: Adapted from Ref. [799].
[a]Projected 1996 sales at a 3% growth rate from 1990.
[b]Projected 1996 sales.
[c]Markets for recycled resins; > 10% penetration.
[d]Recycled PET markets, in addition to remolding/forming to non-food applications and textiles, include chemical conversion applications to UPR, reinforced UPR and PUR.

of new markets, the rate could increase to about 30% for PET, but would not exceed 12% for the other thermoplastics. Some potential markets with more than 10% penetration are presented in Table 8-1. Bennett's market penetration estimates obviously depend on many factors such as: type of market (e.g. for food applications and medical uses zero or very low penetration is assumed); purity of feedstock; characteristics of reclaimed resin; ratio of virgin/recycled, etc. However, it does not appear that Bennett's estimates consider the effects of technological advances in the areas of cost efficient sortation/reclamation methods, or polymer stabilization; such advances could open up new markets or increase the share of recycled materials in existing ones.

8.3.2   Limitations due to Existing Reclamation Methods

Improved and more cost-effective reclamation methods will be able to:

(a) Minimize the concentration of impurities which may adversely affect reprocessing and/or reuse. For example, problems with HDPE PCR that prevent its reuse in original applications are: color, odor, contamination (polymer/ non-polymeric), mixed grades (MFI variation). For bottles, some of these problems are overcome by diluting with virgin resin (new recycle-tolerant grades), or by producing three-layer bottles (pigmented virgin outer-PCR middle-unpigmented virgin inner). It should be noted that in bottles containing PCR, dispersed contaminants may not be a problem if pellets rather than flakes are used in the molding operations, since contaminants can be screened out in the extrusion/pelletizing step. Problems related to color, odor, and purity of feedstock should be minimized through selective dissolution reclamation processes; this reclamation process would produce a mixture of polymers with a broad MWD suitable for specific applications.

(b) Produce PCR that could compete with virgin on a cost/performance basis. This would obviously depend on the type of polymer. For example, present end-uses of PET are mostly fiberfill or carpeting and, thus, economic incentives exist. However, virgin HDPE is presently less expensive than recycled; thus, no economic incentives are apparent for PCR alone. Mixing with virgin resin helps in meeting the industry target for 25% recyclable content and at the same time contributes to maintain desired color and enhance ESCR performance.

8.3.3   Limitations due to Polymer Stability

8.3.3.1   General

Plastics vary a lot in their stability during melt processing and during use. Degradation after repeated recycling is usually accompanied by severe loss in properties; this may be offset or delayed with proper stabilizers and is reduced by combining the recycled material with virgin material. The most important types of degradation are thermooxidative, mechanical, photooxidative/weathering, and hydrolytic/solvolytic.

- Impurities affect stability and, in particular, oxidative stability; examples include the presence of hydroperoxides or weak links in the polymer chain, metallic remnants from Ziegler catalysts. Metals (Fe, Cu, Al, Co, etc.), either in metallic form, or as components of pigments, accelerate decomposition of hydroperoxides, which are the primary products of oxidation.
- In principle, all polymers are susceptible to mechanical degradation, which may occur during processing or end-use. In the former case, it depends on the type of process and magnitude of stresses, temperature, atmosphere, etc. During end-use, it would depend on application.
- Structural irregularities (hydroperoxides, carbonyl, double bonds) or impurities from manufacturing (catalyst residues) may cause light absorption at >290 nm and photodegradation for most saturated polymers including polyolefins. Aging involves the combined action of oxygen, UV, heat, and pollutants such as NO_2, SO_2, O_3 that may cause chain scission or crosslinking; degradation at the surface will be followed by cracking and failure.
- Condensation polymers are mostly susceptible to hydrolytic/solvolytic degradation which may lead to MW reduction.

The stability of specific (unstabilized) polymers to various degradative agencies is summarized in Table 8-2. Criteria for degradation include: loss of mechanical properties; yellowing; changes in solution and melt viscosity; weight loss; loss of transparency; surface changes; change in MW. For example: yellowing is mostly important for styrenics, PUR, PC, PVC; solution viscosity is important for PA, PC, PET; weight loss for POM; embrittlement for polyolefins; mechanical properties and melt viscosity for most plastics. In laboratory tests, degradation is assessed by repeated extrusion (for reprocessing), and oven aging or artificial weathering (for end-use).

Table 8-2 Susceptibility of Unstabilized Polymers to Degradation

Polymer	Resistance to degradative process		
	Thermooxidative (processing/in use)	Photooxidative/ weathering	Hydrolytic (processing/in use)
PE	p	p	e
PP	vp	vp	e
PVC	vp	p	e
PS	f	p	e
PMMA	g	e	e
PET	g	g	p/g
PA	f	f	p/f
PC	f	p	f/g
PPO	vp	f	g

Key: e = excellent; g = good; f = fair; p = poor; vp = very poor
Source: Adapted from Ref. [789 (p. 129)].

8.3.3.2 Importance of Stabilizers

General ranking of commercial plastics according to their degradative stability during processing and end-use is difficult; it should take into account origin of degradation, level and type of contaminants, type of end-use, and, of course, types and concentration of stabilizers. Stabilizers protect against thermal, thermooxidative, photooxidative and in some cases biological and chemical attack. However, during service they may be lost due to migration (leaching), evaporation, or consumption by bacteria. The stabilization requirements of virgin plastics are varied. Polyolefins and styrenics are the biggest consumers of antioxidants whereas polyolefins are the biggest consumers of light stabilizers. PVC processing stabilizers are very specific.

The stabilization requirements of recycled plastics are as varied as those of the virgin resins. Limited information is available on the stabilization requirements of recovered plastics [121, 809 Ch. 10]. Until more information is available, it has been recommended to use stabilizers in amounts which would be used in virgin materials for the same application. Table 8-3 [121] summarizes types and concentrations of stabilizers that are expected to perform also with recycled polyolefins, PS and weathering applications of PVC.

8.3.4 Blending/Recycling Mathematics

In estimating degradation due to repeated recycling it is important to define a critical property that changes with the number of recycles. In recycling industrial scrap, Throne [43] suggested various algorithms for determining final product properties, given single-pass property loss and fraction of recycle in the resin mixture. The single-pass property loss may be related to the mixture property

Table 8-3 Stabilizers and Concentrations Used at Various Stages in Hydrocarbon Polymers

Stage	Stabilizer	Usual concentration
Drying	antioxidant	<250 ppm
Storage	antioxidant	<250 ppm
Compounding	antioxidant +	500–1,000 ppm
	phosphite	500–1,000 ppm
Fabrication	same as compounding	
End-use:		
– Low stress	same as compounding	
– Thermal stress	antioxidant +	1,000–5,000 ppm
	thiosynergist +	1,000–5,000 ppm
	phosphite	500–1,000 ppm
– Weathering	antioxidant +	0–1,000 ppm
	phosphite +	500–1,000 ppm
	hindered amine +	0–10,000 ppm
	UV absorber	0–10,000 ppm

Source: Adapted from Ref. [121].

linearly (tensile strength), in a power-law fashion (impact strength), logarithmically (viscosity and intrinsic viscosity), or in an offset fashion (fire retardancy). Linear, power law and logarithmic algorithms yield closed solutions for steady-state processes; however, the offset case results in a nested series that converges in about 20 steps.

In general, it may be shown that products incorporating recycled materials which have undergone significant degradation per pass, may still retain a large proportion of the original virgin value, even after many passes. This retention is a result of the incorporation of the fresh virgin resin in each pass and the bleed off of old polymer into non-recycled fraction. However, the development of algorithms that can accommodate additional property loss during use (e.g. aging) is a complex task given the variety of existing processes, stabilization levels, contaminants and different products with life spans ranging from less than one year to more than 10 years.

8.3.5   Summary/Research Needs

Higher recycling rates for generic thermoplastics are obviously related to: (a) the existence of economic incentives; (b) the development and identification of new products and applications; and (c) the development of cost efficient sortation/reclamation methods. Markets for post-consumer HDPE will succeed on their own when the price of PCR is less than virgin material. While it is true that the cost associated with the reclamation process is important, the costs of collection, handling and sortation are more important and make recycled HDPE unattractive.

Designing for recyclability and the development of specialized reprocessing equipment (both primary and auxiliary) are definitely important contributing factors to the growth of recycled generic thermoplastics. However, the present low recycling rates may also be related to:

(a) The limited inherent stability of the majority of polymers during reprocessing and in-use; and
(b) The lack of predictive models for property loss after repeated reprocessing and use.

Suggestions for specific research areas are as follows:

- Develop information on the stabilizer requirements of recovered plastics and relate to polymer structure, contaminants and conditions encountered during service life (lives);
- Develop stabilizers that mix well, disperse easily and remain in the resin during many "lives", i.e. no migration, no extraction, not consumed by bacteria;
- Maximize recyclability (regardless of intended original use) of a given polymer grade (as measured by repeated extrusion passes and time in oven aging) through the use of both short and long term stabilizers. Create "recyclable" grades and develop accelerated stability specifications that should be met by each

"recyclable" plastic grade sold. Aim for five "lives" if plastic is recycled 100%; for ten "lives", if diluted with virgin resin;

- Develop and test predictive algorithms for property losses after repeated recycling; apply in the design of prototypes based on recycled material;
- Develop and test the cascade concept that is currently discussed in the automotive industry (e.g. Fiat). According to this concept, recovered plastics could be used in increasingly less demanding applications in terms of appearance and performance, e.g. bumpers to trimmings, trimmings to undercarpets; after several applications the recycled plastics would have lost their properties and be sold as fuels;
- Investigate the effects of repeated recycling, not only on the polymer matrix but also on reinforcement degradation; by contrast to glass and carbon fibers which are normally reduced in aspect ratio during recycling, new thermoplastic composites ideal for automotive applications would be based on LCP that can be reportedly reprocessed seven times without appreciable degradation [791].

8.4   Relevance to Critical Waste Streams

The above assessment of research needs is obviously related to all four critical waste streams from which generic thermoplastics can be recovered by suitable sortation/reclamation methods. Particular attention should be paid to items where moderate or high exposure to sunlight is expected; these items are mostly used in the building industry and certain packaging applications, e.g. PVC, UPR, PC, PE (sidings, door, roofing, liners, glazing, fixtures, agricultural film), etc.

Chapter 9

Melt Reprocessing of Generic Thermosets

9.1   Present Status

Thermoset recycling in the U.S. presents a significant opportunity (thermosets account for 9 billion lb/yr sales). Most thermosets are used in durable applications and as such appear mostly in non-MSW streams. Overall, thermoset recycling has not reached advanced levels; for example, 93% of all rigid PUR foam scrap is currently landfilled. Feedstocks containing potentially recyclable thermosets include mostly industrial scrap, automotive sources or demolition waste. Typical thermoset plastics include PUR foam (flexible and rigid), PUR RIM and cast elastomers, phenolics, UPR SMC and BMC, cross-linked PE and vulcanized rubbers (the latter are not part of this study). Fillers and reinforcements that are commonly present in thermoset formulations, often at high loadings, may add to the complexity of the contemplated recycling process.

Recycling of thermosets may be carried out by reprocessing or chemical conversion (solvolysis and pyrolysis); energy recovery in appropriate combustion facilities is an alternative method. The reprocessing methods for thermosets are different from those employed for thermoplastics since thermosets exhibit only limited or no flow under heat and pressure. Thermoset reprocessing in the melt usually involves the incorporation of the reclaimed/reground material into a new polymer formulation intended for the same or different application. Examples are:

- Addition of reground scrap as filler/extender back into the same uncured thermosetting resin, or in thermoplastics. The regrind normally does not undergo any flow or deformation.
- Thermal reprocessing (e.g. by compression molding of certain PUR scrap) with or without additional binder. The regrind may undergo some flow or deformation.

Applications of recycled thermoset products by reprocessing are today limited; few examples include:

- Recycling of regrind produced cryogenically or otherwise in the original applications. For example, as of November 1992 there were three commercial SMC auto parts in Europe and one in Japan that use SMC plant scrap as filler ($CaCO_3$ replacement); in the U.S., GM scheduled the use of SMC parts containing 8% regrind in the '93 Corvettes [784, 810]; in PUR foams a maximum 10% regrind is used [409].

- Miscellaneous applications, such as rebonded carpet underlay for flexible PUR foam, gardening substrates from rebonded foam scrap and the use of regrind as a blasting medium for paint removal.

9.2   Developments

Most of the recent developmental/experimental work is focused on maximizing the amount of thermoset regrind incorporated in phenolics, epoxies, PUR, BMC, SMC or thermoplastics with a minimum reduction in properties and/or surface appearance [788 Ch. 10]. Examples of related topics are as follows:

- Size reduction equipment necessary to produce fine particles (less than 80 mesh) and minimize effects on part surface quality [809 Ch. 22];
- Recycling of automotive SMC, PUR, and RIM scrap by grinding and adding in virgin [105, 123, 784, 809 Ch. 22];
- Problems in retaining Class-A finish at high SMC regrind contents [810];
- Maximum amounts of phenolic [784] or PUR [105] regrind in virgin;
- Cross-linked PE (25–35%) used as a filler in virgin [390, 565];
- Development of a new RRIM mixing head to incorporate scrap RIM into the same type of part which was originally used without irregular cell formation and surface defects that can result from the absorption of the chain extender by the powdered scrap [794];
- Development of a three stream process to incorporate RIM regrind into fascia, since the regrind is dispersed in the polyol component and it may not interact adversely with the chain extender [809 Ch. 22];
- Development of chemically cross-linked RIM polyureas that can also be thermally reprocessed [784];
- Compression molding of granulated scrap RIM material at 175°C, 2600 psi, for 3 min to form parts with adequate properties for some non-appearance automotive applications [809 Ch. 22];
- Evaluation of compatibilizers/adhesion promoters in polyethylene filled with RIM regrind (up to 25%) to improve properties [809 Ch. 22];
- Development of a multiple stage shredding process to separate the glass fibers from the waste SMC parts [367]; the fibers may be used as a reinforcement while the powder is a filler for new BMC [811].

A proprietary technology (Solid State Shear Extrusion) under development at the Illinois Institute of Technology, Chicago, IL [820] claims to produce fine powders of less than 100 micron size from PUR foam, phenolic resins, rubber tires and a variety of thermoplastics. Examples and potential applications of powders produced by a similar technology (elastic deformation, pulverization) are described in recent publications by Enikolopyan [834] and Shevchenko et al. [835].

In other developments it has been recently reported that organosilicon chemicals can increase the mechanical properties of PP filled with reground SMC scrap[1].

Some new uses and applications are discussed in the following references:

- [38], flexible PUR scrap from furniture;
- [407], sintered panels for construction from reclaimed PUR/binder.

9.3   Assessment

An important research area in the recycling of generic thermosets by reprocessing would be the synthesis of new "thermally processable" materials combining the flow characteristics of thermoplastics with the desirable characteristics of thermosets. Present R&D efforts in the development of thermally processable RIM polyureas should extend to other types of polymers. The development of such materials could open new avenues in the recycling of thermosets and compete favorably with chemical conversion or incineration.

Although thermoplastics may be reprocessed several times, there exist limitations in the number and frequency of remelting/reshaping before properties degrade. Cured thermosets when used as fillers may have an advantage since, in principle, they could be used repeatedly without degradation and loss of performance (unless, of course, degradation occurred as a result of weathering or during end-use). Further research may be required to confirm this important characteristic of thermosets reclaimed from different end-uses.

The advancement of reprocessing technologies based on the reuse of generic thermoset regrind as a filler should also benefit from research in the following areas:

- The development of uncontaminated feedstocks; this is related directly to more efficient reclamation and disassembly methods;
- The economic production of ground powders with controlled particle size and particle size distribution; this may lead to higher loadings and better properties;
- Development of applications where the cost/performance ratio of the thermoset regrind may compete with that of the fillers which will replace;
- Improved compatibility of regrind powders with the matrix, particularly when the matrix is structurally different (e.g. PUR RIM regrind in polyolefins); this may also lead to higher loadings, better surface appearance and improved properties;
- Development of new end-uses of thermoplastic molding compounds containing the reground thermoset.

---

[1]Anonymous, Plastics Technology, p. 35, February 1993.

9.4   Relevance to Critical Waste Streams

Recycling of thermoset waste is highly relevant to the following two critical waste streams:

- Automotive; this stream may include used parts (disassembled, or ground up and present in "fluff") as well as industrial scrap from part production. Estimates are that roughly 22% of the plastics used in automobiles are PUR, and 24% miscellaneous thermosets (notably, polyester-based SMC).
- Wire and cable; cross-linked PE jacketing may be a major component in high voltage cables.

Chapter 10

Melt Reprocessing of Commingled Polymers

10.1 Present Status

10.1.1 General

Collection of post-consumer plastics discards provides a wide variety of polymeric materials. While several generic plastics can be separated from the commingled stream efficiently, a significant fraction remains which cannot be recovered as individual polymers. The residue mixture can consist of:

- Non-recognizable plastic items;
- Minor amounts of specific polymers;
- Multilayer plastic packaging;
- Composite items made of plastics and one or more additional materials;
- Highly contaminated items;
- Highly pigmented or filled generics;
- Different MW grades of the same polymer;
- Waste from reclaiming operations.

Since, at the present time, cost-effective technologies to separate and clean the commingled streams do not exist, these residues or "tailings" are either landfilled or the plastic mixture (predominantly thermoplastic) is melt reprocessed by converting into thick sectioned shapes or products. The presence of unmelted particles and contaminants, and the incompatibility of the different polymers in the mixed waste do not allow the production of thinner wall articles and, thus, limit applications. However, useful articles with acceptable physical/mechanical properties have been produced from the contaminated commingled post-consumer waste plastics stream. While mechanical properties are generally inferior to those of the virgin polymers, these plastics mixtures will perform adequately in specialized or less demanding applications. Classic end products are lumber substitutes such as park benches, decking in marine environments, road markers and highway posts. Unfortunately, the commingled plastics products have not met with significant commercial success and only a small percentage of the potential quantity of commingled post-consumer plastics are currently being processed. The main reason for the slow growth is a lack of competitiveness in cost-performance.

Current commingled plastics processes are capable of utilizing post-consumer waste plastics, a variety of plastic plant scraps, and various percentages of fillers.

The recycling of rigid plastic containers, the most widely available and readily collectable of post-consumer waste plastic, has been the focus of much attention in the U.S.

Some rigid containers such as unpigmented HDPE plastic milk bottles and PET plastic carbonated beverage bottles are easy to identify and separate from a MSW stream. These containers have been "standardized" since a specific polymer is identified with a particular packaged product, e.g. HDPE with milk and PET with soda. Unfortunately, containers for household cleaners, cooking oils, foods and motor oil, can vary in shape, color, and/or polymeric composition from manufacturer to manufacturer. Since these containers are not easily identifiable, separating them by resin type is both difficult and expensive.

To facilitate sortation, legislation in many states has required the use of SPI identification symbols of containers. Many molders have also voluntarily incorporated these symbols on their molds. However, products made from these recycled resins have limited markets because of the great variety of pigmentation, additives and molecular weight grades used within a single SPI code for a polymer. In addition, collection systems across the U.S. have found that when milk and soft drink bottles are collected for recycling, 15 to 30% of other plastic bottles are deposited into the collection system. These containers come in a large array of sizes, shapes, colors, polymer types (including multi-layer products based on several polymers); a very high portion are made of olefinic (e.g. PP and PE) polymers. These factors make it very difficult to process and reclaim them as pure resin feedstocks.

10.1.2   Processing

Several manufacturing processes have been developed specifically for processing commingled plastics feedstocks from household and other post-consumer and post-commercial sources; they are described in detail in Ref. [788]. These processes can be categorized into four basic types: intrusion based on Klobbie's design, continuous extrusion, the "Reverzer" process, and compression molding. Each is capable of producing products from a variety of macroscopically inhomogeneous mixtures of waste plastics containing some degree of contamination. Commingled processes are limited to producing products of large cross-sections, where small internal imperfections may be of little consequence for the mechanical properties. For all these processes, studies on a variety of samples produced using different combinations of commingled plastics as feedstocks have been found to yield properties which are heavily dependent upon the composition.

Klobbie-Based Intrusion Processes   In the 1970s, E. Klobbie of the Netherlands began developing a system for processing "unsorted" thermoplastic synthetic resin waste material into an article having the working and processing properties of wood. His system consisted of an extruder, several long, linear molds of large cross-sections mounted on a rotating turret, and a tank of cooling water into which the turret is partially submerged [846, 847][1].

The extruder works on and softens the thermoplastics mixture; it then forces it into one of the molds without using a screen-pack or an extrusion nozzle. After one mold has been filled, the turret rotates in order to fill the next mold. Eventually, each mold slowly passes underneath the coolant level in the tank, where the plastic is cooled, solidified, and shrinks away from the mold, pulling coolant into the gap between the product and mold surface.

The Klobbie process is a cross between conventional injection molding and extrusion. Therefore, it has been termed an "intrusion" process. While Klobbie never patented his system in the U.S., he did patent the use of foaming agents in his equipment [846]. Several companies have produced variations of Klobbie's equipment (Advanced Recycling Technology of Belgium, Hammer's Plastic Recycling of Iowa, and Superwood of Ireland).

Continuous Extrusion   Variations of the Klobbie intrusion process has been used to produce linear profiles from mixed plastic waste. These continuously extrude molten polymeric material of large cross-sections into cooled dies, in a manner similar to continuous pipe manufacture. Since large cross-sections are produced the extruded material must be made to cool for a fairly long time. Polymers have low thermal conductivity and this results in significant temperature gradients during cooling between the interior and the outer skin. Consistency in raw materials is critical since surging and lack of dimensional stability for the product can otherwise result.

"Reverzer" Process   The earliest U.S. patented process for fabricating products of large cross-section from commingled plastics was developed by Mitsubishi Petrochemical and is known as the "Reverzer" process [848][2]. Commingled waste plastics were softened in a hopper, and mixed in a screw to develop a well-mixed uniform batch. Three systems were utilized for transforming this melt into useful products: flow molding, extrusion, and compression molding. The "Reverzer" process was not limited to linear shapes but was capable of producing different shaped items from commingled plastic waste. The process was capable of accepting a large variety of mixtures of contaminated commingled scrap. Mitsubishi did not successfully market this equipment and manufacture of the "Reverzer" was terminated after only eight units were produced.

Compression Molding   The most successful technology for the compression molding of commingled plastics, Recycloplast [849], was developed in Germany. Batches of thermoplastics (50–70%) and other materials are melted in a plasticator which feeds a heated extruder that produces roll-shaped loaves. The loaves are loaded into compression molds. Products are cooled in the molds and then ejected. Flashing from the molded products is transferred to a granulator for in-house

---

[1]"The Klobbie", REHSIF Bulletin No 400, Rehsif S.A., Switzerland.
[2]"The Reverzer", REHSIF Bulletin No 300, Rehsif S.A., Switzerland.

recycling. Unfortunately, the size of a Recycloplast plant is necessarily large and the capital investment is significant. However, the process is capable of producing finished thick-walled products such as pallets, grates, benches and composting boxes.

10.1.3 Commercial Activities

General information on commercial commingled plastics processing activities (mostly related to plastic lumber) can be found in Refs. [86, 168, 183, 194, 357, 363, 416]. Additional data from worldwide activities are as follows:

U.S.   A number of small business have developed to utilize the tailings of the plastics recycling program. In 1992, at least 30 manufacturers specialized in plastic lumber items such as benches, docks, fences, pallets, pilings, posts, etc. Production capacity per eight-hour shift was usually less than 6,000 lb, although few manufacturers reported capacities exceeding 12,000 lb (source "Resource Recycling").

Europe and Canada   Superwood International Ltd. established plants in England, Ireland, Canada and the U.S. which use a system named "Superflow" to fabricate solid plastic products to be used in applications as substitutes for wood. Based upon modifications of the Klobbie process, Superwood's "Jumboflow" machine is capable of an output of 2.5 times that for the original Klobbie. Feedstocks for Superwood products consist primarily of thermoplastics, HDPE, LDPE, and PP, obtained from both curbside collection programs and post-commercial operations.

About 20 million lb of plastic wastes were processed by Superwood in 1990. In October 1989, Superwood bought Plastics Recycling Ltd. This U.K. company processed supermarket plastics waste into large boards or sheets of plastics, called "Stokbord". In August 1991, Superwood International went into receivership as a result of a fire in its Irish plant. Two Canadian companies, Superwood Ontario Ltd. and Superwood Western Ltd., formed a joint venture and purchased the North American rights to the Klobbie patents from Lankhorst Recycling Ltd.

Wormser Kunststoffe Recycling GmbH (WKR), a privately held German firm, processes post-consumer plastics waste into products that are used in applications as substitutes for wood. This system uses a roller extruder that is capable of handling up to 15% of heterogeneous nonpolymeric material such as sand, glass, stones, and metal parts.

Advanced Recycling Technologies Ltd. (ART) of Belgium utilizes the ET/1 extruder to process mixed plastics waste into objects of bulky cross-section. In 1987, ET/1 machines were operating in 12 plants in Europe and Russia, with many more pending in other locations. Currently, there are estimated to be over 40 machines installed worldwide.

The ET/1 extruder is used as part of a complete waste management/recycling program owned and operated by Städtereinigung Nord (SN) in Flensburg,

Germany. SN has added finishing steps to its ET/1 product line. In addition to the traditional lumber profiles and products, they are fabricating value-added items such as sound-absorbing walls for expressways.

Recycloplast-based recycling systems for processing of mixed plastics waste, such as the Ramaplan facility of Munich, Germany, have witnessed extensive product development since 1986. This has resulted in finished materials of improved strength and appearance over original Recycloplast products.

A continuous extrusion technology developed by C.A. Greiner and Söhne in Austria has provided an efficient and viable recycling system for mixed plastics waste. The process uses commingled material from domestic waste streams to produce a variety of hollow profiles continuously; such profiles enable the production of more length per unit weight[1] and may be cut to the desired length.

10.2   Developments

Most of the current experimental and developmental work in the general area of commingled thermoplastics is focusing on the evaluation of real or simulated mixed plastics waste in terms of properties and processing characteristics; in the absence of further modification mechanical properties are usually poor. In an attempt to identify viable end uses, efforts have been made to upgrade properties through the addition of virgin resins and additives such as fillers, reinforcements, compatibilizers, coupling agents, etc. The potential of compatibilization in improving the properties of mixed polymer waste is discussed in more details in Chapter 13.

The following references contain examples of reprocessing of simulated or real waste mixtures without any further modification through additives:

- HDPE/LDPE virgin blends [27, 140];
- Model PE/PS/PP mixtures representative of those found in MSW [97];
- Mixtures of recycled PET/PBT or PP/HDPE for melt blown nonwoven fabrics production [239];
- Mixed virgin (PP/HDPE/PS) resins extruded and molded [333];
- Mixed plastics from MSW reprocessed by extrusion/injection molding [425];
- Melt filtration of PC/ABS computer casings [542];
- Evaluation of processing of recycled PP/HDPE mixtures [69];
- Mixtures of reclaimed PS with NJ Curbside tailings [364, 788, p. 200].

Examples of references describing attempts to upgrade properties through either optimization of processing parameters or through the use of additives (with the exception of compatibilizers which are discussed in Chapter 13) include:

- Modification of commingled polyolefins with recycled paper [326, 373];
- Mixed thermoplastics with sand for tiles, etc. [222];

---

[1]Greiner Extrusionstechnik, Technical literature, C.A. Greiner & Söhne, Austria.

- Mixed LDPE/PS with foaming agents [24];
- Efforts to improve properties through intensive mixing [788, pp. 200–333];
- Injection molded polyester/cotton waste blends with acceptable properties without the need for nucleating or plasticizing additives [444];
- Use of glass fibers in commingled extruded MSW [788, Ch. 9].

In the area of *coextruded multilayer* products (containers, films), the following are examples of available references:

- New PP-based multilayer film structures incorporating regrind from PP/PVDC barrier films as a distinct layer [788, p. 89];
- Multilayered PP/EVOH bottles without separation used in new multilayered bottles [797].

Additional information is available on coextruded LDPE/adhesive/nylon films [540], on recycled coextruded ABS/HIPS or PA/Surlyn products [139], and coextruded PP/EVOH [783, 103]. Some promising results were obtained with ground ketchup bottles consisting of PP/EVOH/adhesive and wood fiber reinforcement, apparently because of improved adhesion with the EVOH polar groups [809, Ch. 18]; addition of EPDM and additives at 25% produced an interesting TPO formulation which was used to mold experimental rear bumper fascia [809, Ch. 21].

The following are examples of additional references describing efforts to reprocess *complex mixtures* into useful products (often without much success):

- Reprocessing of synthetic leather consisting of PVC facing and PA fibers at temperatures below the M.P. of the PA [18];
- Molding pellets from mixed scrap obtained from junked cars to form utility products [153];
- Commingled automotive carpet scrap with a complex composition processed below and above the M.P. of the PA fibers [796];
- Recovery of the plastics fraction from nonmetallic automotive shredder residue (ASR) and use of the mixed material for low-grade applications [167, 801, 802].

In order to improve performance of the reprocessed material and allow thin sections in the final product, attempts to produce "refined" commingled plastics are described in a series of publications from CPRR Rutgers University (see [788, Ch. 9, 800]). A combination of washing and float separation, degassing and melt filtration with a minimum of polymer degradation should yield commingled products with properties approaching those made from virgin resins. Both improved properties and cost reduction are the goal. Rather than forming heavy thick sections, a "refined" plastic melt can be formed into thin sections where the advantage of complex shape permits an efficient mechanical structure with a minimum cost.

The "refined" commingled plastic process is envisaged to include:

- Wet flaking for reduction of size to feed subsequent stages and to clean surface dirt and food residue;
- Float separation to reduce metal, glass and other heavy contaminations;
- Drying to remove volatile contaminants which cause voids and odors in the final product;

- Fluxing in an extruder with a melt filter to remove infusible particles to noncritical size and number;
- Stripping in a vacuum zone to reduce volatiles and odors;
- Compounding in several stages to make uniform polymer dispersions and compositions coupled with the addition of compatibilizers, reinforcements and additives;
- Forming through a series of dies to make continuous shapes.

Information on upgrading these materials through chemical modification and the addition of compatibilizers and reinforcing agents are included in Ref. [788] and in Chapter 13.

In the area of *plastic lumber*, recent work by CPRR at Rutgers University and Washington and Lee University [850–852], focuses on the understanding of structure/properties relationships through detailed morphological examinations of samples produced in an ET/1 machine [788, Ch. 9]. The commingled feedstock used for the production of samples was obtained from the post-consumer plastic waste streams of several New Jersey communities recycling plastic containers known as New Jersey Curbside Tailings. The composition of New Jersey Curbside Tailings is as follows: HDPE 80%, LDPE 4%, PP 4%, PVC 4%, PET 4%, PS 3%, other 1%.

Examination of the cross-sectional profile of a piece of "lumber" consisting of 100% tailings showed that while the pieces are solid around the perimeter of the cross-section, the area around the center (core) contains numerous pores or voids of varying size. These voids were the result of water vapor and other gases that are not vented during processing, as well as shrinkage. A comparison of the density of the outer region with the overall density of a profile suggested that the void volume fraction due is about 10%. Improved properties were obtained through the addition of 10–30% recycled PS to the tailings. It was concluded that products which possess consistent properties and microstructure may be produced from post-consumer, commingled plastics obtained from curbside collections. Therefore, bulky products made from commingled plastics may offer a possible alternative to the use of tailings, rather than landfilling or incineration.

Additional articles on the analysis, testing, standardization and measurement of long-term properties of plastic lumber through accelerated tests can be found in Ref. 809 (Chs. 8 and 9).

10.3 Assessment

Commercial, institutional and industrial plastic streams yield tailings or residue mixtures that cannot be efficiently recovered by present-day reclamation processes. Processing of mixed thermoplastics to produce marketable products is essential for efficient plastic recycling. At the present time, separation and cleaning of these "commingled" polymers into generic polymers cannot be done in a cost effective manner. Although useful products have been produced from the mixed, unwashed, contaminated, commingled plastic packaging wastes stream that remain after removal of generic resins, the development of profitable operations has been slow because significant markets have not been developed. This reflects the inadequate performance of the products at the present cost.

Commingled processes have been dedicated towards the fabrication of bulky products which in many cases displace products made from wood. For commingled products to compete with wood over a variety of critical applications, it is desirable that they have mechanical properties which are at least equivalent to those of wood. However, economic advantages may not be as important when other benefits such as environmental safety and resistance to rot and bacteria are required.

In general, recycling of commingled plastics through reprocessing should benefit from research in the following areas:

- identification of new products/applications where molding compounds based on commingled streams may be used;
- upgrade properties through compatibilization and/or through reinforcement;
- in the absence of more advanced reclamation technologies, refining of the mixture through chopping, washing, melt filtering etc.

Additional open issues are:

- identification of suitable processing/long-term stabilizers for mixed plastics where partitioning and migration to the different phases may present major problems;
- possible adverse effects of specific additives that may be present in each component of the mixed stream; e.g., if carpets are recycled by remelting, the effects of specific additives such as antistainers need to be considered.

10.4   Relevance to Critical Waste Streams

In the absence of cost effective sortation/reclamation technologies for single polymers, recycling of commingled streams by melt reprocessing is highly relevant to all four critical waste streams:

- MSW tailings including mixed plastics and multilayer containers;
- Automotive "fluff" where reprocessing becomes more complicated due to the presence of mixed thermoplastics/thermosets;
- Textiles/carpets where fibers may not be easily separated from other fibers or backing;
- Wire and cable coverings where PE and PVC may coexist.

Chapter 11

Solvolysis

11.1 Introduction

Solvolysis reactions generally deal with the breaking of C–X bonds, where X represents hetero-(non-carbon) atoms like O, N, P, S, Si, halogen, etc. However, in the context of this chapter, we will consider solvolysis reactions applicable to polymers containing only C–O and/or C–N bonds in their backbone (not as a side group or branching), viz. polyesters, polyamides and polyurethanes. These *step-growth* polymers are often synthesized by reversible reactions and it is feasible to convert them back to their monomers (immediate starting materials) or oligomers/chemicals by various solvolytic processes such as:

- Glycolysis;
- Hydrolysis;
- Methanolysis;
- Aminolysis;
- Transesterification (ester exchange);
- Alcoholysis;
- Hydroglycolysis;
- Acidolysis;
- Transamidation (amide exchange).

The products of these reactions (monomers/oligomers as shown in Section 11.3.4) are valuable and can be used to remake the plastics. On the other hand, plastics such as PE, PP, PS, PVC, etc. (*chain-growth* polymers), are synthesized via irreversible reactions (free radical/ionic polymerization), and can be converted into basic petrochemical components (fuels, gases, chemicals or monomers) through *thermolytic* processes (pyrolysis, thermooxidative degradation, etc.)

Thus, this unique form of recycling—chemical recycling (solvolytic/thermolytic)—which is possible only with plastics, is gaining acceptance and momentum worldwide, since existing reclaim and reuse technologies are not yet adequate enough to handle complex waste streams such as wire and cable, auto-shredder fluff, carpets/textiles, blended and compounded plastics, medical disposables, etc. In general, solvolysis reactions are applicable to step-growth thermoplastics/thermosets (containing hetero-atoms in the backbone) contrary to chain growth thermoplastics, which are amenable to thermolytic and backbone chemical modification

Table 11-1 Chemical Conversion Processes for Plastics

Types of plastics	% U.S. plastic sales (1991)	Common chemical conversion processes for virgin plastics
Thermoplastics		
A. Chain-growth:		
LDPE	20.0%	*** Chemical modification
HDPE	15.1%	** Thermolytic processes
PVC	15.0%	* Solvolysis
PP	13.4%	
PS	8.0%	
Styrenics	1.9%	
ABS	1.8%	
Acrylics	1.1%	
TPE, SAN, Vinyl, other	<1.0% (each)	
B. Step-growth:		
Polyester	4.2%	*** Solvolysis
POM, PC, nylon	<1.0% (each)	** Chemical modification
		* Thermolytic processes
Thermosets		
Step-growth:		
PUR	4.9%	*** Solvolysis
Phenolics	4.2%	** Thermolytic processes
UF, MF	2.4%	* Chemical modifications
Uns. polyester	1.8%	
Epoxies, alkyds	<1.0%	

Note: ***Indicates most applicable, *least applicable.

reactions. Table 11-1 depicts a general breakdown of various thermoplastics and thermosets into chain-growth or step-growth plastics with respect to the % U.S. sales (1991) and corresponding applicable common chemical conversion processes. It can be seen from Table 11-1 that solvolysis, as the predominant conversion route for step-growth plastics, could be applicable to *only* 20% of all plastics sold in the U.S. However, step-growth plastics are more concentrated in specific waste feedstocks and, thus, solvolysis may be a potential alternative chemical conversion method in certain cases.

11.2   Characteristics of Targeted Critical Feedstocks as Related to Solvolysis

During the course of this study, four feedstock categories that are critical in terms of large volume and related total energy content were identified. Table 11-2 shows the general distribution of step-growth and chain-growth polymers in these critical feedstocks, viz.

Table 11-2 Types of Plastics in Critical Feedstocks

- MSW (post-consumer):
  Chain-growth thermoplastics (e.g. PE, PP, PVC, PS).
  Step-growth thermoplastics (e.g. polyester, PET, PUR, nylons).
- Automotive:
  Most thermoplastics (both chain-growth and step-growth) and thermosets [e.g. PUR, SMC (polyester), nylons].
- Wire and cable:
  Chain-growth thermoplastics (unmodified and crosslinked) (e.g. X-LDPE, PVC, elastomers).
- Textile/carpets:
  Chain-growth (e.g. PP, acrylics); and
  Step-growth thermoplastics (e.g. polyester, nylon).

1. MSW (municipal solid waste);
2. Automotive;
3. Wire and cable;
4. Carpets/textiles.

Based upon the current sortation/separation/reclamation technologies, it becomes apparent that three major step-growth plastics, as listed below, could be reclaimed from these critical feedstocks in relatively high purity grades:

1. PET (polyethylene terephthalate);
2. PUR (polyurethanes);
3. nylon 6 and/or nylon 66.

Thus, the scope of this chapter will be limited to the chemistry and applications of various solvolysis reactions of these three types of plastics.

11.3 Synthesis and Solvolysis Reactions of PET, Polyurethanes, and Nylons

11.3.1 Synthesis of PET

PET is a step-growth (condensation) polymer derived from terephthalic acid (TPA) or dimethyl terephthalate (DMT) and ethylene glycol (EG) according to the following chemical reactions:

$$\text{HOC}-\underset{}{\bigcirc}-\text{COH} + \text{HO}-\text{CH}_2\text{CH}_2\text{OH} \rightleftharpoons \text{HO}\left[\text{C}-\underset{}{\bigcirc}-\text{C}-\text{OCH}_2\text{CH}_2\text{O}\right]_n\text{H} + \text{H}_2\text{O} \qquad (11\text{-}1)$$

$$H_3CO-\overset{\overset{O}{\|}}{C}-\langle\bigcirc\rangle-\overset{\overset{O}{\|}}{C}-O\overset{}{C}H_3 + HO-CH_2CH_2OH \rightleftharpoons H_3CO\left[\overset{\overset{O}{\|}}{C}-\langle\bigcirc\rangle-\overset{\overset{O}{\|}}{C}-OCH_2CH_2O\right]_n H + CH_3OH \qquad (11\text{-}2)$$

These are reversible reactions, and polymerization occurs by heating these systems, typically with antimony catalyst, and removing water or methanol in order to shift the equilibrium in the forward direction (product) [788, p. 47]. Copolyesters, which are produced commercially to reduce the crystallinity of PET, are made by replacing a portion of the TPA or EG with another dibasic acid or glycol or both. The step-growth reaction occurs in two steps: first, a low molecular weight precursor is formed, which is then transesterified to form a high molecular weight reactor grade resin.

11.3.2   Synthesis of Polyurethanes

Polyurethanes (PUR) are step-growth polymers synthesized by the reactions of polyols and polyisocyanates, generally in the presence of basic or organometallic catalysts. PUR can be thermoplastics or thermosets, depending on the functionality of the reactants. Both polyols and polyisocyanates are sensitive to moisture. Before mixing polyols and polyisocyanate reactants, additives such as catalysts (often called "activators"), antiaging compounds, antioxidants, plasticizers, dyes, fillers etc. are added to the polyol component; the isocyanates are used "as is". A typical PUR synthesis reaction can be shown as:

$$OCN-R_1-NCO + HO-R_2-OH \rightarrow OCN\left[R_1-NH-\overset{\overset{O}{\|}}{C}-O-R_2\right]_n OH \qquad (11\text{-}3)$$

(diisocyanate)   (diol)   PUR

(a)   Polyisocyanates

Few polyisocyanates are of commercial importance. Examples include the diisocyanates of toluene and of diphenyl methane, as shown below [723, p. 113]:

2,4-Tolylene diisocyanate (2,4-TDI)   2,6-Tolylene diisocyanate (2,6-TDI)

Diphenyl methane diisocyanate
(methylene diphenyl 4,4'-diisocyanate) (MDI)

(b) Polyols

Castor oil (3 hydroxyl groups) has been a proven natural polyol for the synthesis of cross-linked PUR. Synthetically prepared polyols are divided into two groups:

(*i*) *Polyester Polyols*   These are made by esterification of diols with dicarboxylic acids using an excess of alcohol. Bifunctional compounds lead to linear polyester polyols while higher functionality could give branched or cross-linked polyols. Examples of typical starting materials for the synthesis of commercially important polyester polyols are given in Table 11-3.

(*ii*) *Polyether Polyols*   These are made by polymerization of cyclic oxides initiated by an alcohol. Use of diols results in linear polyols while that of triols results in branched polyols. Some commercially important starting materials for polyether polyols are also given in Table 11-3.
    It should be noted here that polyether polyols are thermally more unstable and more easily oxidized than polyester polyols, but they are more stable to saponification (alkaline hydrolysis).

(c) Catalysts for PUR Manufacture

Examples of some important basic as well as organometallic catalysts for PUR manufacturing are given in Table 11-4. Tin containing catalysts have substantially higher activity than basic catalysts.

Table 11-3 Starting Materials for the Synthesis of Polyols

Polyester polyols	Polyether polyols
Adipic acid	Ethylene oxide
Phthalic acid	Propylene oxide
Sebacic acid	Tetrahydrofuran
Ethylene glycol (EG)	Ethylenediamine
Diethylene glycol (DEG)	Diethylenetriamine
Triethylene glycol (TEG)	Aromatic amines
1,2-Propylene glycol (PG)	Ethylene glycol
Dipropylene glycol (DPG)	Glycerin
1,3-Butylene glycol	
1,4-Butanediol	
1,6-Hexanediol	
Neopentyl glycol	
Glycerin	
Trimethylolpropane	
Hexane triol-1,2,6	
Pentaerythritol	

Source: [723].

Table 11-4 Catalysts for PUR Synthesis

Basic catalysts	Metal catalysts
Triethylene diamine	Butyl-tin-IV chloride
Dimethyl benzylamine	Tin-II chloride
Dimethyl aminoethanol	Tin octoate
Piperazine	Tin oleate
Ethylenediamine	Dibutyl-tin-dioctyl maleate
Triethylenetetramine	Tetrabutyl titanate
Ethylmorpholine	Ferric chloride
	Antimony-III chloride
	Cobalt 2-ethylhexoate

Source: [723].

11.3.3   Synthesis of Nylons

Nylon 6 and nylon 66 are the only nylons of importance related to the critical feedstocks for this study.

(*a*)   *Nylon 6*   Nylon 6 is manufactured by various procedures [717, p. 59] using ε-caprolactam as starting material either in a batch reactor or a continuous process. A typical chemical reaction is as follows:

$$\underset{\text{ε-caprolactam}}{\underset{(CH_2)_5-NH}{\overset{C=O}{\diagup}}} + H_2O \rightleftharpoons \underset{\text{Nylon 6}}{H\!\left[HN-(CH_2)_5-\overset{\overset{O}{\|}}{C}\right]_n\!OH} \tag{11-4}$$

ε-Caprolactam has also been made to polymerize through the action of an alkali metal catalyst. The mechanism of anionic polymerization of ε-caprolactam has been described in detail by Kohan [727, p. 458].

(*b*)   *Nylon 66*   A typical reaction for the production of nylon 66 is as follows:

$$\underset{\text{Adipic acid}}{HOOC-(CH_2)_4-COOH} + \underset{\text{Hexamethylene diamine}}{H_2N-(CH_2)_6-NH_2} \rightleftharpoons \underset{\text{Nylon 66}}{HO\!\left[\overset{\overset{O}{\|}}{C}-(CH_2)_4-\overset{\overset{O}{\|}}{C}-NH-(CH_2)_6-NH\right]_n\!H} + H_2O \tag{11-5}$$

Although catalysts are not generally required for the reaction, acid components are occasionally used to hasten the formation of the amide bond [717, p. 36].

11.3.4   Solvolysis Reactions

Various solvolysis reactions as related to chemical conversion of PET, PUR and nylons can be categorized as follows:

11.3.4.1   Hydrolysis

(a)   *PET*

$$PET + H_2O \xrightarrow{\Delta} TPA + EG \qquad (Neutral)$$
(excess) Na-acetate

$$PET + H_2O \xrightarrow[\Delta]{H_2SO_4} TPA + EG \qquad (Acid\ catalyzed)$$

$$PET + H_2O \xrightarrow[\Delta]{NH_4OH} TPA + EG \qquad (Base\ catalyzed)$$

(b)   *PUR*

$$\sim\!\!\sim R'NHCO\!\!+\!\!O\!-\!R\!-\!O\!\!+\!\!CONHR'NHCO\!\!+\!\!OR \sim\!\!\sim$$
$$HO\!+\!H \qquad H\!+\!OH \qquad HO\!+\!H$$
$$\downarrow \Delta$$

$$\sim\!\!\sim R'NH_2 + CO_2 + HOROH + CO_2 + H_2NR'NH_2 + CO_2 + HO\!-\!R \sim\!\!\sim$$

(c)   *Nylons*

$$\sim\!\!\sim NH\!-\!\overset{\overset{\displaystyle O}{\|}}{C}\!\sim\!\!\sim + H_2O \xrightarrow{\Delta} \sim\!\!\sim NH_2 + HOOC\!\sim\!\!\sim$$

11.3.4.2   Methanolysis

(a)   *PET*

$$PET + CH_3OH \xrightarrow[\Delta]{Cat.} DMT + EG$$

(b)   *PUR (alcoholysis, in general)*

$$\sim\!\!\sim R\ NHCO\!\!+\!\!O\!-\!R'\!-\!O\!\!+\!\!CONHRNHCO\!+\!OR' \sim\!\!\sim$$
$$R''O\!+\!H \qquad H\!+\!OR'' \qquad R''O\!+\!H$$
$$\downarrow$$

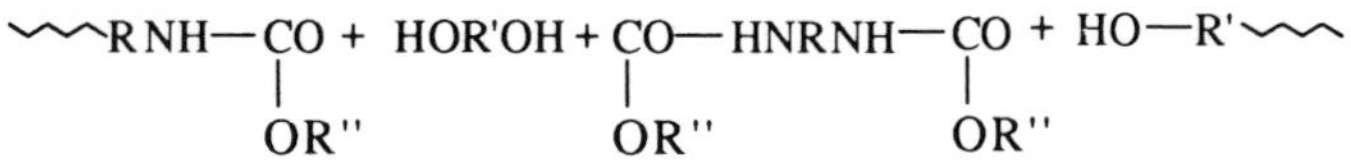

$$\sim\sim RNH-\underset{\underset{OR''}{|}}{CO} + HOR'OH + \underset{\underset{OR''}{|}}{CO}-HNRNH-\underset{\underset{OR''}{|}}{CO} + HO-R'\sim\sim$$

(c)   *Nylon*

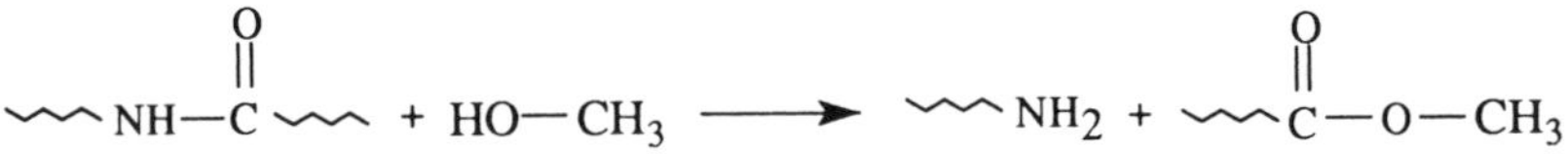

$$\sim\sim NH-\overset{O}{\overset{||}{C}}\sim\sim + HO-CH_3 \longrightarrow \sim\sim NH_2 + \sim\sim\overset{O}{\overset{||}{C}}-O-CH_3$$

11.3.4.3   Glycolysis

(a)   *PET*

$$PET + PG \xrightarrow[\Delta]{Cat.} polyols + PG + EG$$

propylene
glycol
excess

(b)   *PUR*

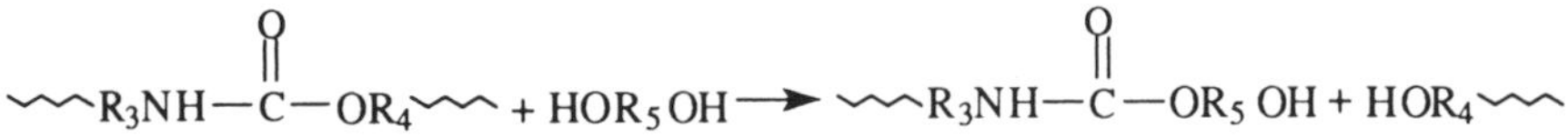

$$\sim\sim\sim R_3NH-\overset{O}{\overset{||}{C}}-OR_4\sim\sim + HOR_5OH \longrightarrow \sim\sim\sim R_3NH-\overset{O}{\overset{||}{C}}-OR_5OH + HOR_4\sim\sim\sim$$

(c)   *Nylons*

$$\sim\sim R_1-NH-CO-R_2\sim\sim$$
$$H O-R_3-OH$$

$$\downarrow$$

$$\sim\sim R_1-NH_2 + HO-R_3-O-CO-R_2\sim\sim$$

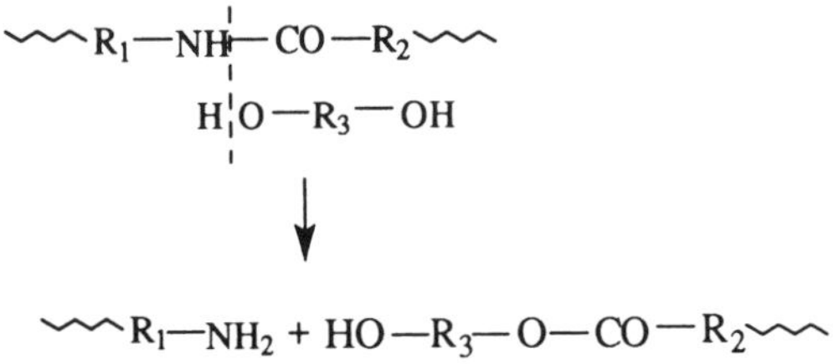

11.3.4.4   Aminolysis

(a)   *PET*

$$R_1-\overset{O}{\overset{||}{C}}-OR_2 + H_2NR_3 \longrightarrow R_1-\overset{O}{\overset{||}{C}}-NHR_3 + HOR_2$$

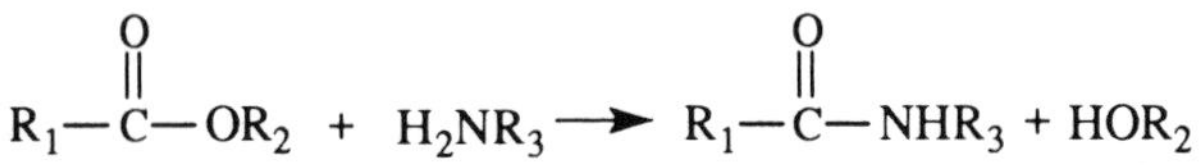

(b) PUR

$$R_1NH{-}\overset{\overset{\displaystyle O}{\|}}{C}{-}OR_2 + R_3NH_2 \rightleftharpoons R_1NH{-}\overset{\overset{\displaystyle O}{\|}}{C}{-}NHR_3 + R_2OH$$

(Equilibrium strongly favors formation of substituted ureas.
Rate is proportional to base strength of the amine.)

(c) Nylons

$$R_1{-}\overset{\overset{\displaystyle O}{\|}}{C}{-}NHR_2 + NH_3 \longrightarrow R_1{-}\overset{\overset{\displaystyle O}{\|}}{C}{-}NH_2 + H_2NR_2$$

$$\text{OR} \quad R_1{-}\overset{\overset{\displaystyle O}{\|}}{C}{-}NHR_2 + H_2N{-}R_3 \longrightarrow R_1{-}CO{-}NH{-}R_3 + H_2NR_2$$

11.3.4.5 Transesterification

(a) PET

$$R_1{-}\overset{\overset{\displaystyle O}{\|}}{C}{-}OR_2 + HOR_3 \rightleftharpoons R_1{-}\overset{\overset{\displaystyle O}{\|}}{C}{-}OR_3 + R_2OH$$

(b) PUR

$$R_1NH{-}\overset{\overset{\displaystyle O}{\|}}{C}{-}OR_2 + HOR_3 \rightleftharpoons R_1NH{-}\overset{\overset{\displaystyle O}{\|}}{C}{-}OR_3 + R_2OH$$

(Equilibrium favoring formation of aliphatic rather
than aromatic urethanes)

11.3.4.6 Transamidation (Amide Exchange)

Nylons

$$R{-}\overset{\overset{\displaystyle O}{\|}}{C}{-}NHR + R_1{-}\overset{\overset{\displaystyle O}{\|}}{C}{-}NHR_1 \longrightarrow R{-}\overset{\overset{\displaystyle O}{\|}}{C}{-}NHR_1 + R_1{-}\overset{\overset{\displaystyle O}{\|}}{C}{-}NHR$$

11.3.4.7 Acidolysis

Nylons

$$\sim\!\!\sim\!\!\overset{\overset{\displaystyle O}{\|}}{C}{-}NH\!\!\sim\!\!\sim + RCOOH \longrightarrow \sim\!\!\sim\!\!\overset{\overset{\displaystyle O}{\|}}{C}{-}OH + R{-}\overset{\overset{\displaystyle O}{\|}}{C}{-}NH\!\!\sim\!\!\sim$$

11.4   Applications of Solvolysis to Waste Polymers

11.4.1   Present Status and Developments

11.4.1.1   PET

11.4.1.1.1   Glycolysis   PET is the only step-growth plastic in critical feedstocks for which solvolytic processes have attained commercial success in view of recovery of chemicals, and repolymerizing them for similar or other product applications. A summary of various solvolysis processes for PET is given in Table 11-5(A). Typical reactants and catalysts reported for glycolysis of PET are listed in Table 11-6(A).

Goodyear recently developed a commercial product trademarked REPETE polyester resin, which incorporates recycled PET along with virgin starting material to make bottle grade polymer [1, 52, 111, 809 p. 196]. Goodyear's commercial glycolysis plant is located in Point Pleasant, WV [563]; recently Goodyear sold the operation to Shell Chemical Company.

Table 11-5 Chemical Conversion by Solvolysis

	Type of reaction	Reaction condition state (bulk/ solution/surface)	Industrial application	References
A.	Polyethylene terephthalate (PET)			
1.	Glycolysis	Bulk/catalytic	Yes	[193, 424, 706, 715, 610, 764, 707, 785, 687, 327, 426, 70, 103, 135, 112, 141, 185, 205, 220, 256, 276, 1, 50, 52, 111, 156, 414, 563, 788 (p. 12, 13, 60), 16, 17, 757]
2.	Hydrolysis	Bulk/catalytic	Not widely practiced	[200, 758, 797, 632, 204, 126, 258, 376, 788 (p. 12)]
3.	Methanolysis	Bulk/catalytic	Yes	[688, 246, 788 (p. 59), 601, 694, 1, 412, 563, 200, 788 (p. 12), 105]
4.	Aminolysis	Bulk	Not practiced	[132 (p. 70–71 cf. 160)]
5.	Transesterification	Bulk	Yes	[68, 209, 406]

Table 11-5 (Continued)

Type of reaction	Reaction condition state (bulk/ solution/surface)	Industrial application	References
B. **Polyurethane (PUR)**			
1. a) Glycolysis/ alcoholysis	Bulk/catalytic	Yes (batch reactors)	[174, 274, 814, 815, 255, 57, 784, 134, 6, 8, 161, 196, 247, 269, 252, 257, 259, 263, 267, 269, 391, 197, 204, 129, 401, 753 (p. 984), 161, 806]
b) Glycolysis	Bulk/catalytic	Yes (continuous)	[134, 11, 250, 247]
2. Hydrolysis	a) Bulk/neutral	Yes	[813, 133, 777, 273, 568, 81, 755, 756, 266, 247, 133, 277, 279, 268, 270, 271, 129, 251, 280, 281, 126, 134, 81, 273, 13, 441, 242, 283, 788 (p. 12)]
	b) Dissolution/ catalytic	Yes	[12, 214, 430]
3. Hydroglycolysis	Bulk/catalytic	Yes	[136, 215, 242, 214]
4. Aminolysis	Bulk/catalytic	Yes	[753 (p. 984), 23, 265, 10]
C. **Nylons**			
1. Alcoholysis/ glycolysis	Bulk/solution/ catalytic	Yes	[717 (p. 40–41), 255, 129]
2. Hydrolysis	Bulk/solution/ catalytic	Yes	[717 (p. 40–41), 727 (p. 70–72) 81, 126, 129, 204, 632, 776, 766, 753]
3. Aminolysis	Bulk/catalytic	Yes	[717 (p. 40–41), 727 (p. 46), 790 (p. 185)]
4. Acidolysis	Bulk/catalytic	Not widely practiced	[717 (p. 40–41), 727 (p. 99), 284, 563]
5. Amidolysis (amide exchange)	Bulk/catalytic	Not widely practiced	[717 (p. 40– 41), 727 (p. 46)]

Table 11-6 Solvolysis of Polyethylene Terephthalate (PET) : Reagents and Catalysts

A. Glycolysis

Reagents [Refs.]	
EG	[16, 17, 103, 112, 135, 141, 424, 610, 687, 706, 715, 764, 785]
PG	[16, 50, 52, 103, 112, 135, 141, 687, 785]
DPG	[687, 707, 785]
Aromatic polyols	[70]
PEG	[687, 707, 785]
PPG	[687, 707, 785]
DEG	[103, 135, 205, 256, 327, 707, 785]
Neopentyl glycol [NPG]	[112]
Butylene glycol	[687, 785]
Thiodiethylene glycol	[185]
Bis[2-hydroxy-ethoxy-ethyl] glutarate	[687, 707]
Oxyalkylene glycol	[205]
[polyethoxylated nonyl phenol] glycerol	[788 p. 60]
Aromatic polycarboxylic acids	[220]
Mixed ether-ester triol	[707]

Catalysts [Refs.]	
Zn-acetate	[103, 135]
Pb, Zn, Mn, Co-acetate	[141, 788 p. 60 cf. 18]
Amines	[788 p. 60 cf. 17]
Alkoxides	[788 p. 60 cf. 17]
Metal acetates	[788 p. 60 cf. 17]
Na-acetate trihydrate	[764]
Benzenesulfonate	[715]
Ti[OBu]$_4$	[256]

B. Hydrolysis

Reagents [Refs.]	
H$_2$O/EG/NaOH	[715]
H$_2$O/NaOH	[632]
CH$_3$OH/DMSO/NaOH	[105]

Catalysts [Refs.]	
Na-Acetate	
H$_2$SO$_4$	[758]
NH$_4$OH	

On December 6, 1991, Goodyear obtained from FDA a "Letter of no objection" to the use of REPETE polyester resin in the manufacture of food packaging [414]. Goodyear selected model contaminants and successfully removed them until the

50–100 ppm level was reached; no further purification was possible. The following represent general classes of contaminants:

- Nonvolatile, nonpolar compounds;
- Nonvolatile, polar compounds;
- Volatile, nonpolar compounds;
- Volatile, polar compounds;
- Heavy metal compounds.

These classes represent potential contaminants in post-consumer PET, such as (i) microbiological; (ii) foreign material (wood from pellets, aluminum from bottle caps, glass); (iii) mixed plastics (PP from bottle caps, HDPE from base cups, PVC from cap liners); (iv) non-food residues (detergents); and (v) contaminants from consumer misuse (pesticides, petroleum products such as motor oil, metal compounds). Presence of such contaminants above FDA limits would render recycled PET unsafe for food packaging applications.

Freeman Chemical Corp. processes PET bottle and film into aromatic polyols used for urethane and isocyanurate formulations [156].

In a patent [707] issued to Freeman Chemical Corp., PET reclaimed from desilvered photographic film is digested with organic diols and triols, and the digested product is further reacted with polyisocyanate to produce a poly-isocyanate-terminated prepolymer. Flexible as well as rigid PUR foams prepared with these prepolymers, obtained by glycolysis of PET film, fiber, bottle, wastes, resulted in unexpected strength properties, and they are used for fire retardant building panels and other applications [687, 785].

The glycolysis of reclaimed PET with PG to polyols suitable for reaction with maleic anhydride to produce unsaturated polyesters was described by Eastman Chemical [50, 788, p. 12, cf. 54].

A patent issued to Du Pont describes the use of aq. NaOH in EG at 90–150°C and at atmospheric pressure to decompose in-plant scrap to disodium salt (95.7% yield) and then to TPA [715]. In an earlier patent also to Du Pont [610], waste fiber PET is reacted with EG and a benzenesulfonate catalyst to give bis-hydroxyethyl terephthalate (BHET). A final polymer made with 45% of recovered monomer gave fiber properties equivalent to that of virgin. A schematic of this glycolysis process is shown in Fig. 11-1. Less formation of DEG and a faster depolymerization of the waste PET fiber (in excess EG) was obtained upon the addition of BHET and sodium acetate trihydrate to the reaction [764].

Vaidya et al. [16, 17, 103, 135] have extensively studied glycolysis of waste PET using EG, PG and DEG as reactants with or without Zn-acetate catalyst to obtain polyols. These polyols were further reacted with (1) maleic anhydride to give unsaturated polyester and (2) adipic acid to give polyester polyols followed by reaction with 4,4′-diphenyl methane diisocyanate (MDI) to give PUR elastomers.

Rebeiz et al. [112, 193] glycolyzed PET waste using EG, PG or neopentyl glycol to obtain monomers and oligomers; oligomers were reacted with unsaturated dibasic acids or anhydrides to give unsaturated polyesters (UP) suitable for use in polymer concrete as replacement for virgin UP. The advantage for this application

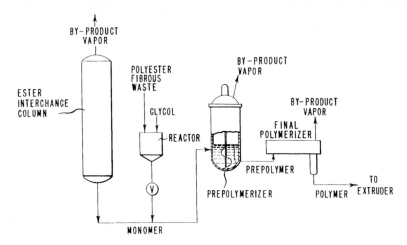

Figure 11-1 Schematic of a continuous glycolysis process for polyester fibrous waste followed by repolymerization, Ref. [610].

is that PET waste materials do not have to be purified extensively, including removal of pigments.

The effect of various metal acetate (Pb, Zn, Co, Mn) catalysts on glycolysis of PET waste bottles with EG at 190°C has been studied. The green pigment in soft drink PET bottles has no effect on the glycolysis reactions [141].

Birt [327] reacted waste PET from bottles with DEG at 300°C to obtain polyols which were reacted with MA at 180°C to prepare UP.

Muhs et al. [424] have described a mild depolymerization process for PET using a small amount of EG, requiring less energy and time.

ICI [256] patented a glycolysis process in which PET waste is digested with excess glycol (DEG) and treated with aliphatic dicarboxylic acid or derivatives, using $Ti(OBu)_4$ as catalyst, to prepare a random polyester polyol for use in the manufacture of PUR foam for shoe soles.

The preparation of rigid isocyanurate foams from a recycled PET polyol modified with polyethoxylated nonylphenol is disclosed by Texaco Inc. [205].

Fiber Industries [706] patented a continuous glycolysis process for scrap PET of fiber formable grade using EG at atmospheric pressure conditions to obtain low molecular weight PET oligomer mixture, which may be employed directly as feed material to make high viscosity PET suitable for films and fibers. A schematic of the continuous glycolysis process is shown in Fig. 11-2.

Petrov et al. [276] examined the factors affecting the glycolysis rates of PET solid wastes at 120–200°C. The glycolysis rate was higher for spinneret cuts than for monofilaments and increased with temperature.

11.4.1.1.2 Methanolysis   By the year end 1991, Eastman Chemical and Hoechst-Celanese Corp. had received no objection letters from the Food and Drug

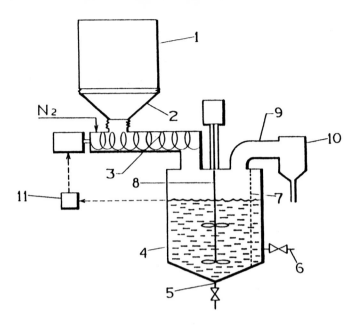

Figure 11-2 Schematic of the continuous atmospheric depolymerization (glycolysis) process for particulate polyester utilizing an extruder, Ref. [706].

Administration (FDA) for their methanolysis processes which depolymerize and then repolymerize PET bottle waste [1, 412].

Coca-Cola bottles contain 25% reconstituted PET from Hoechst-Celanese (N.C.) while Pepsi-Cola bottles contain 25% reconstituted PET from Goodyear [246].

Du Pont is starting up a commercial methanolysis unit in Nashville, TN to recover DMT & EG from PET (and ultimately other polyesters) [563].

Eastman Kodak Co. recently patented a batch methanolysis process for recovering EG and DMT from ground scrap PET bottles including contaminants such as polyolefin bottom cups, aluminum bottle caps, labels, and adhesive by dissolving the scrap in oligomers of the same monomer and passing superheated methanol through the solution [688]. A schematic of the batch methanolysis process is shown in Fig. 11-3.

High purity, colorless, depolymerized PET products were obtained by Eastman Kodak [601] by reacting scrap PET with various alcohols and then catalytically hydrogenating the products.

Cudmore [200] patented a methanolysis process for the efficient, energy conservative, substantially complete depolymerization of granulated PET to DMT and EG.

Hoechst (Germany) patented a process for depolymerizing PET waste in any form (fiber, chips, ribbon, film) by reacting the molten PET with methanol in a two-stage process to obtain DMT in 99% yield [694].

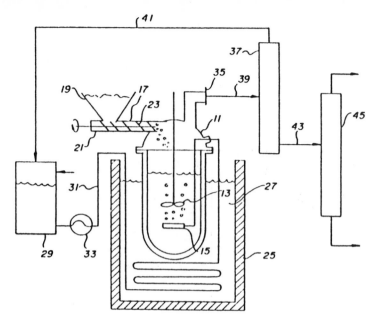

Figure 11-3 Schematic of a batch/semi-continuous methanolysis process for recovering EG and DMT from ground scrap PET bottles, Ref. [688].

11.4.1.1.3 Hydrolysis   Complete depolymerization of PET is also achieved by hydrolysis. Under hydrolytic conditions, waste PET yields crude terephthalic acid (TPA) and ethylene glycol. The TPA can be used directly as a feedstock, or further purified by traditional methods to pure terephthalic acid. Amoco has reportedly patented this process[1].

Barber Colman Co. hydrolyzed waste PET photographic and X-ray films to TPA while reclaiming silver [788, p. 12]. Michigan Technological University held the patents on the technology and adapted it for PET bottles. In this process, PET is reacted with aqueous ammonium hydroxide at elevated temperature and pressure. The diammonium salt is acidified with sulfuric acid to isolate TPA and EG. A 99% pure TPA is claimed [758].

Cudmore [200] patented a process for the efficient, energy conservative, substantially complete hydrolysis of ground PET waste aqueous slurry to TPA and EG.

Celanese (Mexico) patented a continuous neutral hydrolysis process in a twin screw extruder to depolymerize PET waste using high pressure steam at 200–300°C and ~15 atm. (1140 cm Hg) pressure [204]. A schematic of the continuous hydrolysis process is shown in Fig. 11-4.

Michalski hydrolyzed waste PET fibers using PET:H_2O ratio 1:2 at 215°C for 6 hours to obtain TPA and EG [258].

---

[1]Mod. Plast. Encyclopedia 93, p. 55.

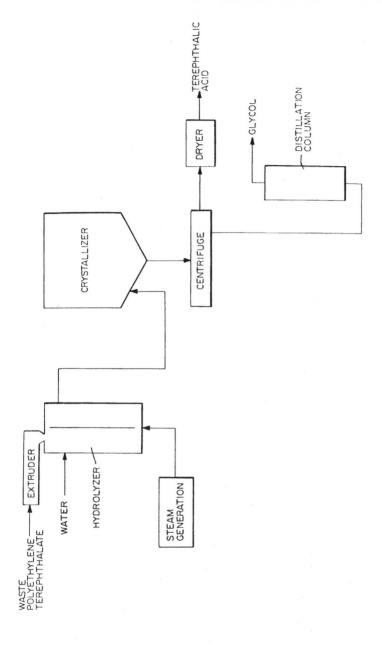

Figure 11-4 Schematic of a continuous neutral hydrolysis process in a twin screw extruder to depolymerize PET waste, Ref. [204].

In a 2 liter batch reactor for the neutral hydrolysis of PET, Campanelli et al. [376] found that the rate of hydrolysis reaction is quite rapid when PET is in the molten phase. The rate constant is shown to be orders of magnitude larger than for hydrolysis reactions of solid PET.

A patent issued to Allied Chemical Corp. [632] teaches the batch hydrolysis process (as described in Section 11.4.1.3.2) for mixed PET and nylon 6 fiber scrap.

Table 11-6(B) lists typical reactants and catalysts reported for hydrolysis of PET. A report from the Textile Research Institute includes additional literature on PET hydrolysis [797].

11.4.1.1.4 Transesterification   Degradative transesterification reaction of PET pellets (from PET bottles) with 2-ethylhexanol (20% excess) at 220°C using a tin catalyst for 4–6 hours resulted in cost effective production of dioctyl terephthalate (DOTP), a plasticizer for flexible PVC. Thus, DOTP produced from scrap PET could be a good replacement for commercial dioctyl phthalate (DOP) [406].

Carlstrom et al. [68] have reported a transesterification reaction to convert high molecular weight waste PET to low MW aromatic polyols useful in urethane and isocyanurate formulations.

In a patent, Texaco, Inc. [209] has described the preparation of mixtures of aromatic polyols containing ester functionalities suitable for use in rigid foams by reacting a dimethyl terephthalate waste stream, containing methyl *p*-formyl-benzoate, over a metal oxide catalyst and subsequently transesterifying the product with polyalkylene glycol in the presence of heat.

11.4.1.1.5 Aminolysis   PET may be degraded with aqueous methylamine. The dependence of rate of aminolysis on the morphology of PET fibers has been reported by Fettes [132].

11.4.1.2   Polyurethanes

While viable recycling technologies for PUR continue to develop, numerous challenges remain. Currently, rigid foam recycling is developing more slowly than flexible foam recycling; almost all flexible foam manufacturing scrap is recovered for use in bonded carpet underlay [183].

The Rigid Foam Task Force of PURRC (Polyurethane Recycle and Recovery Council) has investigated mechanical, energy and chemical conversion as alternatives to landfilling. Currently 93% of all rigid foam scrap goes to landfilling. By 1995, post-industrial and post-consumer rigid foam in the U.S. will amount to 250 million lb. Various solvolytic processes applicable to PUR are summarized in Table 11-5(B).

11.4.1.2.1 Glycolysis/Alcoholysis   The decomposition of PUR foams by hydrolysis and glycolysis to form polyols suitable as partial replacement of virgin polyols in the manufacture of PUR has received considerable attention. The Upjohn Company patented a glycolysis process to convert PUR scrap from a variety of sources into polyols which could be reused to make PUR foams [788, p.

12, 134, cf. 7, 174, 809, p. 273]. This process was licensed to Nippon Soflan, a subsidiary of Toyo Rubber Co. in Japan, which was operating in 1978 a commercial plant with an annual capacity of 1.3 million lb (585 tons). The process is emission (CO_2) free and not sensitive to varying product mixes.

Although a considerable R&D effort has been expended on the hydrolysis/glycolysis of PUR foams [788, p. 253, cf. 87–94] including production facilities at the million pound per year (450 tons) level, the perception remains that the processes are too costly compared to virgin polyol production [788, p. 253, cf. 95]. Recently, the Ford Motor Company, Europe, developed a recovery process which yielded acceptable polyol at claimed costs 30% less than new polyol [788, p. 253, cf. 96, 97].

Bauer has described a pilot facility to recover polyols from car seats by glycolysis [788, p. 253, cf. 98, 99]. The process can utilize the polyester fabric as well.

A pilot plant at a German Technical University carried out the staged glycolysis of flexible foam seat cushion material in a series of reactors at 200–250°C using base catalyst and alkylene or dialkylene glycol as reactant/solvent [6, cf. 9]. Up to 50% substitution of virgin polyol by recycled polyol has been claimed.

In separate patents, Bauer [255] has reported preparation of polyols, by heating waste polyesters, polyamides, and/or PUR with polyols (MW 50–5,000) at 180–250°C, useful in the preparation of semi-rigid PUR foams with low shrinkage. Polyol-containing dispersion is prepared by the reaction of >3:1 mixture of PUR-urea waste with DEG or polyether triol, optionally in the presence of acid or base catalyst, followed by dispersion of the product in primary polyol of MW ≤6,000 [252].

Meister and Schaper [401] have mentioned that the alcoholysis pilot plant at a German Technical University would be an economical one. The polyol mixture obtained is suitable for production of rigid foam.

In a number of publications and patents [247, 250, 274, 814, 815], researchers at the Upjohn Company have explored the glycolysis of polyurethane and polyisocyanurate foam using diols like EG, PG, DEG, DPG with or without 5–10% diethanolamine at 175–250°C in either a batch or a continuous process under a slight N_2 pressure. The polyols obtained could be used to make semi-rigid or rigid foams. The effect of tris-chloroethyl phosphate (TCEP) flame retardant on the acidity and corresponding reactivity of recovered polyols has been discussed.

Painted RRIM automotive parts were granulated and then chemically reduced via a glycolysis process to medium MW liquid components which were reformulated to produce new RRIM parts incorporating up to 30% recycled content. The glycolysis products have also been utilized to make insulating PUR foams for the construction industry [391]

During alcoholysis, the PUR network is broken down at about 200°C with alcohols (glycols), often with some additives, into liquid polyols. There is no need to separate painted and unpainted PUR parts for this procedure. The weight ratio between the PUR scrap and the alcohol can vary between 3:1 and 5:1. The short fibers present in the parts produced by RRIM are little affected by the process and transfer almost unchanged into the recycled product [161].

Goodyear patented a glycolysis process [57] for reclaiming cured flexible elastomeric cellular PUR into a liquid useful to remake articles of commerce.

Bayer [11] patented a continuous high temperature glycolysis process in a screw extruder for polyester based PUR foam waste by reacting the foam with PG at 280°C (residence time ~10 min) to give a polyol used for manufacture of PUR foam.

Koeble et al. [267] described a catalyzed glycolysis of PUR or polyisocyanurate foam waste by reacting with DPG at 200°C using chlorides of Ti, Cr or Zr as the catalysts.

Simioni et al. [197, 263] glycolyzed microcellular elastomeric PUR foam with DPG at 200°C using $Ti(OBu)_4$ as the catalyst, and rigid PUR foam with DEG using potassium acetate as the catalyst. The products were used for PUR formulations.

Asahi Chemicals patented a glycolysis process for PUR [269] using glycerol/KOH/DMSO or glycerol/KOH as reactants at 133–153°C. Glycerol/KOH/DMSO system was found to be better than glycerol/KOH system with less reaction time.

Cellular PUR wastes from the manufacture of shoe soles were degraded by thermocatalytic glycolysis with 1,4-butanediol at 175–185°C using triethylene diamine as the catalyst to give low MW liquid PUR. This, in turn, was used to replace a portion of polyol component in the fresh PUR formulation for shoe soles [257, 259].

Waste PUR foam is reacted with DEG at 100–150°C with Group I–IV metal alkoxide, e.g., Ti(i-Pro)$_4$ as a catalyst. The product can be reacted with polyols or diisocyanates to give PUR with good strength [8].

Jody et al. [806], in a small laboratory scale run, have separated automotive shredder fluff into four potential marketable products, one of them being clean PUR foam. Solvolysis of the reclaimed PUR was discussed briefly.

Shutz [817] has patented both continuous and batch alcoholysis processes for PUR waste using polypropylene polyol at 120–200°C to obtain liquid products which were reacted with polyisocyanates to produce PUR.

Table 11-7(A) is the compilation of typical reagents and catalysts reported for the glycolysis/alcoholysis of PUR.

11.4.1.2.2 Hydrolysis   Flexible PUR foams can be hydrolyzed to diamine, polyol and CO_2 by the action of high pressure steam. The Ford Motor Company and General Motors have developed processes for the hydrolysis of flexible PUR foam to polyols and diamines using superheated steam @ 250–350°C [788, p. 12, cf. 44, 45]. According to the General Motors procedure [788, p. 249, cf. 64, 813], high pressure steam will hydrolyze flexible foam rapidly at 232–316°C. The diamines can be distilled and extracted from the steam and the reclaimed polyols can be recovered from the hydrolysis residue. The optimum foam degradation temperature for the polyol yield and quality was 288°C. On the other hand, Ford studied the hydrolysis of PUR flexible foam seat cushion material at lower temperature than the GM study [788, p. 249, cf. 69]. Formation of 2,4- and 2,6-toluene diamines (TDA) and polypropylene oxide followed first order kinetics. TDAs were isolated from the reaction mixture by vacuum distillation in 65–80% yields.

High pressure steam hydrolysis of PUR flexible foam utilizing DEG as solvent at 190–220°C resulted in reasonable rates of hydrolysis. Use of 0.2% (by weight of

Table 11-7 Solvolysis of Polyurethane (PUR): Reagents and Catalysts

A. Glycolysis/alcoholysis

	Reagents [Refs.]
EG	[6, 8, 134, 247, 250, 814, 815]
PG	[8, 11, 134, 247, 250, 815]
DEG	[6, 8, 134, 136, 174, 247, 250, 252, 263, 274, 814,]
DPG	[197, 247, 267, 814]
Thiols	[8]
DEA	[274]
Diols	[252, 391]
1,2-butane diol	[815]
1,4-butane diol	[257, 259]
1,5-pentanediol	[814]
Polyether glycol	[263]
Polyether triol	[252]
3-methylpentane, 1,5-diol	[815]
1,6-hexane diol	[215]
Glycerol:KOH:DMSO	[269]
Glycerol:KOH	[269]
H2O:DEG:LiOH	[788, p. 250 cf. 70, 71]

	Catalysts [Refs.]
Ti(OBu)$_4$	[197]
Base	[6]
Group I–IV metal alkoxides	[8]
Ti(i-Pro)$_4$	[8]
Catalyzed dissolution	[214]
Acid or base	[252]
Triethylenediamine	[257, 259]
Diethanolamine	[174, 247, 250, 274, 814]
Potassium acetate	[263]
Chlorides of Ti, Cr, Zr	[267]
Ti-butylate	[267]

B. Hydrolysis/Hydroglycolysis

	Reagents [Refs.]
Superheated steam	[133, 242, 279, 280, 281, 283, 788 p. 12 cf. 44–46]
Steam/NaOH	[268, 270]
DEG/steam	[136, 215]
DEG/steam/NaOH	[215]
Glycerol/steam	[215]
H$_2$O	[13, 81, 129, 133, 247, 266, 273, 277, 441, 777]
H$_2$O/DMSO	[430]
H$_2$O/NaOH, H$_2$O/KOH	[136, 214, 215, 270]
H$_2$O/NH$_3$	[271]
DEG/H$_2$O/NaOH,	[214]
Glycerol/H$_2$O/NaOH	[214]
DIPG/H$_2$O/NaOH	[214]

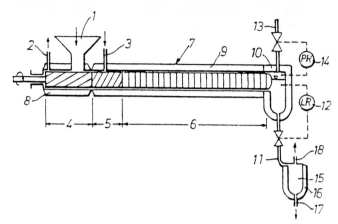

Figure 11-5 Schematic of a continuous hydrolysis process for PUR foam scrap in a specially designed twin screw extruder, Ref. [777].

glycol) LiOH as the catalyst greatly accelerated the rate of hydrolysis (a few minutes at 170–190°C). However, the catalyzed hydrolysis was a complex reaction with two reactions proceeding at different rates, both producing TDA. It was surmised that the faster reaction might be the hydrolysis of the urethane linkages and the slower one that of the urea linkages [788, p. 250, cf. 70, 71]. Even though the glycol solvent complicates the product isolation from the reaction mixture, high quality polyols can be extracted with hexadecane.

Capital and operating cost were estimated for a plant to consume 4 million lb of waste foam per year in a two-shift operation. Approximately 2.4 million lb of polyol could be produced [788, p. 250, cf. 72].

A continuous hydrolysis process for foam scrap using a specially designed twin screw extruder (TSE) was patented by Bayer AG in 1977 [777]. A schematic of the process is shown in Fig. 11-5. PUR waste is shredded, compressed and evacuated to remove air, after which it is mixed with hot water and fed into the extruder at 300°C to give $\sim$100% yield of polyethers and $\sim$90% yield of diamines [81, 273]. Also, a continuous process using a vertical reactor has been designed which yields 60–80% recovery of polyol from scrap at 288°C with residence time of 10–28 min [788, p. 249, cf. 66, 67].

In a number of patents and publications, researchers at Ford Motor Company (U.S., Germany, France, Japan, Belgium) have disclosed batch or continuous hydrolysis processes for PUR wastes with or without catalysts as follows:

• Vapor-phase hydrolysis of scrap PUR foams with superheated steam is improved by using catalytic amounts of basic alkali metal (e.g. NaOH) or alkaline earth metal compounds applied to the foam before hydrolysis. Thus, hydrolysis of PUR pieces containing 0.1 phr NaOH/100 phr foam with superheated steam at 190°C and $\sim$1 atm. ($\sim$76 cm Hg) resulted in 33.6% hydrolysis in 25 min [268].

- The hydrolysis of PUR foam impregnated with 0.1 phr NaOH with superheated steam under pressure at 250°C for 25 min resulted in 94.3% hydrolysis, compared with 64.9% without the NaOH treatment [270].
- PUR foam scraps were hydrolyzed at >185°C/0.1–1.5 atm. (7.6–114 cm Hg) with steam and 0.001–0.2 mol. NH_3/mol H_2O to recover gaseous diamines and polymeric liquid. The ammonia increases the rate of hydrolysis [271].
- Waste PUR foam from automobile headrests was hydrolyzed at 217–400°C in a closed reactor to give an aqueous solution of diamine and a liquid polymer (polyether or polyester) by passing steam into the reaction zone; the exit gases were removed above the reaction zone and cooled to give an aqueous solution of diamine. Liquid polymer was removed at a point below the foam layer [279].
- Hydrolysis of low density PUR foam by steam at 200°C for 15 min gave 66–85% recovery of toluenediamine (TDA) and 90% recovery of dark colored PG. Rate constants and temperature coefficients for the hydrolysis reaction were derived [283].
- Small particle size PUR foam industrial waste was continuously hydrolyzed in a tubular closed hydrolysis zone at 343°C with a stream of N_2 and superheated steam 1–1.5 atm (76–114 cm Hg) to give, in the separation zone at 260°C, a liquid polymer product and an exit vapor which is cooled to give an aqueous solution of diamine [280].
- Continuous hydrolysis of PUR foam waste in a fluidized bed at ~260°C in a closed reactor by passing 10:90 superheated steam-air mixture upwards through the foam bed gave an aqueous solution of diamine above and liquid polymer below the hydrolysis zone [281].

Cambell and Meluch [133] described a technique where a low pressure super-heated steam at 316°C was used to hydrolyze PUR waste into polyol and diamine which can be used to make tolylene diisocyanate.

In a number of patents and publications [13, 266, 277, 441], researchers at Bayer (Germany) have described a continuous hydrolysis process for PUR using a twin screw extruder at 200–250°C and 30–40 bars in the presence of a stream of water to give diamines and polyols; the residence times were relatively short (10–40 min). Separation of diamines and polyols from hydrolyzate is described.

PUR has been hydrolyzed or alcoholyzed; the reaction products are reacted with molten asphalt and/or bitumens in amounts of 1–80% (based on final composition) to give improved hot-rheological and physicochemical properties [251].

Jody et al. [568] have mentioned hydrolysis of PUR in relation to ASR (Auto Shredder Residue) as one of the alternative techniques to recycle ASR.

In a patent, Wyandotte Chemical Corp. [430] has described the hydrolysis of polyether-based PUR using H_2O/DMSO at high temperature, followed by extracting the polyols from the medium with an organic solvent (e.g. petroleum ether) immiscible with the medium.

The effect of alkali on linear polyurethanes has been studied by Dyer and Bartels [756]. PUR foams prepared from aliphatic diols and diisocyanates were unaffected by 1% NaOH at 50°C, although the corresponding phenol analogs were attacked.

Table 11-7(B) compiles typical reagents reported for hydrolysis/hydroglycolysis of PUR.

11.4.1.2.3 Hydroglycolysis   The term "hydroglycolysis" refers to the combined use of polyols (diols, triols, etc.)/alcohols and water as the reagents to bring about chemical degradation of step-growth polymers. Researchers at Ford Motor Company have developed hydroglycolysis processes for PUR foams.

PUR foam was added to the reactor containing DEG and water at 190–210°C. When dissolution was complete, the mixture was either allowed to separate into two phases so the upper polyol layer could be collected, or base catalysts such as NaOH were added and the reaction was allowed to continue. Upon completion of hydroglycolysis, water was allowed to evaporate, hexadecane was added at 160°C, and a clean phase separation of the hexadecane extract occurred [136]. It would be important to note here that:

(a) NaOH was used to base-catalyze the reaction;
(b) Contaminants such as PVC do not react due to mild conditions; and
(c) Up to 50% recovered products can be mixed with virgin PUR.

PUR foam waste was dissolved in EG at 185–220°C under N_2; water and alkali metal hydroxides (e.g. NaOH) were added to the solution, refluxed at 175–220°C to give amines and alcohol [214].

Through the solution of PUR foam waste in glycol ether at 185–220°C in the presence of NaOH, superheated steam was bubbled to produce alcohol and amines. The solution volume is maintained by adding alcohol (EG) to replace that removed by steam. Substantial amounts of polyol are recovered [215]. A schematic of the process is shown in Fig. 11-6.

11.4.1.2.4 Aminolysis   Polyether alcohols were recovered with high space-time yields and low by-product formation by slowly heating the coarsely chopped PUR waste with aniline to 120°C, then reacting it with propylene oxide in the presence of KOH [10].

Rigid PUR foam wastes were simultaneously aminolyzed with NH_3, ethylene diamine, diethylene triamine, hexamethylenediamine, or ethanolamine and alkoxylated by ethylene oxide, propylene oxide, butylene oxide, phenyl glycidyl ether, or styrene oxide optionally in the presence of a hydroxyl containing tert-amine (dimethyl ethanol amine) catalyst at 160–190°C and 4 kg/cm² (294 cm Hg) of pressure for 2.5 hours to give brown polyols [23].

Wastes of cellular, flexible and elastomeric PUR were treated with diethanolamine at 140–190°C to give polyols having diethanolamino groups for use in the manufacture of rigid PUR foams [265].

11.4.1.3   Nylons

Various solvolysis reactions applicable to nylons (particularly nylon 6 and nylon 66) have been summarized in Table 11-5(C). The nylons are among the oldest engineering thermoplastics, dating from the mid-1930s, and contain the amide (–CO–NH–) linkage along the polymer backbone. They are also the largest volume of engineering thermoplastics sold at 570 million lb (257 × 103 tons) in 1990

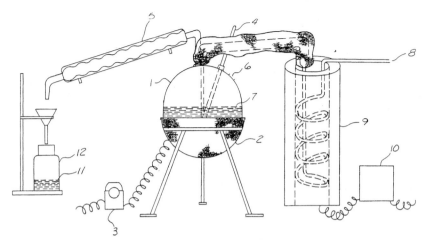

Figure 11-6 Schematic of a batch hydroglycolysis process for PUR foam waste, Ref. [215].

[788, p. 164, cf. 32]. They are widely sold in such diverse applications as transportation, electrical, industrial, consumer, appliances, film, fibers (carpets/textiles) etc.

As mentioned earlier, carpets/textiles is one of the critical feedstocks for this study. Reclamation and chemical recycling of nylons from these feedstocks is still in its infancy, although it has gained much attention as a potential viable alternative to landfilling.

The Du Pont Company, Wilmington, DE, has been working on several nylon recycling technologies that it believes can serve to reuse up to 85% of all nylon used today. In late 1992, Du Pont was testing a proprietary chemical process that would depolymerize either molded parts or fibers made of nylon 6 or nylon 66 into its main ingredients, which would then be repolymerized to make nylon in any form and for any market where nylon is used. Du Pont currently operates a nylon recycling plant in Glascow, DE with a capacity of 500,000 lb/year, and believes that within five years, carpet fiber—or even nylon pantyhose—could be collected and chemically transformed into automobile components[1].

BASF Corporation's Carpet Fibers Division, Williamsburg, VA, has filed patent applications for product and processes that will depolymerize nylon 6 from finished carpets to its monomer caprolactam. For 30 years, BASF has been recovering caprolactam from process water and nylon solid waste at its plant sites in Enka, NC, and Arnprior, Ont., by using a procedure which converts the material back into usable products[2]. In a patent assigned to BASF [888], a process for the continuous recovery of caprolactam from nylon 6 fibers containing carpet waste has been described. Nylon 6 fiber scrap obtained from the carpet separation is fed to a depolymerizing reactor at temperature of at least the melting point of nylon 6 in the presence of catalyst and superheated steam to produce caprolactam

---

[1](a) Plaspec News, October 12, 1992; (b) Plastics News, November 2, 1992, p. 10.
[2]Plaspec News, November 18, 1992.

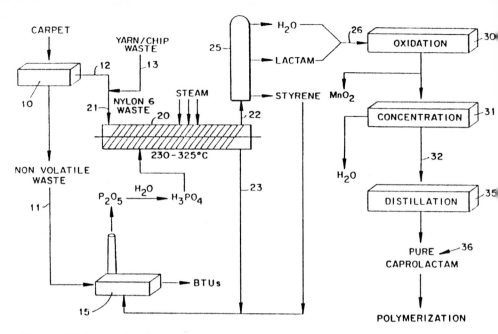

Figure 11-7 Schematic of a continuous process for reclaiming ε-caprolactam from nylon 6 carpet, Ref. [888].

containing distillate which is separated from other volatiles and purified. A schematic of the process is shown in Fig. 11-7.

11.4.1.3.1 Hydrolysis   Among the various solvolysis reactions applied to nylons, as listed in Table 11-5(C), hydrolysis appears to have gained wide acceptance followed by alcoholysis/glycolysis. A two-stage process for depolymerizing nylon 6 (including scrap polymer) was patented by Allied Chemical Corporation in 1965. The ground scrap nylon is first solubilized with high pressure steam at 125–130 psig (646–672 cm Hg) at 175–180°C for 0.5 hours in a batch mode in the presence of H_3PO_4 (as the catalyst) and ε-caprolactam. The solution thus prepared is then continuously hydrolyzed with superheated steam at 350°C and 100 psig (517 cm Hg) to ε-caprolactam at an overall recovery efficiency of 98% [776]. Later patents also issued to Allied deal with the recovery of ε-caprolactam monomer from:

(i) Nylon 6 oligomers using steam at 200–300°C and 10–250 torr (760–1900 cm Hg) [766];

(ii) Process residues using steam at 180–235°C in the absence of H_3PO_4 (753) as shown in a schematic in Fig. 11-8, and

(iii) A liquid process stream of organic and inorganic materials containing 40–60% caprolactam [666].

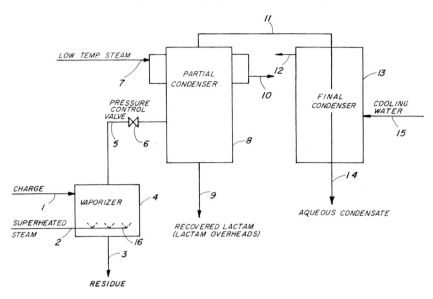

Figure 11-8 Schematic of a process for the recovery of ε-caprolactam from process residues, Ref. [753].

Caprolactam was prepared by depolymerization of oligomeric and polymeric nylon wastes by using H_3PO_4 at 150–210°C/4–18 atm. (405–1823 kPa) (304–1368 cm Hg) and steam at 210–260°C/0.1–5 atm (7.6–380 cm Hg) (284).

Celanese (Mexico) has patented a continuous neutral hydrolysis process using a twin screw extruder to depolymerize nylon 6 and nylon 66 using high pressure steam at 200–300°C and ~15 atm (1140 cm Hg) (204). Caprolactam is recovered in ~80% theoretical yield from nylon 6. Hexamethylene diamine and adipic acid are recovered from nylon 66.

In laboratory scale experiments, Kinstle et al. [126] obtained ~79% caprolactam from nylon 6 by neutral hydrolysis (using water) in a sealed tube at 260°C for 4 hours.

Steiner [81] has mentioned the use of a specially equipped twin screw extruder for the continuous neutral hydrolysis of nylons by injecting water at 300°C.

11.4.1.3.2 Hydrolysis of Mixed PET/Nylon 6 Fiber Scrap   Allied Chemical, in a patent [632], has described a batch hydrolysis procedure using $H_2O/NaOH$ at 230°C and 250 psig (1292 cm Hg) for 10 hours for the simultaneous depolymeriza-tion of mixed PET/nylon 6 fiber scrap to obtain ~97% theoretical yield of terephthalic acid, ~80% caprolactam and ~75% ethylene glycol upon isolation.

11.4.1.3.3 Alcoholysis/Glycolysis of Single/Mixed Polymers   Ford, in Germany, has initiated industrial scale investigation into the alcoholysis of seat cushions and covers. Production waste consisting of polyamide/polyester and PUR provided the model mixture for alcoholysis trials. At reaction temperatures of ~200°C for ~90 min, in the presence of glycols and catalysts, a viscous homogeneous mixture of polyols was formed [129]. In a discontinuous process, alcoholysis of Ford's waste mixtures can be completed in less than 2 hours. Continuous depolymerization of the mixtures using an extruder has been tried. It was possible to make rigid PUR foam from this polyol under normal conditions.

In a separate patent, Bauer [255] has described the depolymerization of 1/1/1 mixture of waste nylon 6 fibers/flexible PUR foam/PET fibers using dipropylene glycol (DPG) and calcium acetate (as catalyst) at 230°C for 3 hours to give viscous polyols.

11.4.1.3.4 Aminolysis/Acidolysis/Transamidation   These solvolysis reactions are not widely practiced in the industrial world. However, Zimmer AG (Frankfurt, Germany) has developed a process that converts nylon 6 from worn-out carpets containing 40–80% nylon to caprolactam. The Zimmer process uses an acid-catalyzed reaction at 536–752°F (280–400°C) to produce a caprolactam product that is filtered and purified by chemical treatment and distillation. By adding a proprietary shredding and pretreatment step, Zimmer has demonstrated the process' feasibility in the lab. A semicommercial plant with 10–20,000 metric tons/yr capacity has been planned [563].

11.4.1.4   Miscellaneous Step-Growth Polymers

Even though this chapter has been limited to applications of solvolysis to PET, PUR and nylons, it would be appropriate at this point to mention that solvolytic processes could be extended to other step-growth polymers such as polycarbonates (PC), polyureas (PU), and crosslinked polyester (e.g. SMC) from specific potential feedstocks, such as compact discs, disassembled automotive parts, etc.

11.4.1.4.1 Polycarbonate   Polycarbonates are susceptible to solvolytic reactions through their carbonate ($-O-CO-O-$) functionality to produce monomeric/oligomeric compounds. As reported in a patent [105] issued to Eastman Kodak, carbonate or ester bonds could be hydrolyzed by being contacted with a mixture of (i) an alcohol, such as methanol, or glycol; (ii) a polar aprotic solvent such as N-methyl-pyrrolidone or dimethyl sulfoxide (DMSO); and (iii) alkoxide or hydroxide such as NaOH. Thus, PC (bisphenol A based) was hydrolyzed in 3 min by refluxing with 1:4 (vol.) mixture of $5M$ NaOH in methanol:DMSO to produce monomeric compounds.

Li and Buese [544] hydrolyzed PC in THF under N_2 over CaH_2 by KOH or CsOH to obtain cyclic carbonates by precipitating the soluble products into excess hexane.

During the water sorption and hydrolytic stability study of polycarbonates, Golovoy and Zinbo [889] found that the decrease in weight-average molecular weight was a first order process under a constant relative humidity and temperature. Both phenolic end groups and additives, such as fire retardants and thermal stabilizers, are known to accelerate hydrolytic degradation.

11.4.1.4.2 Unsaturated Polyesters   One of the large-volume applications of unsaturated polyesters (UP) is in sheet molding compounds (SMC) used for body panels and other automotive parts such as General Motor's APV, Ford's mini vans, trailers, etc. According to SMC Alliance's (association of 30 companies) 1993 report, SMC is being used in greater quantities in the auto industry's 1993 model year than ever before. The report identifies about 300 different SMC components on nearly 100 vehicle lines from 28 manufacturers for this model year[1]; with SMC being a thermoset, it was considered a challenge to recycle this huge amount of it. At present, SMC is recycled only by grinding, and auto parts incorporating ground SMC into virgin SMC (up to 30%) were used in 1993 models of GM's Corvette in the U.S., Audi and Volkswagen in Europe, and Toyota in Japan [810]. SMC Alliance is working on pyrolysis of SMC, but no commercial process has been developed yet. Another potential approach for SMC would be in chemical recycling by solvolysis.

Kinstle et al. [126, 788, p. 250] hydrolyzed cured unsaturated polyester resin (with no fillers) under neutral conditions at 225°C for 2–12 hours. Filtration of the solids remaining after hydrolysis yielded isophthalic acid (60% of theoretical), styrene-fumaric acid copolymer, and unhydrolyzed starting material. The copolymer could be recovered by acetone extraction in high yield. Propylene glycol recovery was below 50%.

In a recent study sponsored by the U.S. Department of Energy, Tesoro et al. (201, 545) have described neutral hydrolysis of model cured UP (no fillers) in mixed solvent systems (e.g. butanone/water) in an autoclave at 220–275°C for 2–6 hours. After hydrolysis, the products separated into two layers. The upper layer (butanone) contained primarily oligomer (62–75% yield); the lower layer (water) contained phthalic acid (66–85% yield). Thus, technical feasibility of recovery of value from model cured UP has been shown.

In another study, also sponsored by the U.S. Department of Energy, on the actual SMC automotive body panels (containing $CaCO_3$ and glass fibers), Patel et al. [812] have described hydrolysis of ground SMC using 30% methanolic KOH in dioxane under reflux conditions. The complexity of the steps involved in the isolation of the products from the mixture containing glass fibers and $CaCO_3$, and poor yields does not make hydrolysis an economically viable recycling method for SMC.

11.4.1.5   Other Relevant Literature

For more information related to solvolysis of the above mentioned and other polymers, refer to the following references: [64, 66, 84, 113, 115, 175, 198, 226, 227, 232, 253, 254, 260–262, 264, 272, 275, 278, 282, 285, 313, 353, 355, 359, 360, 367, 440, 751, 784, 789, 799, 816].

---

[1]Plastics News, February 8, 1993, p. 9.

11.4.2   Assessment of Technologies

11.4.2.1   PET

Among the various PET products such as beverage bottles, photographic- and X-ray films, fibers etc., the recycling of beverage bottles by means of solvolytic processes has been well advanced. Commercial success of methanolysis and glycolysis processes has reached the point that the recycled PET is now used for food contact packaging applications. Methanolysis has been found to be *more tolerant* to contaminants than glycolysis (1), however, both processes are economically successful, provided clean raw material is available at low cost. Neutral hydrolysis of PET in the molten state has shown some promising results on a developmental basis. Exploration of this technology for further evaluation would be worthwhile. Aminolysis and transesterification of PET have not been practiced in the industry.

While exploring any solvolytic process for PET, e.g. hydrolysis, the effect of contaminants present in the feedstock is a prime consideration. Therefore, *specifications* on feedstocks from various sources become important. Typical flake specifications for Goodyear's pcPET (post-consumer PET), and typical metals content along with their probable function in representative samples of pcPET are given below [111]:

Goodyear Flake Specification for pcPET

	Maximum (ppm)
Label	7
Green PET	960
EVA	10
HDPE, PP	15
Aluminum	1
PVC	non-detectable

Typical Metals Content in pcPET

Metal	Conc. (ppm)	Function
Sb	220–240	PC
P	6–110	
Stabilizer Co	50–100	PC
Mn	20–60	
TE Ti	0–80	PC
Fe	0–6	From wash water
Na, Mg, Si	trace	Various

PC = Polycondensation catalyst
TE = Transesterification catalyst

In summary, there is a need to establish specifications on PET feedstocks in order to determine which solvolytic process is more suitable for a given feedstock. There is also a need to have specifications on recycled PET used for food or non-food applications. Finally, neutral hydrolysis of PET in the molten state needs further exploration.

11.4.2.2   Polyurethanes

As mentioned earlier, rigid PUR foam recycling is developing more slowly than flexible foam recycling. Several recycling/recovery methods that PURRC (Polyurethane Recycle and Recovery Council) is evaluating for rigid PUR foam include [183]:

(i)   Using PUR scrap with methylene diisocyanate binder to product boards and other parts;
(ii) Using ground PUR as a filler for roof and wall insulation, and bun stock;
(iii) Flexible bond underlay (carpet underlay), a very active business nowadays;
(iv) Paint sludge removal with rigid foam particles (using rigid foam dust for detackifying paint);
(v)   PUR recovery by appliance dismantling.

Thus, PURRC does not report any significant solvolysis technologies being tried for rigid PUR foam. However, considering the huge amount of feedstock available, it would be worthwhile to explore solvolysis as an alternative recycling method provided, of course, that collection economics become favorable.

Hydrolysis of PET merely reverses the polycondensation reaction which formed the polymer initially. On the other hand, by hydrolysis of PUR, one of the monomers, the diisocyanate, is not obtained but rather its reaction product with water, the diamine, is obtained along with the polyol [788, p. 247, cf. 56, 57, 59–61; 134]. The presence of other hydrolyzable groups in PUR, such as urea in flexible foams and isocyanurate in some rigid foams, further complicates the reaction, yet both groups are hydrolyzed to amines. Thus, irrespective of the type of PUR (different chemical structures), hydrolysis can convert them to di- or polyamine plus polyol(s). The major disadvantage is that both the diamine(s) and polyol(s) should be separated before they are reused.

Glycolysis of PUR (only urethane groups) converts everything to a mixture of polyhydroxy compounds (polyols) which can be used directly without further separation. However, the presence of ureas or isocyanurate groups in PUR could lead to formation of amines [134]. Separation of amines from polyols can be avoided by converting the amine groups to hydroxyl with ethylene or propylene oxide, resulting in increase of total hydroxyl groups. Glycolysis of rigid PUR is an efficient process for chemical conversion of waste products into raw materials. The choice of catalyst is an important factor in selecting the type of reaction as well as controlling the reaction rate. The best results are obtained with DPG (dipropylene glycol) and potassium acetate, giving raw materials that can be used without further treatment for the production of rigid PUR foams [196]. Foam reconstruction using an organic binder is an effective method for flexible foams, but it is not applicable to rigid foams because of high processing cost and inferior properties of the end products. Glycolysis temperature is also an important factor; at 195°C or higher, simultaneous pyrolysis of urethanes and ureas also takes place. It should be noted that the glycolysis of rigid foams, containing a flame retardant such as tris-chloroethylphosphate (TCEP), was found to evolve hydrochloric acid and the final products were insoluble [196, p. 283, cf. 11]. However, soluble products from

TCEP based foams were obtained using a base as catalyst in relatively high concentration. Thus, the effect of the *presence of additives* such as flame retardants should be taken into account during the selection of reagents/catalysts for any solvolytic process for PUR.

Bauer [129] has compared hydrolysis vs. acidolysis/glycolysis of PUR, polyesters and polyamides, and notes that:

(i) Hydrolysis of PUR gives unsatisfactory results;
(ii) Hydrolysis requires drastic reaction conditions and long reaction times;
(iii) During alcoholysis of PUR, the composition of the reaction mixture can be controlled;
(iv) Alcoholysis of polyesters and polyamides is preferable to hydrolysis; and
(v) The alcoholysis of PUR is analogous in principle to the way hydrolysis proceeds. The difference in reaction conditions arises from the fact that the alcoholysis products, in contrast to those of hydrolysis, are stable and do not split off carbon dioxide.

In summary, recycling activities for PUR through solvolytic processes have been limited to small scale industrial scrap. There seems no large scale commercial plant in existence even though significantly large feedstocks are available. The reasons apparently are related to problems with collection, sortation and overall economics; to some extent the applicable technologies appear also to be controlling factors.

According to PURCC's Rigid Foam Task Force [183], rigid PUR foam recycling is developing more slowly (93% of all rigid foam being landfilled) than flexible foam recycling. Therefore, among other alternatives (e.g. mechanical reprocessing, energy conversion), more research efforts would need to be focused on chemicals recovery through solvolysis of rigid PUR foams. Other important areas of research that need attention: a) development of technologies to separate PUR foams from halogen-containing flame retardants, and b) development of catalysts to tolerate these flame retardants during solvolysis. In case of hydrolysis and aminolysis of PUR, the chemicals produced (amines and polyols) need to be isolated before reuse or be further reacted with cyclic oxides to obtain a mixture of polyols that do not need separation prior to reuse. There is a need to explore the economical feasibility of aminolysis of PUR foams.

11.4.2.3   Nylons

From the available embodied energy data for various plastics, nylons appear to be the top candidates in terms of recovering the total embodied energy by recycling rather than incinerating or landfilling. Recovery of monomers/chemicals by solvolytic processes provides an excellent route to serve the purpose. Yet, there exists no large scale commercial plant in the U.S. largely because of the lack of an infrastructure for collection/reclamation of the critical feedstock—carpets/textiles. Serious consideration should be given to making collection/reclamation economical.

At present, industrial activities have been very limited to small scale depolymerization of mainly in-plant scrap nylons.

It should be noted that carpets are complex structures. Recycling nylon from used carpets is not a simple process because of the various components present in the finished carpet, e.g. dyestuff, latex, jute, rubber, stain-resist chemicals, antisoiling chemicals, plus the contaminants that are added during the use such as ground-in-dirt, pet hair, food etc. Nylon fibers account for 25% of all synthetic fibers produced, and 27% of nylon fibers used in carpets in 1987 contained various types of "stain blockers" such as (i) phenolics, (ii) thiophenolics, (iii) dihydroxy-diphenylsulfones, and (iv) nonaromatic sulfonic acids. While exploring any of the solvolytic reactions for nylons, the effect of the presence of these additives should be studied [234].

Only a limited study that appears in literature has shown the feasibility of hydrolysis of mixed PET/nylon 6/PUR mixture. More efforts are needed in the study of mixtures of step-growth polymers. No study appears on solvolysis of nylons/chain-growth polymers, e.g. nylon 6/PP (as in many carpets). Thus, the effect of other chain-growth polymeric contaminants should be considered.

Alcoholysis of polyamides and polyesters would appear more attractive than hydrolysis since the latter requires drastic reaction conditions and longer reaction times. In the alcoholysis of polyamides, removal of amide groups proceeds relatively slowly and incompletely; this might be desirable if the aim is to get polyol rather than monomer by complete depolymerization [129].

Assessment/feasibility of aminolysis, acidolysis, and transamidation reactions for nylons should also be considered.

11.4.3   Relevance to Critical Waste Streams

The commercial success of methanolysis and glycolysis processes for PET beverage bottles from MSW reflects the importance and technical feasibility of these processes for step-growth polymers that are present in other critical feedstocks such as carpets/textiles and automotive. Of course, it should be pointed out that PET bottles are collected economically because of mandatory collection programs and deposit laws; without these, there would be an inadequate supply of PET for secondary or solvolytic recycling. Feedstocks other than bottles must meet certain specifications with respect to contamination levels for solvolytic recycling. The technical feasibility of applying solvolytic processes such as hydrolysis and glycolysis has already been demonstrated on small scale experiments for such complex mixtures as PUR foam/nylon fibers/PET fibers or PET/nylon 6, which are among the prime recoverable candidate polymers from these critical feedstocks. In addition to PET, PUR, and nylon considered in detail in this chapter, the applicability of solvolytic processes could be extended to other potential feedstocks containing other step-growth polymers such as polycarbonates (PC), and polyureas (PU) and cured unsaturated polyester compounds (SMC).

Abbreviations

ABS	Acrylonitrile-butadiene-styrene plastic
ASR	Auto shredder residue
BHET	Bis-hydroxyethyl terephthalate
DEA	Diethanolamine
DEG	Diethylene glycol
DIPG	Diisopropylene glycol
DMSO	Dimethyl sulfoxide
DMT	Dimethyl terephthalate
DOP	Dioctylphthalate
DOTP	Dioctyl terephthalate
DPG	Dipropylene glycol
EG	Ethylene glycol
FDA	Food and Drug Administration
HDPE	High density polyethylene
LDPE	Low density polyethylene
MA	Maleic anhydride
MDI	Methylene diphenyl 4,4′-diisocyanate
MF	Melamine-formaldehyde resin
MW	Molecular weight
NPG	Neopentyl glycol
PC	Polycarbonate
PE	Polyethylene
PEG	Polyethylene glycol
PET	Polyethylene terephthalate
PG	Propylene glycol
POM	Polyoxymethylene
PP	Polypropylene
PPG	Polypropylene glycol
PS	Polystyrene
PU	Polyurea
PUR	Polyurethanes
PVC	Polyvinylchloride
RRIM	Reinforced Reaction Injection Molding
SAN	Styrene-acrylonitrile plastic
SMC	Sheet Molding Compound
TCEP	Tris-chloroethylphosphate
TDA	2,4- or 2,6-toluene diamine
TDI	Tolylene diisocyanate
THF	Tetrahydrofuran
TPA	Terephthalic acid
TPEL	Thermoplastic elastomer
UF	Urea-formaldehyde resin
UP	Unsaturated polyester

Chapter 12

Pyrolytic Processes

12.1 Status

Pyrolytic processes that convert plastic wastes to monomers, chemicals, and liquid and gaseous fuel products have been studied and practiced over the past 50 years [75, 226]. The scope of the studies carried out with polyethylene, polypropylene, polystyrene, polyvinyl chloride, and nylon feeds are summarized in Table 12-1.

In pyrolytic processes, the plastic feeds derived from waste streams are only feedstocks. Their economic attractiveness compared to other feedstocks (for a given process technology) will depend on the relative selectivity to the desired products and the cost structure. The embodied energy (Chapter 3) content of the plastic waste is *not* relevant, only the heat of combustion of the plastic feed is relevant. In most instances the recovery of embodied energy in a pyrolytic process will be lower than combustion in waste-to-energy facilities. The only exception is pyrolytic processes involving polymers with high selectivity to monomers, e.g. pyrolysis of nylon 6 of carpets to caprolactam; that cannot be produced in one-step petrochemical processes.

All published studies and our approximate calculations indicate that the maximum value of the plastic feeds for most fuel and petrochemical processes will be in the range of 5–10¢/lb; this is equivalent to a crude oil price range of $15–30/barrel. Moreover, it seems reasonable to believe that the value of plastics (of a purity acceptable as a feedstock for pyrolytic processes) will fluctuate with the price of crude corrected for any difference in the heat of combustion. Therefore, it is highly unlikely that plastic wastes will be economical for many pyrolytic processes unless their use is subsidized or legislatively mandated.

A large variety of reactors are available for pyrolysis; many have been tested at significant scales of operation. Significant work has been done on molten media and fluidized bed reactors. Extruders may be particularly attractive at low throughputs.

Overall yield data of variable quality can be widely found in the literature. Only limited data are available on reaction pathways, and there are few modeling studies. This deficiency should be corrected following the principles established in pyrolytic petroleum refining processes.

The National Renewable Energy Laboratory (NREL) studies on pyrolysis of nylon 6 carpet scrap to caprolactam showed 85% selectivity to the monomers. The results could be commercially interesting.

Table 12-1 Pyrolysis of Polyethylene, Polypropylene, Polystyrene, PVC and Nylon

Type of reaction	Reaction conditions	Potential industrial application	Effect of polymeric impurities/ contaminants (metals, etc.)
Polyethylene			
Catalytic gasification	Bulk	Yes	Likely
Catalytic cracking	Bulk	Yes	Likely
Partial oxidation	Bulk	Yes	Likely
Fixed-bed pyrolysis	Bulk	Yes	Likely
Circulating-bed pyrolysis	Bulk	Yes	Likely
Catalytic hydrogenation	Bulk	Yes	Likely
Polypropylene			
Catalytic gasification	Bulk	Yes	Likely
Catalytic cracking	Bulk	Yes	Likely
Partial oxidation	Bulk	Yes	Likely
Fixed-bed pyrolysis	Bulk	Yes	Likely
Circulating-bed pyrolysis	Bulk	Yes	Likely
Polystyrene			
Catalytic gasification	Bulk	Yes	Likely
Catalytic cracking	Bulk	Yes	Likely
Partial oxidation	Bulk	Yes	Likely
Fixed-bed pyrolysis	Bulk	Yes	Likely
Circulating-bed pyrolysis	Bulk	Yes	Likely
Polyvinyl chloride			
Catalytic gasification	Bulk	Yes	Probable
Catalytic cracking	Bulk	Yes	Probable
Partial oxidation	Bulk	No	Probable
Nylon			
Catalytic gasification	Bulk	Yes	Likely
Catalytic cracking	Bulk	Yes	Likely
Partial oxidation	Bulk	No	Likely
Fixed or circulating-bed pyrolysis	Bulk	No	Likely

12.2 Developments

Pyrolytic processes involve the heating of plastics to produce gases, liquids, and solid residues, chars, and inorganic fillers. However, to be pyrolytic, the decomposition of the plastic occurs at elevated temperatures, during which oxygen is *largely excluded*. Consequently, it is not combustion that occurs but rather a complex set of reactions that depends both on the plastics involved and the precise nature of the pyrolytic process used [131, 862, 863, 864]. The possible reaction pathways are:

- Decomposition into monomers, e.g. PMMA and PTFE;
- Fragmentation of the principal chains into organic moieties of variable size, e.g. PE and PP;
- Simultaneous decomposition and fragmentation [302], e.g. PS and PIB;
- Elimination of simple inorganic moieties leaving charred residues, e.g. PVC;
- Elimination of side chains, followed by crosslinking.

In addition, the course of the pathways can be modified by addition of controlled quantities of hydrogen or oxygen or the presence of catalysts [137].

Pyrolysis, therefore, can be utilized to recover *materials* (monomers and other organic chemicals), *fuels* (liquids and gases), or *both* materials and fuels.

12.2.1   Pyrolytic Pathways

12.2.1.1   General

The thermal degradation of plastics follows a variety of pathways that are significantly influenced by the reaction temperature. As a broad generalization, higher temperatures favor the production of gaseous products and lower temperatures liquid products. However, the pyrolysis reactions can be significantly influenced by the presence of additives such as stabilizers, plasticizers, and pigments.

A few pyrolysis pathways are relatively well understood:

- Poly(methyl methacrylate) and styrene/methacrylate polymers produce essentially monomers by unzipping of the polymers chain;
- Polyvinyl chloride eliminates hydrochloric acid and produces cyclic structures;
- Cyclization reactions are common in polysiloxanes and polyesters;
- Polyolefins undergo random scission to produce homologous alkanes, olefins, and diene fragments.

However, the suppression of volatile degradation products [865–867] and the influence of additives [868] can modify the degradation pathways and, therefore, the product distributions. These interactions are not well understood or quantified.

While pyrolysis has been widely practiced in a variety of reaction-processing sequences[1] (Table 12-2), one cannot be certain of duplicating the reported product distributions (except in a gross overall sense) in some other experimental apparatus. In many published studies, the reaction time was determined by the requirement to heat a polymeric mass to some reaction temperature. Therefore, the temperature-time history of the polymer in these studies is not well established, nor can it be readily duplicated in another reactor-processing sequence (even if it is identical in nature but larger in size).

---

[1]HDR Engineering, Lake County (IL), Solid Waste Management Plan, Vol. III, Appendices A1–A5, Report prepared for Lake County Joint Action Solid Waste Planning Agency, April 1989.

Table 12-2 Typical Pyrolytic Reactor Systems

Reactor system	Investigators	Reference
Conveyors	Wayne Technology	[411]
Extruders	APV	[359, 360]
	Union Carbide	[847]
	Japan Steel Works	
	Voest-Alpine	
Fluidized beds	Japan Gasoline Co.	
	Nippon Zeon	[882]
	Occidental	[231]
	Sumitomo Machinery	[882]
	Toyo Engineering	[882]
	Tsukishima Ebara	[312, 315]
	University of Hamburg	[234, 244]
	University of Waterloo	[321, 344]
	West Virginia Univ.	[847]
Molten salt	Ruhrchemie	[881]
reactors	Univ. of Tennessee	[310]
Rotating drum/	Fischer Menges	
furnaces	Kobe Steel	[880]
	Kohnle-Fichtner	
	Monsanto Landgard	[884]
	Sanyo Electrical	
	Veba Oel Technologie	
	Dr. Otto Noell	[881]
Stirred tank	Mitsubishi Heavy Industries	[18]
reactors	Mitsui Engineering	
	KWU	[881]
Vertical retorts	Andco-Torrax	[881]
	Firestone	[881]
	Union Carbide	[883]

Yields are also often influenced by how the feedstock is prepared and fed to the pyrolysis reactor [308]. If the feed has been shredded into small particles, the temperature, residence time, and heating rate can be more readily controlled [339]. For a given set of conditions (including temperature, residence time, and heating rates), the smaller the particle, the lower the amounts of solid and liquid products, and the higher the amounts of gas generated [869].

12.2.1.2   Recovery of Embodied Energy

Pyrolysis, unlike combustion, is an endothermic process; therefore, heat must be supplied (directly or indirectly) to the reactor. Some of the heat can be supplied by combustion of the pyrolysis products. This requirement and the distribution of possible products will determine the fraction of the embodied energy in the discarded plastic products that were recovered by a pyrolytic process.

The heat balance for the pyrolysis of one pound (1 lb) of polystyrene objects (e.g. cups) can be developed in a straightforward manner if we assume:

- 50% yield of styrene;
- 40% yield of coproducts;
- Heat of combustion of polystyrene, styrene, and pyrolysis coproducts is 18,000 BTU/lb.

The embodied energy of the polystyrene cups is, of course, not relevant to the heat balance for the pyrolysis.

Pyrolysis heat balance for one pound of polystyrene cups		
0.5 lbs styrene:	0.5 (18,000)	9,000
0.4 lbs coproducts:	0.4 (18,000)	7,200
0.1 lbs char:	0.1 (0)	0
Required process heat & losses		(1,000)
	Net energy "recovered":	15,200

The difference between the heat of combustion of the styrene and coproducts (16,200 BTUs) and the net energy recoverable (15,200 BTUs) is a result of the need to supply energy for the pyrolytic process and losses. The char has been assumed to have *no* heating value that may (if the char is not combustible, e.g. glass fibers) or may not be correct in specific circumstances.

The possible "value" of the char has been ignored. In practice, its recovery and disposal (there are most likely no significant uses) may present significant environmental issues.

To estimate what fraction of the embodied energy of the polystyrene cups can be recovered by pyrolysis, it is useful to think in terms of the incremental embodied energy over the heat of combustion.

Incremental embodied energy (BTU/lb) of polystyrene cups and styrene		
	Cups	*Styrene*
Embodied energy	47,250	37,000
Heat of combustion	18,000	18,000
Incremental embodied energy	29,250	19,000

If we ignore for the moment the coproducts and char, the recovery of the embodied energy of the polystyrene cups in a pyrolysis process is:

Incremental embodied energy of 0.5 lbs styrene	+	Net energy recoverable from process	=	Total revovery of energy
0.5 (19,000)	+	15,200	=	24,200 BTU/lb

Only the incremental embodied energy of styrene is used in these calculations since its heat of combustion was accounted for in the pyrolysis heat balance.

Therefore, if we focus only on the styrene and the net energy recoverable (24,200 BTU), pyrolysis will recover potentially 51.2% (24,200/47,250 (100)) of the embodied energy of the polystyrene cups.

Most likely, the recovered 0.5 lb of styrene would be polymerized into more cups. This would require the expenditure of energy for purification of the styrene polymerization, fabrication of the cup, and transportation. To simplify the calculations, the energy required for purification of styrene has been ignored.

Embodied energy recovered if styrene is converted to cups		
Total recovery of energy		24,200 BTU/lb
Polymerization	0.5 (3,200 BTU/lb)	(1,600)
Fabrication of cup	0.5 (1,750 BTU/lb)	(875)
Transportation	0.5 (95 BTU/lb)	(48)
	Net recovery of embodied energy	21,677 BTU/lb

No allowance has been made in these calculations for the energy flows associated with collection, sortation, and washing of the cups. While these requirements are small, they are not insignificant; they could be as high as several thousand BTU/lb of cups.

Now if our focus of interest is using the recycled styrene to make more cups, the recovery of the embodied energy of the original cups drops to 45.9% (21,677/47,250 (100)). Our calculations up to this point have ignored the coproducts, e.g. benzene, toluene, substituted benzenes, etc. (except for tracking their heat of combustion in the pyrolysis heat balance calculation).

Depending upon the values (embodied energy) assigned to the coproducts, the recovery of the embodied energy of the polystyrene cups can be significantly different, as shown in Table 12-3. Where the coproducts have been given a value, i.e. there is a use for them other than as a fuel, the heat for pyrolysis would have to be supplied by some other fuel. Therefore, the assessment of what fraction of the embodied energy of the plastic feed is recovered will always depend on the uses and, therefore, the values assigned to all the products.

Table 12-3 Recovery of Embodied Energy from the Pyrolysis of Polystyrene Cups

Recovered styrene as	Value of coproducts	Recovery of embodied energy %
Monomer	Heat of combustion	51
Cups	Heat of combustion	46
Monomer	Zero value[a]	35
Cups	Zero value[a]	29
Monomer	Embodied energy[b]	66
Cups	Embodied energy[b]	60
Combustion of cups		30

[a]Assigning a zero value to the coproducts is equivalent to not being able to burn them (presumably for some environmental/safety issue).
[b]This assumes that the coproducts have some valuable use. For these calculations, the embodied energy of the coproducts and styrene has been assumed to be equal.

12.2.2   Pyrolytic Reactor Systems

Pyrolysis as a commercial process has been used for many years in the production of methanol, acetic acid, and turpentine, as well as charcoal from wood. Moreover, it is widely applied for the production of liquids and gas from low rank coals in Europe and throughout the world for the production of coke. More recently, it has been widely used on both a commercial basis and in pilot plants in the U.S., Europe, and Japan with municipal solid waste, plastics, and tires as feeds [304]. Significant studies have also been done on thermal oxidation and hydrocracking of plastic wastes.

A large number and variety of reactors and associated systems have been tested to a significant degree for use with plastic streams (Table 12-2). The characteristics of the reactors that have been utilized are compared qualitatively in Table 12-4[1]. The reactors (per pound of throughput) differ quite widely in their cost, an extruder being the most expensive [84].

A reactor system involves in addition to the reactor(s):

- Feeding system for moving the plastic waste into the reactor;
- Systems for the treatment of gases and liquid products;
- Removal systems for solids.

If sheet molding compounds (SMC) are processed as part of the solid stream, the degree of success attained in recycling the fillers [123) will depend on:

- Average particle size and particle distribution of the recovered filler;
- Compatibility of the recovered filler with new matrix materials;

[1]HDR Engineering, Lake County (IL), Solid Waste Management Plan, Vol.III, Appendices A1–A5, Report prepared for Lake County Joint Action Solid Waste Planning Agency, April 1989.

Table 12-4 Characteristics of Pyrolytic Reactors

| | Direct heating | | Indirect heating | | | |
| | | | Wall transfer | | Circulating medium | |
	Operational simplicity	High heating rates	Operational simplicity	High heating rates	Operational simplicity	High heating rates
Vertical shaft	+	o	+	−	−	+
Horizontal shaft	o	o	−	−	−	+
Rotary kiln	+	Possible	+	−	−	+
Fluidized bed	−	+	None	None	−	+
Extruder	−	Possible	−	−	Not relevant	
Molten salt	−	+	o	+	+	+

Note: A plus (+) entry indicates a benefit while a minus (−) indicates a debit.

- Cost structure for intended application (the cost of the recovered filler must be equal to or less than that of the fillers which it will replace);
- Residual mechanical properties of the recovered filler.

The limited information available suggests that properties of many fillers are not significantly degraded at pyrolysis temperatures below 500–600°C [161]. However, sufficient experience is not available to judge the broad applicability of recycling fillers. Some of the fillers recovered from pyrolytic processes may have to be discarded.

12.2.3   Predictive Models for Pyrolytic Processes

Predictive kinetic descriptions of fluid catalytic cracking and thermal cracking developed in the petroleum industry can be applied to pyrolysis of mixtures of plastic wastes. The state of the art on modeling chemical reactions in complex mixtures, where all reactants undergo irreversible reactions, is summarized in Ref. [870].

Both the methodology and data are available to "predict" the yield pattern to be expected from hydrocarbon waste polymer feeds in different reactor systems. "Limited" quantities of nitrogen in the waste polymers can also be accounted for with the available models. The use of these models is desirable to permit predictions to be made from limited experiment data.

The modeling methodology can handle pyrolysis of polymers containing oxygen and nitrogen; however, data are lacking to test the models. Unfortunately, neither the methodology nor the data exist for thermoset plastics.

Small scale studies should be directed at uncovering the reaction pathways including crosslinking reactions and interactions with fillers/contaminants rather than just determining gross yields. Studies by Serio et al. at Advanced Fuel

Research (pyrolysis of phenol formaldehyde) [872] and Klein et al. at the University of Delaware (thermal reactivity of 2,2-diphenylpropane) [871] are good examples of what should be done on a broader scale. The American Plastics Council is sponsoring a limited program on pyrolysis of polyolefins at the University of North Dakota. Hopefully, the data obtained will be suitable for modeling studies.

12.2.4   Pyrolysis to Monomers

12.2.4.1   General

The thermal degradation of polymeric compounds can follow, as discussed previously, a variety of pathways. For those polymers where the degradation proceeds by unzipping of the polymer chains, as is the case for poly(methyl methacrylate), styrene/methacrylate copolymers, and other 1,1 disubstituted vinyl polymers, essentially only monomers are produced [873]. However, since the monomers will contain trace impurities (either from depolymerization or the waste) purification will be required. Extensive commercial experience on the pyrolysis of poly(methyl methacrylate) is available.

Monsanto and Du Pont have both studied the depolymerization of nylon 6 and nylon 66. The Monsanto studies were done in the mid-1960s. At the time, it was concluded that, on a total cost basis, pyrolysis would be two to three times the cost of incineration[1].

The National Renewable Energy Laboratory (NREL) has been studying the pyrolysis of nylon 6. Using scrap material without prior separation of the fiber from the polypropylene backing selectivities to caprolactam of 85% have been obtained [878].

Studies are underway in a number of organizations to extend depolymerization to recovering [30, 226]:

- Terephthalic acid esters from the PET bottle resins;
- Styrene from polystyrene in residential plastics;
- Diisocyanates from polyurethane in automobile parts.

Small facilities for the recovery of diisocyanates are believed to be operating in France and Japan.

When pyrolysis is applied to mixed polymers wastes a number of reactions in addition to depolymerization to monomers can occur. For example, it is well known that thermal degradation of polyvinyl chloride (PVC) releases HCl; indeed, hydrogen chloride generation begins at temperatures as low as 130°C. In inert atmospheres and at temperatures ranging from 160 to 700°C, more than 75 pyrolysis degradation products have been identified, including olefinic hydrocarbons, benzene, toluene, xylenes, ethylbenzenes, aliphatic, naphthalenes, and methy-

---

[1]J.L. Dickerson, Monsanto Technical Center, Pensacola, FL, personal communication.

Table 12-5 Production of Ethylene from Recycled Polyethylene

Waste polyolefin feed	720.00 M lb/yr
Ethylene production	300.00 M lb/yr
By-product production	
Hydrogen (90%)	6.00 M lb/yr
Propylene (chem. grade)	147.00
Butadiene	51.00
Butylenes	45.00
Benzene concentrate	21.00
Steam cracked naptha	72.00
Steam cracked naptha polymer	24.00
Tar	18.00
Fuel gas	57.00

Note: Yields have been extrapolated from data on steam cracking of C_{20} linear paraffins

lated species. Some condensed aromatics, such as biphenyl and anthracene, have also been identified [874].

While many reaction products have been identified, the major products of PVC pyrolysis are hydrogen chloride and benzene. In some cases, other chlorinated compounds have been identified at higher temperatures; for example, ethylene chloride at 400°C, chlorobenzene, di- and trichlorobenzenes at 500–700°C, and vinyl chloride and ethyl chloride at 500°C. The presence of trace quantities of many chemical species significantly complicates the purification of the desired products.

Battelle has reported the development of a process that can produce monomers from mixed polyethylene, polystyrene, and polyvinyl chloride wastes[1]. Little information is available about the nature of the Battelle technology. However, to obtain high yields of olefins without the production of liquids and chars requires that the pyrolysis be carried out under "fast pyrolysis conditions".

Pyrolysis to monomers (depolymerization) will be of primary interest for those polymers which have a high selectivity to monomers synthesized in a multi-step process, e.g. styrene, adipic acid, caprolactam, methyl methacrylate, tetra-fluorethylene, and diisocyanates. For monomers produced in a one-step petrochemical process, e.g. ethylene and propylene, polymer wastes will be regarded as just an alternative feedstock to other hydrocarbon streams.

12.2.4.2   Steam Cracking of Polyolefins

Polyolefins are an excellent feedstock for production of olefins in a steam cracker. The product yields at commercial conditions (800°C outlet coil temperatures, 0.4 lb steam/lb feed) should be similar to C_{20} linear paraffins [304, p. 177] (Table 12-5).

---

[1]Plastics News, May 27, 1991, p. 3; Battelle Perspective, Development Opportunity: Ethylene Recovery from Waste Plastics, Battelle, Cleveland, OH.

Moreover, the endothermic heat of cracking for the polyethylene will be about 70–80% that of ethane. The total energy requirements (including distillation) for cracking polyolefins will be about 5,600 BTU/lb ethylene as compared to 6,200 BTU/lb for ethane.

The attractiveness of steam cracking will be highly dependent on the cost of mixed polyolefin wastes and sales price for product [see Tables 12-6 (A, B, C, D)]. With ethylene at 20¢/lb, the maximum value at the plant gate (no profit) for the waste polyolefins is 11¢/lb for a 300M lb/yr ethylene facility. The value of the waste polyolefins would be higher if the waste was incremental to hydrocarbon feeds in an existing one billion lb/yr cracker; under these circumstances, the value of the waste might be as high (not considering any profit) as 13–14¢/lb.

To earn limited income with ethylene at 20¢/lb the value of mixed polyolefins wastes would have to be less than 6¢/lb. However, the operator/owner of a steam cracker could value waste plastics by the ratio of their heat of combustion to that of ethane. This ratio is in the range of 80–85%; at parity, plastic wastes would be valued at less than 4¢/lb.

No allowance has been made in "estimating" these values for purification of the waste polyolefin feed. If purification beyond that achieved by sortation and wash-float reclamation process is required, the values would be significantly lower. Reportedly, BP Chemicals has developed a proprietary thermal cracking unit to prepare feed and remove deleterious impurities such as hydrochloric acid from PVC containing wastes.

All published process and economic studies suggest that:

- Stand alone cracking plants are not feasible;
- Feed preparation units, e.g. hydrocrackers, will be required;
- Some subsidy, e.g. a tipping fee, may be required for steam cracking to be financially attractive.

Not surprisingly, the values assigned to the plastic wastes (under the most optimistic assumptions) are *not* higher than the price of crude (at a given time), and they may be significantly lower.

Table 12-6A Basis For Investment Estimate

Literature studies on naphtha cracking, typical study results:	
Capacity	500 M lb/yr
Onsite	192 M$
Offsite	96 M$
Exponent for scaling investment	0.75
Projected investment for 1993 startup of steam cracker using waste polyolefin feed:	
Onsites	167 M$
Offsites	84 M$
Fixed capital	251 M$

Note: Steam cracker is located in a large petrochemical complex, minimal utilities are included in offsites.

Table 12-6B Raw Material, By-Product Credits and Utility Costs

	Unit Cost ¢/lb	Consumption lb/lb ethylene	¢/lb
Polyolefin wastes	C	2.4 lb	2.4C
By-products credits	Unit Cost ¢/lb	Production lb/lb ethylene	¢/lb
Hydrogen (fuel)	12.1	0.02	0.24
Fuel gas	5.6	0.19	1.06
Propylene (poly grade)	19.9	0.49	9.75
Butadiene	18.0	0.17	3.06
Butylenes	10.8	0.15	1.62
Benzene concentrate	10.0	0.07	0.70
SCN	7.9	0.24	1.90
SCN polymer	8.0	0.08	0.64
Tar	4.0	0.06	0.24
	By-product credits		18.97
Utilities	Unit cost	Consumption per lb ethylene	¢/lb
Cooling water[a]	5.3¢/k gal	35.55 gal	0.19
Process water[a]	6.7¢/k gal	0.21 gal	0.01
Electricity[a]	3.4¢/kW	0.0216 kWh[b]	0.07
Natural gas	2.35$/MBTU	0.0056 MBTU	1.31
	Total utilities		1.58
Catalyst & chemicals			0.2¢/lb

Note: [a]At 90% of ethane cracking requirements; [b]Lower energy requirement than ethane for polyolefin feed.

Cracking of polyolefins will require a shorter residence time than ethane (<0.6 seconds) to minimize byproducts reactions. There are no published data at these short residence times. Unfortunately, much of the published data on cracking polyolefin wastes are at long residence time (chips added to a reactor); these data may be misleading.

Energy requirements will be dominated by the ethylene yield and product gas composition obtained from cracking waste polymers. (Heating the feed, generating steam, and purification of impure ethylene consumes significant amounts of energy.) The available data on pyrolysis of mixed plastic wastes, i.e. wastes containing plastics other than polyolefins, suggest that product gas composition will be "poorer" than that obtained from cracking ethane. If this is correct, the energy requirements for purification of the ethylene will be higher for mixed plastics wastes than for ethane.

The product distributions obtained from cracking mixed polymer wastes will most likely be the result of parallel molecular and free radical pathways. The mixtures should behave largely as individual components cracked separately. How-

Table 12-6C Total Production Costs

Total variable operating cost (TVOC)
    From Table 13-6(B):
    TVOC $= (¢/lb - 2.4C + 1.58 + 0.2 - 18.97 = 2.4C - 17.37)$

Fixed costs @ capacity operation

	¢/lb	Basis
Operating labor	1.00	10 operator posts
Operating supplies	0.10	10% of operating labor
Laboratory	0.07	Three professionals @ 65K$/yr
Technical	0.33	Five engineers @ 200K$/yr
Maintenance labor	1.25	1.5% of fixed capital
Maintenance mat'ls	1.25	1.5% of fixed capital
Taxes	1.05	1.25% of fixed capital
Fixed costs (excluding depreciation)	5.05	
Allowance for administration, sales and R&D	0.83	5% of (fixed + variable + byproducts credits)
Depreciation	5.58	6.67% of fixed capital
Total fixed costs	11.46	
Total production cost	2.4C−5.9	

ever, it is likely that polyethylene cracking will be accelerated at low conversions and retarded at high conversions.

At low conversions and pressures, high molecular weight polyolefins (judging from the available data on cracking of high molecular weight paraffins) will crack selectively to olefins, methane, and ethane. Straight chain polymers will produce only alpha olefins, but branched polymers will also yield both branched olefins and linear olefins.

The presence of PVC will alter both cracking rates and the relative selectivities to products. The limited data available suggest that the yields will be poorer in the presence of PVC. Of course, any hydrochloric acid that is generated will undoubtedly contribute to stress cracking of the unit's materials of construction.

Table 12-6D Value of Mixed Polyolefin Wastes at an Ethylene Price of 20¢/lb

Breakeven cost:
    Total production cost $= 20 = 2.4C - 5.9$
        $C = 10.8¢/lb$
Cash generation ratio of 15%:
    Requires cashflow of 37.65 M$/yr or 12.45¢/lb ethylene.
        $20 - 12.45 = 2.4C - 5.9$
        $C = 5.6¢/lb$

There is considerable interest among petrochemical producers who also manufacture polyolefins in steam cracking mixed polyolefin wastes as an alternative to the recycling of generic polyolefins. BP Chemicals has developed a steam cracking process for mixed polyolefins that has a proprietary pretreatment step for the removal of unspecified impurities [387].

The embodied energy of the plastic waste is not recovered to a significant degree in steam cracking (as is the case for most pyrolytic processes). Since steam cracking is not highly selective, a plastic waste is just an alternative feed. What is important is the yield, selectivity, and price of the plastic wastes as compared to conventional hydrocarbon feeds. Mixed plastic wastes are a *poorer* feed than mixed polyolefin wastes which can be considered as being "equivalent" to high molecular weight paraffins; therefore, their value will be lower than that of polyolefin mixtures.

Under some circumstances and most likely only with some subsidy, small pyrolysis units (circa 200M lb/yr) might be of interest for preparation of a feed that could be processed in the light end purification system of a steam cracker. Liquid phase pyrolysis units have been proposed for such an application. However, since the cracking and termination rates are faster in the liquid phase, longer residence time than those used in steam cracking will be necessary. The longer times at elevated temperatures may result in byproduct formation, particularly when mixed plastic wastes are the feed.

12.2.5   Pyrolysis to Fuel Products

The yields of specific products from any pyrolytic process that uses plastic wastes as a feed depend on a variety of factors: residence time, temperature, particle size of waste feed and atmosphere (oxygen, air, oxygen-free, steam) [232, 353]. Depending on the combination of conditions chosen, varying amounts of gas, liquid, and solids can be produced from a feed. The gas and liquids will be fuels, and their quality will be significantly influenced by the impurities in the feed [210].

As a broad generalization to obtain significant quantities of liquids that are potentially useful as liquid fuels requires operation at temperatures of about 700°C [241, 350]. Hydrocracking tends to produce significantly larger quantities of liquids than thermal cracking as shown below [323, 343]:

| | Thermal cracking 700°C | | Hydrocracking 300–500°C | |
	PE %	PP %	PE %	PP %
Products				
Gases	51	43	10	17
Oils	42	27	90	65
Chars	6	30	1	18

However, hydrocracking will result in significantly higher costs and potential operating difficulties. Whether these can be justified depends on the value assigned to liquid fuels.

In a recent process developed in Japan, zeolite catalysts are used to reduce the thermal cracking temperature to 200–400°C. However, no information is available about the quality of the liquid products that are produced [169, 563, 879].

12.2.6   Refinery Processes

12.2.6.1   General

Mixed polymer wastes are an excellent feed for fuel processes provided the PVC content has been reduced to an acceptable low level [100]. The value of the polymer waste will be determined by its performance "parity" with crude to the desired products. Therefore, the value of the wastes will fluctuate with the price of crude and the relative process credits and debits.

There is a range of possible alternatives for the use of mixed plastics in refinery processes [368]:

• Boiler Feed;
• Fluid Catalytic Cracker Feed;
• Coker Feed.

From an energy recovery point of view (if only BTUs are of interest), the most efficient use of plastic wastes is combustion in a boiler, i.e. waste-to-energy. In refinery processes, the mixed plastics will replace (or supplement) hydrocarbon streams that have some advantages relative to feeds containing plastics. Moreover, all pyrolytic refinery processes produce mixtures of gases and liquids.

While process energy requirements will vary depending on whether plastics waste or conventional feedstocks are used, the incremental embodied energy of a plastic waste will not be recovered. Only the heat of combustion of the plastic wastes is relevant in fuel processes. As a result, one billion lb/yr of plastic wastes with a heat of combustion of 20,000 BTU/lb are equivalent to the heat of combustion of 9,630 barrels of crude.

For all fuel units some form of pretreatment will be required. Pretreatment processes are under development by Shell Petroleum and the American Plastics Council [386].

Cracking of plastic wastes to gasoline and fuel oil in fluid catalytic cracker (FCC) should be more attractive than other pyrolysis processes except when the pyrolysis process is highly selective to high valued monomers. Most likely the presence of fillers in the waste can be compensated for by catalyst additions. However, this has not been demonstrated to date.

Studies at Amoco [386] have shown that, in an FCC unit, the following significant product yields are obtained:

- Polystyrene   Aromatic Naphtha;
- Polypropylene   Aliphatic Naphtha & Distillate;
- Polyethylene   LPG and Aliphatic Naphtha.

The performance of the catalysts will limit permissible hydrogen chloride concentrations. However, there are no published data that show what the technical issues might be. For present-day catalysts the permissible maximum chloride level is about 200 ppm. Most likely one can develop nonzeolitic cracking catalysts that have a higher tolerance to chlorides.

The impurity levels in the liquid fuel products will be critical in determining the future uses for the liquid. Treatments of the liquid products may be required depending on the nature and level of the impurities.

A coker should be able to crack all polymer wastes provided they can be slurried in a suitable form. However, data on the yields pattern are not available. The American Plastics Council is planning to get these data in future programs.

The value of mixed plastics as coker feed should be greater than that as a fuel. The presence of fillers should not upset operation of the coker, but they may degrade the quality of the coke. Not surprisingly, the presence of PVC or the chlorides derived from PVC is unacceptable.

12.2.6.2   Hydrocracking/Hydrogenation

Hydrocracking of plastic liquids will also remove heteroatoms, e.g. (Cl, N, O). The process is feasible and has been demonstrated on both a pilot plant scale and in commercial tests [425]. Rheinische Braunkohlen Kraftstoff has demonstrated the feasibility in bench scale tests. Pilot plant and commercial tests have been planned. However, these have been delayed as a result of the unfavorable economic climate.

Veba Oel's Bottrop Refinery treated in 1992 about 70 tons (equivalent to 300–400 barrels of oil) in a commercial test[1]. Newspaper stories suggest that treatment of 50,000 tons of mixed packaging wastes (primarily polyolefins) is planned in 1993–1994 by German authorities. HDs/HDN catalysts (Co-Mo-S on alumina) can be used to hydrocrack plastic wastes at chloride levels of about 200 ppm. Rheinische treated plastic wastes with PVC level in plastic waste of about 0.1%; however, little is known about catalyst deactivation rates [876]. At chloride levels above 500 ppm a polyfluoroethylene support may have to be used.

Hydrogenation is an acceptable first step in preparing a feed for a refinery process such as thermal cracking [884]. However, the process must be done in two steps since the activity of the hydrogenation catalyst will be damaged at thermal cracking conditions.

There are no known commercial activities in hydrocracking or hydrogenation of plastic wastes in the U.S.

---

[1]Plastics News, September 14, 1992, p. 18; Plastics News, May 18, 1992, p.15; Chem. Engineering, October 1992, pp. 27–28.

12.2.7   Thermal Oxidation

12.2.7.1   Early Work

Thermooxidative degradation of waste plastics must be distinguished from inciner-ation (complete combustion to CO_2 and H_2O) and pyrolysis (thermal cracking in the absence of oxygen). Products obtained by thermal decomposition in an oxygen-deficient atmosphere are either gases containing mostly CO, H_2 and various hydrocarbons, or low MW liquids.

Chemical conversion of waste polymers by thermooxidative degradation is poten-tially applicable to mixed plastic streams containing mostly hydrocarbon polymers and could be a useful complement to pyrolytic processes. Although significant experimental and developmental work on thermooxidative degradation of virgin and waste plastics has been conducted over the past 20 years worldwide, particu-larly in Japan and Germany, no significant commercial operations exist to our knowledge.

Thermooxidative degradation systems for converting urban refuse, with little or no emphasis on plastics, to fuel gas were developed in the U.S. in the 1970s. We are not aware of how economically viable these systems were projected to be. Examples disclosed in the literature include:

- A partial oxidation process (PUROX) using oxygen for converting municipal solid waste to fuel gas and inert slag was developed in the early 1970s by Union Carbide [143]. The fuel gas that was produced was low in sulfur and ash. One ton of refuse (after being reprocessed to remove iron) required 0.2 tons of oxygen, and produced 0.7 ton of medium BTU fuel gas, 0.22 ton of sterile residue, and 0.28 ton of waste water. The gas consisted of H_2, CO, CO_2, and light hydrocar-bons with a heating value of 370 BTU/ft^3 The slag contained $>50\%$ SiO_2. The energy balance from the PUROX facility in million BTU/ton was:

  - Energy in refuse, 9.5;
  - Energy loss in conversion, 2.0;
  - Energy in fuel gas, 7.5;
  - Energy for in-plant electric power generation, 1.0;
  - Net energy produced, 6.5.

- In the "Landgard System" (Monsanto), partial oxidation of MSW produced an off-gas having a heating value of about 120 BTU/ft^3 [160].
- Carborundum Environmental Systems developed a system called -"Torrax" that yielded an intermediate quality fuel as having a heating value of 170–190 BTU/ft^3 [160].

A process applicable to plastics waste is described in an expired patent from Japan [431]. A special fluidization setup was used for complete combustion of part of the waste hydrocarbon plastics and thermal oxidation ($>600°C$) of the remain-der was carried out by using the heat generated in the combustion. The products consisted of hydrocarbon gases (CH_4, C_2, C_3, C_4) and oils ($>50\%$ C_2O).

12.2.7.2   Developments

The following are examples of basic studies on the partial oxidation of materials that are representative of polymer wastes:

- Bockhorn and coworkers [199, 303, 341] studied the partial oxidation of poly-olefins and polystyrene in fuel-rich spray flames as a complement to pyrolytic processes. Model fuels representative of polymer wastes were converted into a gas mixture containing H_2, CO, and a mixture of smaller hydrocarbons (CH_4, C_2H_4, C_2H_6) by atomizing the molten feed with a gas mixture of 1:1 H_2:CO; this was converted with a quantity of oxygen insufficient for complete combustion in a spray flame. The conversion depended on the C:O ratio and the atomizing conditions. For polymers, about 30–45% of the carbon was converted into C_2 hydrocarbons. PS exhibited the lowest hydrocarbon yields, although the yields were improved by mixing with PE or PP.
- Levie et al. [339] conducted basic studies on the degradation (without and with oxygen) of pellets of refuse derived fuel containing paper, plastics, metal, binder, and moisture. The contributions of composition, type of plastic, oxygen concentration and temperature on heat and time for the process and ash yield were studied.

Partial oxidation as a gasification process *per se* or as part of refinery processes has been considered in a variety of R&D programs. For example:

- Shell International [385] proposed a chemical recycling scheme for MSW consisting of a feed preparation unit and the Shell downstream *gasification* process. The feed preparation unit involves mechanical treatment, thermal cracking (preferably noncatalytic) to shorter molecular length, and removal of impurities that could affect adversely the gasification. The actual gasification is a noncatalytic partial oxidation process converting the hydrocarbon feedstock into synthesis gas, which can be used either directly or as feedstock for manufacture of methanol, acetic acid, ammonia, etc.
- According to publications from Argonne National Laboratory [806, 568], gasification could be used to convert auto shredder residue (ASR) into low BTU gas containing CO, H_2, and light hydrocarbons. The product gas could be used as fuel or as feedstock to produce products such as methanol. Experiments conducted in a high temperature gasification unit on mixtures of ASR with waste oils or waste plastics produced a low BTU industrial fuel gas (≈ 100 BTU/ft^3).
- Research in Germany [564, 367] suggests that degradative extrusion of mixed waste polyolefin plastics in the presence of oxygen can be used as the first step for the production of suitable feedstock for hydrogenation or gasification and production of synthesis gas. Polyolefins and more complex mixtures corresponding to compositions of household refuse were degraded in a twin screw extruder at 400°C by injecting O_2 or compressed air downstream. The products were waxy and brittle at room temperature, but they were of low viscosity and could be pumped as the feed to a gasification unit. The mixed waste plastics could also be fed into a gasifier to produce synthetic gas after size reduction and iron removal.

12.3   Assessment of Technologies

Most of the open issues related to the use of pyrolytic processes as an alternative recycling process are controlled by the overall economics of the process under consideration. These are related to:

- Capital investment;
- Thermal efficiency (i.e. heat requirements);
- Purity and composition of the resulting products;
- Selectivity to desired products;
- Transportation costs for both the feedstock and the degradation products;
- Variability in feedstock composition;
- Scope of preliminary physical separation.

With the exception of wastes that produce high valued monomers, i.e. monomers that are synthesized in a multi-step process, the value of a polymer waste will be determined by its performance relative to crude and hydrocarbon gases (e.g. ethane and propane).

A significant fraction of the incremental embodied energy above the heat of combustion will be recovered only in highly selective processes to high value monomers. For all other pyrolytic processes, the heat of combustion of the wastes is the major controlling factor. Therefore, ranking of potential pyrolytic processes is determined primarily by the state of the technology and the policy goal as shown below:

Maximize recovery of total heat (BTUs):
   Fluid bed boiler $\gg$ FCC $\approx$ Coker $>$ Hydrocracker.
Maximize production of electricity:
   Two-stage pyrolysis $>$ FCC $\approx$ Coker $>$ Conventional Boiler.
Maximize production of liquids:
   FCC $>$ Hydrocracker $\approx$ Visbreaking $>$ Coker $\approx$ Thermal Cracking.

To maximize the production of electricity, it has been assumed that the gas and liquid products produced in the identified processes are combusted in a combined cycle unit. The combined thermal efficiencies for combustion in a combined cycle unit of the products from a two-stage pyrolysis unit, FCC or coker differ by about 10% (relative). However, the thermal efficiency of the conventional boiler is substantially lower.

12.4   Relevance to Critical Waste Streams

In the absence of cost-effective sortation/reclamation technologies, pyrolytic processes are potentially applicable to commingled streams containing mostly hydrocarbon polymers. Therefore, in principle, pyrolytic processes may be applicable to MSW tailings, ASR fluff, and perhaps mixed textiles. However, the limitations imposed by PVC contamination and other impurities will significantly limit the applicability of a specific process or require a pretreatment process.

Chapter 13

Polymer Modification/Compatibilization

13.1 Introduction

Polymers may be chemically modified in order to meet specific cost/performance/processability characteristics. Due to the limitations of unmodified resins, chemically modified products have found commercial applications in end-uses which could have been otherwise unattainable.

Modification may involve single polymers or mixtures of two or more polymers. Reactive modification of single polymers may be accomplished through a variety of reagents or through radiation. Modification of polymer blends is usually accomplished through agents commonly known as compatibilizers that may be added separately or formed in situ during mixing/compounding. In general, reactions are carried out in polymer solutions, in bulk (e.g. in the melt) or on the surface of the plastic part or pellets; furthermore, reactions may be promoted or retarded by a variety of foreign substances.

Recent advances in the technology and economics of modification reactions for single polymers and polymer blends (particularly in the absence of solvents, as in reactive extrusion) suggest that this route of chemical conversion could also be applicable to polymer wastes. Note that polymer wastes may contain polymeric or other contaminants; thus, modification reactions may be affected accordingly to different degrees.

13.2 Modification Reactions of Single Polymers

Tables 13-1 to 13-7 provide a summary of the types of reactions applicable to seven common polymers: four commodity thermoplastics (PE, PP, PVC, PS), two engineering thermoplastics (PET, Polyamides) and PUR which may be available in either a thermoplastic or a thermoset form. In addition to the type of reaction (e.g. bulk, solution, surface, catalytic), information is also supplied on its industrial applications. Solvolysis reactions have been discussed in an earlier part of this book and are not discussed here. References in Tables 13-1 to 13-7 describe reactions of virgin polymers. The same reactions could be, in principle, applicable to recyclable streams although in this case the effects of impurities would need to be carefully analyzed.

Table 13-1 Modification Reactions of Polyethylene (PE)

Type of reaction	Reaction conditions (Bulk/Solution/Surface/Catalytic)	Industrial application	References
1. Chlorosulfonation, then crosslinking by: (a) Metal oxide and carboxylic acid (b) Diepoxides (c) Diols (d) Diamines	Bulk	Yes (as an elastomer)	[723 (p. 174–176)] [132 (p. 263)]
2. Chlorination	Dispersion/Solution	Yes (adhesion promoter)	[725 (p. 692), 132 (p. 254–271)[a]]
3. Sulfonation	Bulk	Yes (dyeing, cement adhesion)[b]	[132 (p. 249), 703 (p. 186)]
4. Fluorination	Bulk	Yes (gasoline tanks)	[132 (p. 257)]
5. Bromination	Bulk	No	[132 (p. 259)]
6. Oxidation by acids or oxidants	Surface/Bulk	Yes (hydrophilic surface)	[722, 790 (p. 204)]
7. Cross-linking by electron beams	Surface	Yes (foams, insulator for high voltage cables)	[723 (p. 154)]
8. Cross-linking by UV-light	Surface/Catalytic	Yes (films)	[723 (p. 156)]
9. Thermal cross-linking by free-radical generators	Bulk/Catalytic	Yes (any size articles)	[723 (p. 158), 190]
10. Silane cross-linking	Bulk/Catalytic	Yes (extruded pipes and foams)	[723 (p. 161)]
11. Cross-linking by microwave energy	Bulk/Catalytic	Yes (high voltage cables, insulators)	[723 (p. 163)]
12. Cross-linking by sulfur	Bulk	Yes	[c]
13. Monomer grafting (a) X-rays (b) peroxide	Surface Solution/Bulk	Yes (compatibilizers) Yes	[132 (p. 1016–1041)] [132 (p. 726), 702, 703 (Ch. 3, 4)]
14. Ozonization	Bulk/Surface	Yes (surface etching, grafting)	[132 (p. 702)]
15. Phosphorylation	Bulk/Catalytic	Yes	[132 (p. 267)]
16. Controlled degradation	Bulk (extrusion)	Yes	[703 (p. 183)]

[a]See also: ACS-PMSE, 68, 28 (1993).
[b]See also: Plastics Technology, February 1993, p. 35.
[c]See also: Makromol. Chem., 76/77, 25–38 (1979).

Important modification reactions of PE and PP (Tables 13-1 and 13-2) involve functionalization with various polar groups (e.g. halogenation, chlorosulfonation), monomer grafting, and cross-linking or degradation through the action of peroxides or radiation. Some important PVC and PS reactions also include grafting and functionalization (Tables 13-3 and 13-4). Chemical modification reactions of PET

Table 13-2 Modification Reactions of Polypropylene (PP)

Type of reaction	Reaction conditions (Bulk/Solution/ Surface/Catalytic)	Industrial application	References
1. Chlorosulfonation	Bulk/Solution	Yes	[132 (p. 266)]
2. Chlorination	Bulk/Solution/ Catalytic	Yes (adhesion promoter)	[748, 132 (p. 261),[a] 703 (p. 186)]
3. Bromination	Bulk/Solution	Not practiced	[703 (p. 186), 132 (p. 261)]
4. a) Ozonization	Surface/Bulk	Yes (less degradation than in O_2, surface etchings)	[132 (p. 702 cf. 574), 839 (p. 196)]
b) Oxidation by atomic oxygen	Surface	Yes (more effective than ozonization)	[839 (p. 197)]
5. Phosphorylation	Bulk/Catalytic	Not practiced	[132 (p. 267)]
6. Peroxidation	Bulk	Yes	[839 (p. 189) 132 (p. 1037)]
7. Oxidation by acids or oxidants	Surface/Bulk	Yes (hydrophilic surface)	[752, 132 (p. 1042)]
8. Photooxidation	Surface/Catalytic	Yes	[132 (p. 1057)]
9. Cross-linking by electron beams	Surface/Bulk	Yes (modified surface)	[132 (p. 733)]
10. Cross-linking by γ-rays	Bulk	Yes (modified bulk)	[132 (p. 733)]
11. Cross-linking by thermolysis and sulfur	Bulk	Yes	
12. Graft copolymerization	Bulk/Surface/Solution	Yes	[132 (p. 858–865), 177, 703 (Ch. 1, 3, 4)]
13. Surface-grafting (chemical/thermal/ radiative)	Surface	Yes	[132 (p. 1030–1040)]
14. Treatment with amines	Surface	Yes (a base for photographic gelatin coatings)	[132 (p. 1044)]
15. Deuteration	Bulk/Catalytic	Not practiced	[132 (p. 249)]
16. Peroxide-controlled degradation	Bulk	Yes	[703 (Ch. 1, 2, 4)]

[a]ACS-PMSE, 68, 28 (1993).

and polyamides (Tables 13-5 and 13-6) include chain extension through their reactive terminal groups and, hence, increase of MW ("upgrading" degraded resins). Important modification reactions of PUR are chain extension, grafting and cross-linking. Surface modification through methoxymethylation for improved thermal and barrier properties has been also practiced (Table 13-7).

Table 13-3 Modification Reactions of Polyvinylchloride (PVC)

Type of reaction	Reaction conditions (Bulk/Solution/ Surface/Catalytic)	Industrial application	References
1. Chlorination	Bulk/Solution	Yes (paints/lacquers, improved thermal stability)	[132 (p. 255, 262)]
2. Photochlorination	Aqueous suspension, Bulk	Yes	[132 (p. 262), 839 (p. 203)]
3. Epoxidation	Bulk/Solution	Yes	[219, 132 (p. 156)]
4. Dechlorination	Solution/Catalytic	Yes (to produce unsaturation)	[243, 132 (p. 80)]
5. Dehydrochlorination (chemically or by radiation (γ-rays, electrons) or thermal)	Solution/Catalytic/ Bulk	Yes	[692, 693, 132 (p. 81, 749)]
6. Oxidation	Bulk	Not practiced	[132 (p. 1077)]
7. Ozonization	Bulk	Yes (for grafting)	[132 (p. 1040), 790 (p. 189)]
8. Mechanochemical block copolymerization with: a) MMA b) Methyl vinyl ketone c) Phenol aldehyde resin d) Polychloroprene	Bulk	Yes	[132 (p. 850, 853, 1103)]
9. Grafting a) (Cationic) styrene, indene, indole b) (Free-radical) MMA, AN	Solution/Catalytic Bulk/cat. emulsion	Yes Yes	[132 (p. 869)] [132 (p. 839)]
10. Surface grafting (by radiation)	Surface	Yes	[695]
11. Grafting with MA in extruder or Brabender	Bulk/Catalytic	Yes	[701, 703 (p. 121)]
12. Reactions with: a) Ethylene diamine b) Hexamethylene diamine c) Thiosorbitol	Surface	Yes (anion exchange membranes)	[696–698, 132 (p. 268)]
13. Friedel-Crafts reaction with: a) Benzene b) Toluene c) m-xylene d) Mesitylene	Solution/Catalytic	Yes (make copolymers, not obtainable otherwise)	[132 (p. 86)]

Table 13-3 (Continued)

Type of reaction	Reaction conditions (Bulk/Solution/ Surface/Catalytic)	Industrial application	References
14. Displacement reactions in extruder a) Na-benzenethiolate b) Na-benzothiazole-2-thiolate c) Na-2-ethyl -hexyl -thiosalicylate	Bulk	Yes	[703 (p. 196), 705]
15. Carbonization by lasers and UV	Bulk	Yes	[839 (p. 203)]
16. Crosslinking (γ-rays in air)	Bulk/Solution	Yes	[132 (p. 748)]
17. Reduction by $(n\text{-Bu})_3\text{SnH}$	Solution	No	[839 (p. 370)]

Table 13-4 Modification Reactions of Polystyrene (PS)

Type of reaction	Reaction conditions (Bulk/Solution/ Surface/Catalytic)	Industrial application	References
1. Sulfonation	Bulk/Solution	Yes (ion-exchange resins)	[132 (p. 280), 730]
2. Nitration	Bulk	Yes	[132 (p. 283), 731, 730]
3. Amination a) Diazotization (phenoles and amines coupling)	Bulk Bulk/Solution/ Catalytic	Yes Yes (very insol. dyes)	[733]
b) Diazotization (hydroquinone or ferrocene coupling)	Bulk/Solution/ Catalytic	Yes (electron exchange resins)	
4. Chlorination	Bulk/Solution	Not practiced	[132 (p. 273, 287), 730, 745]
5. Bromination followed by grafting with vinyl acetate	Bulk/Solution/ Catalytic	Yes (grafted, soluble PS)	[132 (p. 843, 854)]

Table 13-4 (Continued)

Type of reaction	Reaction conditions (Bulk/Solution/ Surface/Catalytic)	Industrial application	References
6. Chloromethylation reaction with: $(CH_3)_2S$, $KSCH_3$, RCOONa, KCN, NR_3, $SC(NH_2)_2$, NH3, $LiPPh_2$, $AlBr_3$, $P(OEt)_3$	Bulk/Catalytic	Yes (intermediates for many other derivatives)	[132 (p. 274), 734]
7. Metalation with I_2, Li, Hg, K, Tl	Solution/Catalytic	Yes	[132 (p. 285), 736]
8. Alkylation (p-i-propyl, p-nonyl, etc.) followed by autoxidation	Bulk/Catalytic	Yes (polymeric peroxide for grafting)	[730, 739, 740]
9. Acylation followed by oxime prepn, condensation with benzaldehyde, or side chain bromination	Bulk/Solution	Yes	[730, 742, 743, 132 (p. 279)]
10. Oxidation by acids or oxidants	Bulk/Surface	Yes (antifogging lenses, coloring with basic dyes, antistatic properties	[132 (p. 1044, 1059)]
11. Ozonization	Bulk/Solution	Yes	[132 (p. 594, 701)]
12. Grafting	Bulk/Surface	Yes	[132 (p. 835–867, 1033)]
13. Cross-linking (chemical) a) via chlorination b) via sulfonation	Bulk/Solution/	Yes	[692, 693, 745, 132 (p. 274)]
14. Cross-linking by thermolysis	Bulk/Catalytic	Yes	
15. Cross-linking by electrostatic forces	Bulk	Yes	
16. Cross-linking by γ-rays	Solution	Yes	[132 (p. 740)]
17. Deuteration	Solution	Not practiced	[132 (p. 253)]
18. Block copolymerization by mechanochemical Rxns—with: Acrylonitrile, Isoprene, MMA, Starch, Vinylidene chloride	Bulk/Catalytic	Yes	[132 (p. 850–871, 1107)]

Table 13-5 Modification Reactions of Polyethylene Terephthalate (PET)

Type of reaction	Reaction conditions (Bulk/Solution/Surface/Catalytic)	Industrial application	References
1. Chain extension, using:			[290, 703 (p. 168)]
(a) Oxazolines	Bulk	Yes (Developmental)	
(b) Bisacyllactams		Yes (Developmental)	
(c) Polycarbodiimides		Yes (Developmental)	
(d) Phenolic esters		No (Phenol by-product)	
(e) Dianhydrides		Yes (cause branching,	
(f) Diisocyanates		thermally unstable	
(g) Bisepoxides		linkages in chain)	
(h) Polyphthalimides			
2. Controlled degradation by EG	Bulk (extrusion)	Yes (for fiber-grade production	[703 (p. 184)]
3. Grafting by			[132 (Ch. XII)]
(a) γ-rays	Surface	Yes (antistatic properties	
(b) UV-light	Surface	Yes	
(c) Ozone	Surface	Not practiced	[695]
(d) Chemical	Surface	Yes (antistatic fabric)	[132 (p. 1046)]
4. Degradation by			[132 (p. 750)]
(a) γ-rays (>50 Mrad)	Bulk	Not practiced	
(b) UV-light	Bulk	Not practiced	
5. Cross-linking by γ-rays (<50 Mrad)	Bulk	Not practiced	[132 (p. 750)]

13.3   Compatibilization of Polymer Blends

The majority of polymers found in commingled waste plastics streams are immiscible, i.e. when melt blended a phase separated morphology is formed. Blend composition, viscoelastic properties of the components and interfacial adhesion are among the parameters known to control the size and morphology of the dispersed phase and its stability to coalescence. Heterogeneous blends of technological importance are termed "compatibilized" and constitute the majority of the commercial blends introduced in the past 20 years. In such blends, satisfactory physical and mechanical properties are related to the presence of a finely dispersed phase and resistance to gross phase segregation.

Polymer compatibility may be enhanced by various methods. Co-crystallization and co-cross-linking can often result in stable morphologies that are resistant to coalescence. Strong interactions such as acid-base or ion-dipole, hydrogen bonding and transition metal complexation have also been shown to enhance thermodynamic miscibility of suitably functionalized components and result in improved compatibility in a variety of systems of technological importance. More commonly,

Table 13-6 Modification Reactions of Nylons

Type of reaction	Reaction conditions (Bulk/Solution/ Surface/Catalytic)	Industrial application	References
1. Oxidation	Bulk	Not practiced	[132 (p. 1080)]
2. Photo-oxidation	Bulk	Not practiced	[132 (p. 1080)]
3. Ozonization	Surface	Yes (for grafting)	[132 (p. 1040)]
4. Surface grafting by irradiation	Surface	Yes	[132 (p. 1024– 1036), 695]
5. Chain extension using (a) polyepoxides (b) polyisocyanates (c) polycarbodiimides (d) polylactams	Bulk (extruder)	Yes	[290, 703 (p. 166)]
6. Degradation (a) γ-rays/vacuum (b) UV/O_2	Bulk Bulk/Surface	Not practiced Not practiced (discoloration)	[132 (p. 751, 1010)]
7. Sulfation (a) conc. H_2SO_4 (b) Chlorosulfonic acid	Bulk	Not practiced	[132 (p. 387–389)]
8. Reaction with formaldehyde (N-Alkoxymethyl substitution)	Bulk/Solution	Yes (nylon 800)	[132 (p. 405), 717 (p. 17)]
9. N-Alkyl substitution	Bulk/Solution	Yes (lower melting nylons)	[716, 717 (p. 16, 44)]
10. Cross-linking (thermal)	Bulk (absence of O_2)	Yes	[717 (p. 41)]
11. Reactions of amino end groups with (a) Epoxy (b) Acrylic (c) Acids (d) Phenolic resins (e) Glyoxal	Bulk/Catalytic	Yes	[717 (p. 50–53)]
12. Melt condensation (a) Diff. nylons (b) Diff. nylon salts	Bulk	Yes	
13. Controlled degradation	Bulk (extrusion)	Yes	[703 (p. 184)]

compatibility is promoted through copolymers (e.g. block, graft) with segments capable of specific interactions and/or chemical reactions with the blend components. The copolymers may be added separately, or formed in situ by blending suitably functionalized polymers. Compatibility may also be enhanced through the addition of specific low MW compounds promoting copolymer formation and/or cross-linking.

Table 13-7 Modification Reactions of Polyurethane (PUR)

	Type of reaction	Reaction conditions (Bulk/Solution/ Surface/Catalytic)	Industrial application	References
1.	Isocyanate prepolymer	Bulk/Chain Extension	Yes (sheets for carpet underlay	[123, 822]
2.	"Rebonding"	Bulk/Chain Extension	Yes (substrate for horticulture or cultivation)	[38]
3.	Grafting	Surface/reactive foam extender	Yes (extender in PUR slabstock)	[147]
4.	Blocked isocyanates	Bulk/Catalytic	Yes (wire enamels)	[132 (p. 993)]
5.	Cross-linking: (a) Diisocyanates and their dimers (b) Peroxides	Bulk	Yes	[723 (p. 173)]
6.	Methoxymethylation	Surface	Yes (Improved thermal stability and barrier properties)	[PMSE-ACS, 68, 327 (1993)]

Tables 13-8 to 13-18 summarize recent literature data on the compatibilization of binary blends having as one component PE (Table 13-8), PP (Table 13-9), miscellaneous polyolefins (Table 13-10), PVC (Table 13-11), PS (Table 13-12), PET (Table 13-13), PBT (Table 13-14), polyamide 6 (Table 13-15), polyamide 66 (Table 13-16), and various polyamides (Table 13-17). Table 13-18 contains miscellaneous polymer blends. In addition to information on the type of the compatibilizing agents/reactions, available data on the types of polymers used (virgin or waste) are given.

Compatibilization of waste polymer mixtures containing two or more components can be, in principle, attained through melt processing techniques that have been used successfully for neat polymers. The following is a summary of our present knowledge on the types and function of compatibilizers of melt blended polymer mixtures:

a) In situ formed copolymers

During melt blending of a pair of suitably functionalized polymers A and B, interchain block or graft copolymers may be formed at various concentrations through covalent or ionic bonding. The in situ formed compatibilizers have segments that are chemically identical to those in the respective unreacted homopolymers and are thought to be located preferentially at the interface, thus, lowering interfacial tension, and also promoting mechanical interlocking through interpenetration and entanglements. Examples of some important compatibilizing reactions that can take place easily across polymer phase boundaries involve functionalities such as anhydride or carboxyl with amine (e.g. PP-g-MA/ PA 6), epoxy with anhydride or carboxyl (e.g. PPE + SMA/EVA-co-GMA), oxazolin with carboxyl (e.g. OPS/EAA), isocyanate with hydroxyl or carboxyl (e.g. PBT/isocyanate terminated polymers), carbodiimide with carboxyl (e.g.

Table 13-8 Compatibilization of Polyethylene (PE) Blends

2nd polymer	Compatibilizing agents/reactions	References
cellulose	epoxidized soybean oil, maleated PP wax, potato starch	[549[a]]
EVA	talc	[529]
EVA (saponified)	polyolefin functionalized with –OH, –COOH	[508]
EVA (saponified)	PE functionalized with MA and/or unsaturated carboxylic acid	[524]
EVACO	HMDAC, DOTG	[661]
EVOH	PE-g-MA	[462]
NR	PE-g-MA/ENR, EPDM, sulfonated-EPDM, PE-g-MA, CPE	[99]
NR	peroxide/coagent	[656]
PA6	EAA, CPE	[604]
PA6	SEBS-g-MA, PP-g-MA, PE-g-MA	[575, 576, 578, 581]
PA6	photooxidized PE	[579]
PA6	PE-g-BA	[580]
PA6	ionomer	[293, 582]
PA6	SAN, SMA, PP-g-MA	[576]
PA6	PP-g-MA	[369]
PA6,PA66	PE functionalized with COOH, MA	[577]
PA66	PE-g-FA	[490]
PA11	PP-g-MA	[576]
PBT	ionomer	[493]
PET	styrenic block copolymer, EAEGMA, EPDM	[102, 429[a]]
PET	EGMA	[457, 559]
PET[a]/PP[a]/PS[a]/PVC	EPR, modified EPR, styrenic block copolymer, modified SEBS	[619[a]]
PET[a]/PS[a]/PVC	styrenic block copolymer, anhydride modified styrene block copolymer	[213[a]]
PP	NR/NBR/IPR/vulcanizing agents	[805[a]]
PP	peroxide, EPR	[297, 658–660]
PP	SEBS, EAA precoated GRT, EAA	[375[a]]
PP	SEBS, BR, EPR, EPDM	[429[a]]
PP	PP-g-PE	[467]
PP	2,5-dimethyl-2,5-bis-(t-butyl-peroxy)hexyne	[297, 558]
PP/PS	EVA, SEB, SEBS, PP-g-AA	[186[a]]
PP/PVC/(PET,PA)	ionomer	[445]
PPE	carboxy- or epoxy-functionalized PPE, functionalized PP or PE with carboxylic acid or carbamic ester group	[470]
PPE	hydrogenated PS-b-BR	[475]
PS	SEBS/BM	[535]
PS	PS-g-PE	[682]
PS	vinylaromatic grafted polyolefins	[528]
PS	hydrog. SBR, PS-g-LDPE, SEBS	[188,[a] 429,[a] 581]
PS	SEP, SEBS, SBS, SB, PS-g-EPDM	[368, 570]
PS	dicumyl peroxide, triallyl isocyanurate	[294]
PS	LDPE/cross-linked rubbers	[527]
PS/PVC	MA/dicumyl peroxide, EVA/dicumyl peroxide	[804[a]]
PVC	CPE	[337, 338, 765 (p. 53)]
PVC	PE-g-MMA , ECO, EVACO, EVA, CPE	[288, 429[a]]
PVDC	PE-co-EMA	[463, 482[a]]
TPUR	polyolefin funct. with carboxylic acid, ester, salt, anhydride, hydroxy, or acyloxy	[466]

[a]Marked references include information on waste polymer.

Table 13-9 Compatibilization of Polypropylene (PP) Blends

2nd polymer	Compatibilizing agents/reactions	References
ABS	PP-g-MA, (PAN-co-2-hydroxypropyl methacrylate-co-PS)	[515]
EPC	OH funct. EPC, PP-g-MA	[178]
EPDM	dimethylol-phenolic curative	[662]
EPDM	peroxide	[663]
EPR	(iPP-g-SA)-g-(OH or NH$_2$ funct. EPR)	[586]
EPR	hydrog. poly(dimethyl-1,3 butadiene-b-IPR)	[516]
EVA (saponified)	EDTA salt	[501]
EVA (saponified)	Mg stearate	[503]
EVA/EPR	terpene resin	[484]
EVOH	EA-MMA-PP graft copolymer	[455]
EVOH	PP-g-VPD	[458]
NBR	NBR-b-PP	[91]
NBR (7% -COOH)	PP-g-2-isopropenyl-2-oxazoline	[555]
NR	peroxide, bismaleimides	[664]
NR	PP-g-MA/ENR, CPE, EPDM	[99]
PA	EGMA-co-VA	[511]
PA	PE-co-MAA-co-IBA	[293]
PA, PA6	PP-g-MA	[535]
PA6	modified polyolefin	[526]
PA6	PP-g-AA	[108]
PA6	organofunctional zirconate, peroxide	[682]
PA6	PP-g-MA, PP-g-AA	[108, 429, 587]
PA6	olefin copolymer grafted with reactive amine monomers and oligoamides	[522]
PA6	PBVE-g-PMOX	[588]
PA6, PA66	EPDM-g-MA/EPR, SEBS-g-MA, PP-g-MA	[429]
PA66	PP-g-MA, PP-g-AA	[369, 429, 507]
PA66	maleated SBR/trimellitic acid modified hydrogenated butadiene copolymer	[512]
PA66/ADA-co-MXDA	PP-g-MA	[517]
PBT	ionomer	[493]
PBT	PP-g-MA/2,2′-bis(oxazoline)	[521]
PBT	PP-g-GMA, EAEGMA	[429^a]
PC	PET/EGMA, PBT/EGMA	[92]
PET	PP-g-MA	[514]
PMMA	PP-g-MMA	[471]
PPE	(PP-g-MA + OH funct. PPE)	[523]
PPE/HIPS	maleated PP-g-MA reacted with OH-terminated PS	[518]
PPS	PP-g-PS	[460]
PS	RPS/PP-g-AA, PP-g-PS	[429^a]
PS	PS-b-PB	[487, 488]
PS	SEBS	[138]
PS-co-PMS	EPDM-g-(PS-co-PMS)	[480]
PVC	bismaleimide (PDM, CP)	[665]
SMA	SBR	[459]

^{a}Marked references include information on waste polymer.

Table 13-10 Compatibilization of Miscellaneous Polyolefin Blends

1st polymer	2nd polymer	Compatibilizing agents/reactions	References
EGMA	carboxy-terminated SAN	glycidyl/carboxyl	[520]
PE/PP	NBR	PP-g-MA/amine terminated NBR	[91]
PE-b-PP	PA-PI elastomer	specific interaction	[509]
polyolefins	bitumen	maleated PP, ferric oxide	[182]
polyolefins	EVOH	MA modified olefinic copolymer	[682]
polyolefins	PA	EVOH contg. unhydrolyzed VA groups	[478]
polyolefins	PA	block copolymer of polyoxazoline & polylactone	[461]
polyolefins	PA6	polyamide-polyalkylene	[525]
polyolefins (chem.mod.)	PA6	reactive mixing	[609]
polyolefins	PA6-co-PA66/PVOH	PE-g-FA	[472]
polyolefins	PC	PP-g-polyester	[349]
polyolefins	PC	PET/EGMA	[502, 506]
polyolefins	PS	LLDPE/cross-linked rubber	[527]
polyolefins	TPUR	polyolefin funct. with carboxylic acid, ester, salt, anhydride, hydroxy or acyloxy	[466]
polyolefins	PUR	PUR as filler	[161, 809 (Ch. 22)]

Table 13-11 Compatibilization of Polyvinyl Chloride (PVC) Blends

2nd polymer	Compatibilizing agents/reactions	References
ABS	PVC-g-ABS	[757]
CPE, EVA	partly miscible	[757]
DOP/CPVC, PCL/CPVC,	partly miscible	[372]
PAMA/PBMA EEACO, EVACO,	partly miscible	[757]
EVA-co-PVC, MSAN, NBR, PCL, Poly(butylene] adipate), PVC-b-PBT-b-PTMEGT		
MBS, SBR	impact modification	[757]
PB	mechanochemical interactions	[757]
PEA, PMA	partly miscible	[597]
PMMA	hydrogen bonding	[757]
PMMA, SAN	miscible	[761]
PUR	miscibility depends on the structure of PUR	[757]
SMA	α-hydrogen of PVC/carbonyl functional group	[757]

Table 13-12 Compatibilization of Polystyrene (PS) Blends

2nd polymer	Compatibilizing agents/reactions	References
EPDM	dicumyl peroxide, triallyl isocyanurate	[557]
PA	PS-g-PA	[682]
PA6	SMA, SAN	[576, 667]
PA6	SMA, SEBS-g-MA, SAN	[581]
PA66	SMA, SGMA	[595]
PBT	PS-b-PBT, PS-b-PET	[684]
PET	PS-b-PET, PS-b-PBT	[581]
PET	PS-co-PCL	[686]
PMMA	OH end group PS/PMMA-co-MA	[535]
PMS	PS-b-PB	[765 (p. 47)]
PPE	GMA funct. PS	[505]
PPE	phosphonated EP, phosphonated EPDM, Zn sulfonated PS, zinc stearate, triphenyl phosphate	[435]
PPE	S-EPDM, S-PS	[644, 645]
PPE	PPE-g-EAA	[655]
PVC	MS-co-MAN, SAN	[757]
PVC	PS-g-PVC	[188[a]]
S-EPDM, SVP	pyridine group, sulfonate group	[646]

[a]Marked references include information on waste polymer.

PBT/ carbodiimide functionalized polymers); transesterification (e.g. PC/PBT), macroradical recombination in polyolefins, and interchain ionic salt formation in sulfonated PS-EPDM/PPE blends are other examples of compatibilizing reactions.

b) Copolymers added separately

Non-reactive copolymers   Interfacially active graft or block copolymers of the type A-B or A-C may compatibilize the immiscible polymers A and B provided that C is also miscible or capable of strong interactions with B. Examples include styrene/butadiene or isoprene diblock and triblock copolymers in blends of PS with polyolefins, EPM or EPDM in PE/PP blends, PS/PMMA block copolymers in PVDF/PS-PMMA mixtures.

Table 13-13 Compatibilization of Polyethylene Terephthalate (PET) Blends

2nd polymer	Compatibilizing agents/reactions	References
EEAGMA, EEAMA	reactive mixing	[623]
EGMA	reactive mixing	[92, 502, 506]
EGMA, SGMA	reaction of PET end groups with epoxy groups	[354]
EIBAMAA, EMAA	reactive mixing	[628]
EPR	EGMA	[559[a]]
EVAGMA	reactive mixing	[628]
PA66	p-toluenesulfonic acid	[592]
PC	transesterification	[631, 532[a]]
PEN	transesterification	[354]
PPE	PET-b-PPE, SGMA	[584[a]]

[a]Marked references include information on waste polymer.

Table 13-14 Compatibilization of Polybutylene Terephthalate (PBT) Blends

2nd polymer	Compatibilizing agents/reactions	References
EAEGMA, EAEMA	reactive mixing	[602, 623]
EEAGMA, EEAMA	reactive mixing	[623]
EGMA	reactive mixing	[92]
EMeAGMA, EVAGMA	PTMO, PA oligomer	[679]
PE-g-FA, PP-g-FA EPDM	EPDM-g-GMA	[685]
EPDM (epoxized)	reactive mixing	[624]
PA6	PS-co-MA-co-GMA, PBT-g-PA6, PS-co-PCL-co-GMA	[672]
PC	transesterification	[625, 626]
PC/phenoxy	interchange reaction	[636]
PS/PPE	PS-b-PBT, PS-b-PET	[684]
SMA	proprietary compatibilizer	[674]

Table 13-15 Compatibilization of Polyamide 6 (PA6) Blends

2nd polymer	Compatibilizing agents/reactions	References
ABS	HISMA	[429ª]
ABS	ABS-g-MA, ABS-g-FA	[599, 667]
ABS	SAN-g-MA	[600]
ABS, PC	PGA copolymer	[532]
acrylic elastomers	PB-g-(PS/AA), SBR-g-(MMA/AA)	[670]
EAEMA	reactive mixing	[602]
EMAA	reactive mixing	[605]
EMeAMAA	amine/carboxylic acid	[497]
EPDM	EPDM-g-MA	[433, 671]
EPDM	impact modification	[606–608]
EPR	EPR-g-ACL, EPR-g-MACL, EPR-g-MA	[667]
EPR	EPR-g-lactam	[614]
EPR	EPR-g-MA	[571]
EPR	EPR-g-SA	[611, 612, 615, 690]
EPR, EVA, EPDM	hydroxy func. EPR, EVA, EPDM	[668]
EVA	reactive mixing	[573]
EVA (saponified)	PA6/(PE-b-PP)-g-MA	[500]
EVACO	reactive mixing	[497]
PC	amide-ester exchange	[594]
PC	HIPS-g-MA	[429ª]
PPE	brominated PPE-g-PA	[617]
PPE	PPE-g-MA, PPE-anhydride	[296]
SAN	SMA or RPS	[600]
SAN	SMA	[618]
SAN-g-EPDM	SAN-co-MA	[456]
SEBS	SEBS-g-MA	[596]
SEBS-g-MA	grafted MA/amine	[598]
S-EPDM/PA11	partly compatible	[613]
SMA	MA/amine	[674]

ªMarked references include information on waste polymer.

Table 13-16 Compatibilization of Polyamide 66 (PA66) Blends

2nd polymer	Compatibilizing agents/reactions	References
BA-co-2-hydroxyethyl methacrylate,	SMA	[668]
EAA, EIBAMAA, EMeAMAME, EVA, EVACO, EVAMAA EPDM-g-MA, EPDM-g-MAME, EPDM-g-BASA, EPDM-g-PASA, EPDM-g-FA, BR-g-PASA IBR-g-PASA, SBR/PE-g-MA, caprolactam oligomer -g-MA-g-EPDM, EPR-g-PASA	amine, carboxylic acid, ionomer	[497]
EAEMA	reactive mixing	[602]
EPR	EPR-g-MA	[620, 621, 433]
PPE	grafted MA/amine	[675]
PPE	EPR-g-MA/EGMA-co-VA	[676]
PPE	SEBS-g-MA	[598]
PPE	organofunctional groups	[677, 678]
PPE	PPE-g-MA, PPE-co-PA	[296]
SEBS	SEBS-g-MA	[596]
SMA	MA/amine	[674]

Reactive copolymers   Reactive copolymers or functionalized polymers of the type A-C (where C is a long reactive segment or a functional group attached to the main chain) may compatibilize a polymer pair A and B provided that C is capable of chemically reacting with B. The non-reactive segment of the polymeric compatibilizer often has different chemical and structural identity from component A, but is still capable of specific interactions leading to a certain degree of miscibility. The majority of blends in this category employ polyamide as the constituent that may react with compatibilizers containing anhydride or carboxyl functionalities to form amide or imide linkages. Other copolymers may

Table 13-17 Compatibilization of Miscellaneous Polyamide (PA) Blends

1st polymer	2nd polymer	Compatibilizing agents/reactions	References
PA	ABS	maleated SAN	[532]
PA	ABS, PA6-co-PA66	SAN-co-MA	[591]
PA	PPE	MA/EPDM grafted with PS-MMA mixture	[454]
PA6, 10	EAEMA	reactive mixing	[602]
PA11	SAA	amine/carboxylic acid	[622]
PA12	EIBAMAA	ionomers	[497]
PA12	PUR	EMeAMAME, EIBAMAA ionomer	[497]

Table 13-18 Compatibilization of Miscellaneous Polymer Blends

1st polymer	2nd polymer	Compatibilizing agents/reactions	References
ABS	epoxy	ABS functionalized with -COOH	[433]
ABS	PA6-co-PA66	SAN-co-MA	[591]
ABS	PA, polyolefin, PVC	RPS	[682]
EAEGMA	SAN	carboxy-terminated SAN	[520]
Epoxy	ATBN	epoxide/amine	[648]
Epoxy	CTBN	epoxide/carboxyl groups	[651, 652]
Epoxy	HTBN	TDI, hydroxyl & epoxy group	[649]
Epoxy	PSn	epoxide/hydroxy(terminal)	[433]
EPR	SBR	block SBR	[464]
EVA	EVACO	EVACO curatives/HMDAC/DOTG	[661]
EVA(sapond)	EPR	grafting oligomer PA6 on PE-g-MA	[504]
NBR	FPM	triazine dithiol complex	[681]
NBR-co-AA	HIPS	RPS	[653]
PAr	phenoxy	terminal hydroxyl	[654
PC	PAr	transesterification reaction	[433, 633, 634]
PC	phenoxy	interchange reaction	[635]
PCL	CHR, chlorinated polyester, CPP, polychlorostyrene	miscible	[757]
POM	acrylic	organofunctional titanate	[682]
SMA	CPVC	miscible	[674]

contain the highly reactive oxazoline, epoxy, isocyanate, or carbodiimide groups discussed earlier.

c) Low MW Compatibilizing Compounds

The addition of low MW compounds in a polymer blend may promote compatibility through the formation of copolymers (random, block, graft) or through the combined effects of copolymer formation and cross-linking. Low MW compounds are usually added at relatively low concentrations (typically 0.1–3 % by wt.); thus, they may offer economic advantages vs. polymeric compatibilizers that are usually effective at higher concentrations. Examples include compounds such as p-toluene sulfonic acid or phosphites that catalyze transamidation melt reactions in blends containing polyamides and polyesters, peroxides (often in combination with coagents), that may promote compatibilization through the recombination of macroradicals in a variety of polyolefin-based systems, cross-linking additives in "dynamically vulcanized" thermoplastic elastomers, common curatives in co-cross-linkable rubbers, etc.

13.4   Applications of Modification/Compatibilization to Waste Polymers

13.4.1   Present Status

Although chemical modification of industrial scrap (e.g. by upgrading the MW of single polymers or by compatibilizing polymer mixtures) is currently practiced for both in-house and external use, there exist a large number of non-exploited technologies that could be applicable to wastes originating from other sources. The following are some examples of commercial/developmental technologies described in the recent literature:

Single Waste

- Reaction of reclaimed PET with acid and glycol to form UPR [5];
- Reaction of DMT from PET waste with polyols to form new polyols for rigid PUR foams [209];
- PUR or polyurea may flow under the combined influence of temperature, pressure and shear and be reused; or, after grinding they can be mixed with additional isocyanate and compression molded [401];
- Grind flexible PUR scrap and mix with polyol to form new foam [147];
- Chain extension of waste nylon 6 fibers in the presence of TiO_2 [426];
- Biodegradability, composting of polycaprolactone, polylactic acid, PHBV [124].

Mixed Waste

- Mix powdered reclaimed resin with glass fibers and additives to form stampable sheet [99];
- Mix commingled stream consisting primarily of waste PE with bitumen [216];
- Diblock and triblock styrene compatibilizers for mixtures of HDPE-PS-PP-LDPE [186];
- Addition of blowing agent and peroxide in a commingled stream to upgrade properties [286];
- Molding compounds from waste plastics through the addition of flame retardant fillers and coupling agents [348];
- Injection molding (at low cylinder temperatures) of mixed plastics from domestic refuse to produce parts with good surface quality and properties [425];
- Mix waste polyolefins/PVC/polyester with compatibilizer (grafted EPDM), fillers, optional impact modifiers and blowing agents in extruder and shape to produce construction materials (lumber substitutes) [445];
- Degradability, photodegradability [355].

13.4.2 Developments

Most of the recent experimental/developmental work on chemical modification focuses on upgrading single polymers through MW increase or functionalization, and improving properties of mixtures through compatibilization and reinforcements. In the area of polymer blends, virgin polymers are often used to assess the applicability of the selected technology to waste streams. A complete list of compatibilizing systems that are available for experimentation with waste polymers is included in Tables 13-8 to 13-19 and in the bibliography. The following are some literature examples of recent developments with waste polymers:

Single Waste

- Shear modification of cross-linked waste LDPE agricultural film; increase MFI, decrease elasticity [101];
- Modification of flow characteristics of waste polyethylenes through peroxides [190];
- Use of recycled PET to synthesize UPR for impregnating concrete structures [374, 384];
- Upgrading of MW of waste nylon 6 and polyester fibers through thermal treatment [83];
- Biodegradation [119].

It was recently announced that sulfonated HDPE waste could replace part of the aggregate in concrete[1]; the resulting good adhesion between the recycled plastic and the matrix helps to improve impact resistance.

Mixed Waste

- Review of potential compatibilizers for industrial scrap [188, 429, 212];
- Compatibilizers for nylon and PP fibers from carpets to develop moldable materials [108, 417, 796];
- Wood fibers from newsprint and other sources as reinforcements for virgin or waste thermoplastics with optional adhesion promoters [328, 419–423, 547, 549];
- Wood fibers combined with multilayered PP from recycled ketchup bottles [110];
- Evaluation of compatibilizers for refined commingled post-consumer plastics from Rutgers University reclamation plant [213];
- Feasibility study for compatibilization of PS/PE/PMMA through graft copolymers [238];
- Evaluation of compatibilizers for waste LDPE/HDPE [233, 289];
- Evaluation of coupling agents for waste PE/PP filled with ground rubber tires [375];
- Compatibilization of PET/PPE industrial scrap [584];
- Use of reinforcements in order to overcome the lower properties of reprocessed plastics [700];
- Functionalization of refined commingled post-consumer plastics for better adhesion with reinforcements/fillers [213];
- HDPE/LDPE/PS/PVC waste mixtures compatibilized through maleic anhydride/peroxide and EVA [804];
- PP/Plasticized PVC industrial scrap compatibilized with CPE or bismaleimide [665];
- PE/PVC waste compatibilized with CPE, EVA [25, 288, 338, 765];
- Photooxidized PE from waste films melt blended with nylon [579];
- Compatibilization of PP/PS waste with styrenic block copolymers [138];
- Compatibilizers for automotive fluff [801];
- Mixed polymers with compatibilizers for melt blowing into nonwovens [541];
- Biodegradation [191].

---

[1]Anonymous, Plastics Technology, p. 35, February 1993.

A proprietary technology—Solid State Shear Extrusion—under development at the Illinois Institute of Technology, Chicago, IL[1], claims to produce fine powders of less than 100 micron size from a variety of thermoplastics, thermosets and commingled plastics. Heterogeneous mixtures are claimed to be pulverized better than homogeneous [820]. In an earlier communication[2] from Northwestern University's Industrial Research Laboratory (BIRL) on a similar technology, it was proposed that mechanochemical reactions occuring during the pulverization process may facilitate the formation of compatibilizing graft and block copolymers between the immiscible polymers of the commingled feedstock. BIRL is currently under contract with DOE's INCOR program to demonstrate that commingled plastics can be pulverized without sortation.[3] In a recent publication [834] on a similar Russian technology—(elastic deformation, pulverization)—details are given on the properties of LDPE/rubber mixtures processed by co-pulverization in the presence of unspecified modifiers; mechanical properties of the thus produced blends were significantly higher than those of blends produced by melt mixing or co-pulverizing without modifiers.

The availability of developmental polymeric compatibilizers for PS/PE, PS/PP and ABS/PP waste mixtures has been recently announced [821] by BASF Corp., Parsipanny, NJ. These pelletized products are mixtures of two or three different polymers and are recommended for use at 5–10% levels.

13.4.3   Assessment of Technologies

The advancement of recycling of single and mixed waste plastics through chemical modification/compatibilization should benefit from research in the following areas:

- Investigation of the precise effects of *impurities* on a particular modification reaction; this may be related to "refining" of the waste stream through chopping, washing, melt filtering, etc., or through more advanced reclamation technologies;
- Analytical methods for compositional analysis of mixed polymer waste (preferably on line);
- Optimize compatibilizing systems for a particular binary mixture; design *compatibilizers* for more complex multicomponent mixtures;
- Upgrade properties of reprocessed materials through *reinforcements* and evaluate products for load-bearing applications;
- Identification of suitable processing/long term *stabilizers* for mixed plastics where partitioning and migration of additives in the different phases may be a major problem.

---

[1]T. Shutov, Literature on SSSE, CEPSE, Illinois Institute of Technology, December 1992.
[2]K. Khait, Proposal from BIRL Industrial Research Laboratory, Northwestern University, Evanston, IL on "Novel Pulverization Process for Commingled Plastics Waste Recovery", June 1992.
[3]K. Khait, Personal communication, February 1993.

However, the most important issue to be addressed when considering chemical modification/compatibilization as an alternative recycling method is the identification of *applications* for products based on modified single or mixed plastics.

For single *plastics*, several technologies listed in Tables 13-1 to 13-7 could be applicable to waste feedstocks of variable purity. The following are examples of potential applications for modified single polymer wastes:

- Chlorinated polyolefins as adhesion promoters for paints; highly chlorinated (70%) PE for abrasion resistant traffic paints;
- Vulcanized chlorosulfonated PE as an elastomer having a wide range of properties depending on the type of vulcanizing agents;
- Functionalized polyolefins or PS through sulfonation or monomer grafting to promote adhesion in cement, dyed polymers, fillers, reinforcements, etc.;
- Peroxide modified PE with upgraded MFI in replacing virgin resins; similarly, crosslinked PE for a variety of applications;
- Cracked polyolefins through thermooxidative degradation to produce functionalized waxes;
- Chain extended condensation polymers (e.g. Nylons, PET) with upgraded MW in replacing virgin materials; isocyanate extended waste PUR for use as sheets for carpet underlay;
- Surface modified ground PUR for improved addition in PUR foam matrix.

Mixed plastics, modified through compatibilizers and, perhaps, additional fillers and reinforcements, could find uses in thin-walled, load-bearing applications that currently utilize neat resins or commercial molding compounds. Potential applications could involve long life cycle products in consumer durables, automotive, appliances, etc. "Breadth" of specifications and performance characteristics will be critical in selecting targets to be matched with recycled materials. The potential use in thin-walled applications is in contrast to the current limited utilization of unmodified commingled plastics (described in an earlier part of this report) in thick sectioned shapes or products. With increasing thin-walled applications, however, an important question needs to be answered: how does one recycle products from the increasingly more complex materials which, eventually, will become a significant portion of the total waste stream?

13.4.4   Relevance to Critical Waste Streams

Chemical modification of single and mixed plastics is highly relevant to all four critical waste streams. Reclaimed single resins recovered mostly from MSW and textile waste streams may be upgraded through MW increases. Other sources of mixed plastics for which presently there are no cost-effective sortation/reclamation technologies for the single components are:

- MSW tailings including post-consumer, industrial scrap and multilayer containers;

- Automotive "fluff" or refined fractions thereof, where a variety of difficult to separate polymers may coexist;
- Textiles/carpets where fibers may not be easily separated from other fibers or backing of different chemical nature;
- Wire and cable where PE, PVC and other polymers may coexist.

For these waste streams, the development of compatibilization technologies combined with the identification of suitable end-uses and applications may present a viable alternative to pyrolysis or incineration.

13.5   Additional References

In addition to the references listed in the text, the following articles should be consulted for further information on the chemical modification of both neat and waste plastics:

Single Plastics
[20, 21, 69, 78, 98, 161, 181, 184, 192, 198, 200, 201, 206, 208, 221, 225, 226, 291, 292, 295, 299, 335, 336, 356, 362, 388, 389, 395, 427, 428, 437, 442, 447, 448, 452, 456, 519, 537, 550–554, 559, 616, 627, 657, 695, 701, 702, 710, 713, 714, 720, 726–728, 736, 744, 754, 762, 767, 769, 770, 772, 775, 784, 788, 789, 797, 820].

Mixed Plastics
[20, 25, 69, 79, 109, 163, 164, 176, 179, 180, 198, 223, 224, 226, 244, 245, 248, 299, 370, 427, 428, 432, 450, 453, 468, 469, 473, 474, 479, 481, 483, 486, 489, 491, 492, 494, 495, 498, 499, 510, 513, 538, 546, 548, 556, 559, 583, 588, 589, 593, 629, 630, 637, 643, 647, 648, 650, 663, 669, 680, 681, 683, 708, 709, 711, 719, 721, 724, 728, 729, 732, 735, 737, 738, 741, 746, 747, 750, 755, 759, 763, 768, 769, 771, 775, 780, 786, 788, 789, 797, 820, 821].

Abbreviations of Monomers/Polymers

AA	Acrylic acid
AAS	Poly(acrylonitrile-co-acrylate-co-styrene)
ABR	Acrylate-butadiene rubber
ABS	Poly(acrylonitrile-co-butadiene-co-styrene)
ACL	Acryloyl caprolactam
ADA	Adipic acid
AE	Acrylic ester
AN	Acrylonitrile
ATBN	Amine terminated butadiene-acrylonitrile rubber
BA	Butyl acrylate

BASA	Benzoic acid sulfonyl azide
BM	Bis-maleimide
BR	Butyl rubber
CHDM	Cyclohexane dimethanol
CHR	Polyepichlorohydrin elastomer
co	Copolymer
CO	Carbon monoxide
CP	Chlorinated polyolefin
CPE	Chlorinated polyethylene
CPP	Chlorinated polypropylene
CPVC	Chlorinated polyvinyl chloride
CTBN	Carboxyl terminated butadiene-acrylonitrile rubber
DIMAE	Dimethylaminoethanol
DOP	Di(ethyl-2-hexyl)phthalate
DOTG	Di-(o-tolyl) guanidine
E	Ethylene
EA	Ethyl acrylate
EAA	Poly(ethylene-co-acrylic acid)
EAC	Ethylene acrylate copolymer
EAEAA	Ethylene acrylic ester acrylic acid terpolymer
EAEGMA	Ethylene acrylic ester glycidyl methacrylate terpolymer
EAEMA	Ethylene acrylic ester maleic anhydride terpolymer
EAMMA	Ethyl acrylate methyl methacrylate copolymer
ECO	Ethylene carbon monoxide copolymer
EDTA	Ethylene diimine tetraacetic acid
EEACO	Ethylene ethylacrylate carbon monoxide terpolymer
EEAGMA	Ethylene ethylacrylate glycidyl methacrylate terpolymer
EEAMA	Ethylene ethylacrylate maleic anhydride terpolymer
EG	Ethylene glycol
EGMA	Ethylene glycidyl methacrylate copolymer
EIBAMAA	Ethylene isobutyl acrylate methacrylic acid terpolymer
EMAA	Ethylene methacrylic acid copolymers
EMeAMAA	Ethylene methyl acrylate methacrylic acid terpolymer
EMeAMAME	Ethylene methyl acrylate monoethyl ester of maleic anhydride terpolymer
ENR	Epoxydized natural rubber
EPC	Ethylene-alpha-olefin copolymer
EPDM	Poly(ethylene-co-propylene-co-diene)
EPR	Poly(ethylene-co-propylene) elastomer
EVA	Poly(ethylene-co-vinyl acetate)
EVACO	Poly(ethylene vinyl acetate carbon monooxide)
EVAGMA	Ethylene vinyl acetate glycidyl methacrylate terpolymer
EVAMAA	Ethylene vinyl acetate methacrylic acid terpolymer
EVOH	Poly(ethylene vinyl alcohol)
FA	Fumaric acid
FAME	Monoethyl ester of fumaric acid
FPM	Poly(vinylidenefluoride-co-fluoropropylene)
g	grafted
GMA	Glycidyl methacrylate
GRT	Ground rubber tires
HDPE	High density polyethylene

HDT	Heat distortion temperature
HIPS	High impact polystyrene
HISMA	High impact SMA
HMDAC	Hexamethylene diamine carbamate
HTBN	Hydroxyl terminated acrylonitrile-butadiene rubber
IBA	Isobutyl acrylate
IBR	Isobutyl rubber
iPP	Isotactic polypropylene
IPR	Isoprene rubber
LLDPE	Linear low density polyethylene
MA	Maleic anhydride
MAA	Methacrylic acid
MACL	Methylacryloyl caprolactam
MAME	Monoethyl ester of maleic anhydride
MAN	Methacrylonitrile
MBS	Poly(methyl methacrylate-co-butadiene-co-styrene)
MeA	Methyl acrylate
MMA	Methyl methacrylate
MMAVP	Poly(methyl methacrylate-co-vinyl pyridine)
MS	Methyl styrene
MSAN	α-methylstyrene-acrylonitrile
MVE	Methyl vinyl ether
MXDA	m-xylene diamine
NBR	Poly(acrylonitrile-co-butadiene) rubber
NR	Natural rubber
PA	Polyamide
PAMA	Poly(n-amyl methacrylate)
PAN	Polyacrylonitrile
PAr	Polyarylate
PASA	Phthalic anhydride sulfonyl azide
PB	Polybutadiene
PBA	Poly(butyl acrylate)
PBMA	Poly(n-butyl methacrylate)
PBT	Poly(butylene terephthalate)
PBVE	Poly(butyl vinyl ether)
PC	Polycarbonate
PCL	Polycaprolactone
PDM	N,N'-m-phenylene bismaleimide
PDPA	Poly(neopentyl glycol adipate)
PE	Polyethylene
PEA	Poly(ethyl acrylate)
PEN	Poly(ethylene naphthalene 2,6-dicarboxylate)
PEO	Poly(ethylene oxide)
PET	Poly(ethylene terephthalate)
PF	Phenol formaldehyde resin
PG	Propylene glycol
PGA	Poly(glutarimide)
PMMA	Poly(methyl methacrylate)
PMOX	Poly(2-methyl oxazoline)
POE	Poly(ethylene-co-octene) elastomer

POM	Polyoxymethylene
PP	Polypropylene
PPE	Poly(phenylene ether)
PPGMA	Poly(propylene glycidyl methacrylate)
PPMA	Poly(n-propyl methacrylate)
PPS	Polyphenylenesulfide
PS	Polystyrene
PSn	Polysulfone
PTFE	Polytetrafluoroethylene
PTMEGT	Poly(tetramethylene ether) glycol terephthalate
PTMO	Poly(tetramethylene oxide)
PTMT	Poly(tetramethylene terephthalate)
PUR	Polyurethane
PVA	Polyvinyl acetate
PVBE	Poly(vinyl butyl ether)
PVC	Poly(vinyl chloride)
PVDC	Poly(vinylidene chloride)
PVOH	Poly(vinyl alcohol)
RIM	Reactive injection molding
RPS	Poly(styrene-co-vinyl oxazoline)
S	Sulfonated
SA	Succinic anhydride
SAA	Poly(styrene-co-acrylic acid)
SAN	Poly(styrene-co-acrylonitrile)
SB	Poly(styrene-b-butadiene)
SBR	Poly(styrene-co-butadiene)
SBS	Styrene-butadiene-styrene block copolymer
SEB	Styrene-ethylene/butylene diblock copolymer
SEBS	Styrene-ethylene/butylene-styrene triblock copolymer
SEP	Styrene ethylene propylene block copolymer
SEPDM	Zinc salt of sulfonated Poly(ethylene-co-propylene-co-diene)
SGMA	Styrene glycidyl methacrylate copolymer
SMA	Poly(styrene-co-maleic anhydride)
SPS	Zinc salt of sulfonated polystyrene
SVP	Poly(styrene-co-vinyl pyridine)
TETA	Triethylenetetramine-modified
TPE	Thermoplastic elastomer
TPEs	Thermoplastic polyesters
TPUR	Thermoplastic polyurethane
UPE,UPR	Unsaturated polyester
VA	Vinyl acetate
VCVA	Poly(vinyl chloride-co-vinyl acetate)
VDC	Vinylidene chloride
VL/ULDPE	Very/ultra low density PE
VOH	Vinyl alcohol
VP	Vinyl pyridine
VPD	Vinyl pyrrolidone
VPP	Vinyl propionate

Part IV

Research Needs and Market Opportunities

Chapter 14

Research Needs

14.1 The Analytical Process

The following process was used to collect and analyze the research needs in plastics recycling:

(a) the criteria for prioritization were developed;
(b) the waste plastics to be analyzed were identified;
(c) a Peer Review Panel was assembled;
(d) a list of research needs was collected;
(e) an iterative review process was employed to analyze and prioritize the research needs.

14.1.1 Development of Criteria

In this study, we focused on recovering energy through plastics recycling over what could be obtained by burning the plastic in waste-to-energy (WTE) incinerators and converting the heat to steam and/or electricity. The source of this "excess energy" over that recoverable through incineration is discussed in Chapter 3.

Our initial focus was on what has been called "tertiary recycling"; that is, conversion of the waste plastic to chemicals or petrochemical feedstocks, but subsequently the scope of the study was extended to cover research in any area of plastics recycling that could result in a significant energy savings.

Through an iterative process, the following criteria were developed:

(1) To be of interest, a given research need should save at least 10^{12} BTU over WTE conversion, which is equivalent to the embodied energy in 100–200 million lb/yr of waste plastic.
(2) Research would be favored that:
   a. Impacted on many areas of plastics recycling;
   b. Had a good probability of success;
   c. Was not unreasonable in terms of cost and time to commercialization.
(3) Important economic issues were:
   a. Long term, the use of the research results should not require subsidies;
   b. Private capital should implement commercialization;

c. Joint or cost-shared activities between government and industry should be encouraged.

(4) Any research should also result in positive impacts on health and the environment.

14.1.2   Waste Plastic Streams of Interest

Instead of analyzing research needs by focusing on individual plastics— polyethylene, polypropylene, etc.—a decision was made to focus instead on waste streams containing significant quantities of plastic, whatever the plastic composition was. However, to be consistent with the criteria outlined above, the sources of waste plastic had to meet certain requirements; in particular, the waste streams had to be:

(1) Available in large quantities, since the threshold of interest was 100–200 million lb/yr and it was desirable to have at least twice that quantity potentially available;
(2) Presently collected or if not collected, readily collectable in principle;
(3) Concentrated in plastic content;
(4) Currently having no attractive alternate to WTE or landfilling.

As described in Chapter 2, four sources of waste plastic have been identified that meet these requirements:

1. Automotive shredder residue (ASR);
2. Carpets (used and industrial scrap);
3. Wire and cable plastic waste (fluff from metal recovery);
4. Tailings from recycle operations on municipal solid waste (MSW).

These streams also encompass a wide range of polymer types, especially those with a high ratio of embodied energy to energy recoverable from combustion.

	Composition
Stream	*Major Polymers Present*
ASR	Thermosets, Polyolefins, Nylon, Styrenics
Carpet	Nylon, Polypropylene
Wire & Cable	Polyvinyl chloride, Polyethylene
MSW tailings	Polyolefins

	Embodied Energy
	% Potential Excess Energy over WTE
Nylon	430
Thermosets	210
PVC	170
Polyurethanes	50
Styrenics	50
Polyolefins	40

For each of these streams, estimates have been made of the volumes and compositions currently occurring and projected through the year 2010. Information on the streams is given in Chapter 2 and the Appendix.

14.1.3 Development of a Peer Review Panel

An important resource was the Peer Review Panel—a group of 28 people of diverse backgrounds but with extensive experience and interest in plastics recycling. Help from the Panel members was obtained through questionnaires, through individual communications and in a two-day conference in early 1993. Information on the composition of the Panel and the results of the questionnaires and conference is given in the "Contributors" section of this book and in Appendix II of the report to DOE.

The Panel served several functions:

(a) As a sounding board to review the quality of the information being generated and used by Study Team and to critique the preliminary conclusions of the panel;
(b) As a resource for information on plastics recycling and a source of research needs;
(c) As an aid in the final prioritization process, both by providing advice during the priority-setting process and in critiquing the final product of the study.

14.1.4 Assembling a List of Research Needs

Three principal sources were used to identify research needs:

(a) The literature on plastics recycling was searched and research needs were identified. A data base of over 850 references was generated and computerized (see Bibliography).
(b) The Study Team was composed of individuals with extensive experience in all aspects of plastics recycling. Many research needs were identified from their collective experience.
(c) Research needs were suggested by the Peer Review Panel through correspondence, through individual conferences, and a face-to-face meeting.

14.1.5 The Analytical Process

The analytical process involved ongoing interactions (1) within the Study Team, (2) between the Study Team and outside resources, especially members of the Panel,

(3) between the Study Team and DOE representatives and finally, (4) in a two-day session involving about half of the Panel and the Study Team.

The Study Team originally intended to have the Peer Review Panel provide the major input to prioritization, forcing a consensus on priority through an interview process (Delphi Technique) and then ranking the top 3–5 research needs using Decision Analysis. This approach was abandoned in favor of arriving at a general consensus on priorities at the meeting with the Panel and the Study Team; the Study Team then recommended priorities on research needs using all of the inputs obtained in the 14 months of the study.

As the study proceeded, key information generated by the Study Team was presented to the Panel for review and comment, both through individual meetings and through questionnaires.

Individual contacts were made with Panel members on the important topics: carpets, wire and cable, automotive, embodied energy, and pyrolysis. Early in the study, the Panel was asked to review the statistical information generated by the Study Team, including projections through the year 2010, and their comments were incorporated into the program.

The two most critical items used in analyzing the information assembled by the Study Team were the comprehensive questionnaire sent to the panelists in early December 1992 and the meeting of the panelists with the Study Team in January 1993.

There was an excellent response to the questionnaire. Of the 28 questionnnaires mailed, 23 responses were received. Many of the respondents included extensive comments covering all aspects of recycling (technology, economics, regulatory and societal) so a rather comprehensive perspective on recycling issues was obtained.

Before analysis of the research needs was undertaken several critical issues were to be settled with the help of the Peer Review Panel:

1. Were there other areas that should be studied instead of or in addition to the ones selected by the Study Team? (That is, automotive, wire and cable, carpets and tailings from municipal solid waste).
   - The Panel agreed that these were the most important, with some suggestion that waste film was of equal interest to those selected. A few were not convinced that carpets were important.
2. Was the assumption that Waste-to-Energy was the most probable alternative to plastics recycling believable?
   - The Panel felt that WTE was a reasonable option for plastics disposal into the indefinite future (with a few strong dissents). They also felt that landfilling was going to become increasingly more costly and less available.
3. What are the characteristics of the plastics recycling industry that need to be kept in mind in assessing its research needs?
   - The Panel felt that in order to progress, the economics of plastics recycling needed major improvements, both in the costs of the processes and the markets for the products.
   - The Panel was not optimistic that these improvements would occur, and so felt that government action was needed if recycling was to progress.

- The Panel did not hold out much hope that technological breakthroughs would make a significant difference in the near term.

Further information on the Peer Review Panel's comments is given in Appendix II of the report to DOE.

During the last two weeks of January 1993, all of the research needs that had been collected from the various sources were reviewed both at the meeting with Panel members and then subsequently by the members of the Study Team. Needs were grouped in 10 Research Areas, with the Research Areas themselves being prioritized and then the needs within each Area also prioritized. The results are discussed in the following Section.

14.2 Prioritization

Using the process described in Section 14-1, the following analysis of the research opportunities involved in managing plastic wastes was conducted from the point of view of energy conservation. *It is quite likely that had there been a different focus, the list of technology opportunities would have been very similar, but the priorities presented below might have been different.*

All of the needs addressed in this list are worthy of serious consideration; there is nothing suggested that the Study Team is uncomfortable about recommending for financial support and further study. However, some are of higher priority than others based on the criteria outlined in Section 14-1. Ten Research Areas were defined and two to four Research Needs were described for each area. The Research Areas were ranked in order of priority, as were the Needs in each area. Illustrative examples are given for each Need, although these are not prioritized. Whether the lowest ranked Research Need in a high priority Research Area is more important than the highest ranked Need in a lower priority Research Area has to be determined in the context of an overall research strategy elected for a research portfolio. For example, given that all of the needs impact reduction of energy use, what importance should be given to short (5–10 yr) vs. long (10–20 yr) term results, good payout/fairly certain success vs. very high payout/uncertain success, etc.

Altogether, a total of 26 Research Needs were identified, illustrated by 45 examples and grouped in 10 prioritized Research Areas.

14.2.1 First Priority

The Research Areas in the First Priority Group share the following characteristics:

(1) They all retain the embodied energy involved in producing the polymer structure;

(2) They are applicable to all of the waste plastic streams;

(3) They are directed toward using the recovered plastics in applications of the highest possible value, and

(4) The chances for technical and commercial success are generally fair to good.

Four Research Areas: (A) Separations/Reclamation; (B) Analytical Methods and Devices; (C) Compatibilization; and (D) New Uses/Applications are ranked first priority; of these, the first two are related and almost equally important, followed by Compatibilization and New Uses/Applications.

Research Area (A): Separations/Reclamation

This research area covers all of the activities that are conducted on a polymeric material after it has been collected and the part containing it has been sorted and separated from other material, and prior to its being processed into a pellet or part. The activities include disassembly if the plastic is in an assembled article (bottle with label, carpet, insulated wire, automotive part, etc.), preparation (such as grinding, washing, etc.), and finally, purification (separating polymers from each other in a polymer mixture or separating polymers from other non-polymeric material such as color or odor bodies, additives, contaminants, etc.). A common need throughout this Research Area is technology to determine through markers or analytical techniques what polymers or other materials are present in the object undergoing separation and reclamation, and the physical and/or chemical processes by which the separation/ reclamation is to be effected.

Separations is the most important technical area to promote in plastics recycling. Low cost and efficient processes are badly needed to separate polymer-containing material from other material; polymers from each other and finally non-polymeric impurities from a given polymer. Provided that a plastic is not chemically altered in use, the availability of these processes would permit recovery of plastics and their reintroduction into the economy in essentially the same uses as the virgin resins.

Successes in the various categories of separations will provide the greatest conservation of embodied energy and result in the highest values for recycled products.

The chances for technical success for programs in this area cover a wide range, for example, separations of polymers with very different properties (such as nylon/PP or PVC/PE) may be quite feasible, while separation of similar polymers (such as the various polyolefins) would be quite difficult. Separations of high valued polymers such as nylon (from carpet waste) and nylon/PC/ABS (from automotive waste) could have attractive economics.

This Research Area would also have an impact on all the polymer waste streams studied.

Need #1: Polymer/Polymer Separations   Of the Research Needs in the Separation/Reclamation area, Polymer/Polymer separations are the most important. If individual polymers can be efficiently recovered from polymer mixtures, they can then be purified, reformulated and in many cases substituted for virgin resins.

If the polymers cannot be separated, the mixtures have much more limited use due to variability of their composition and properties and the generally inferior properties of the mixtures compared with those of the neat polymers.

As a general rule, the more unlike the polymers in a mixture are, chemically and physically, the easier the separation is to effect, and the greater the improvement in utility of the separated polymers as compared with the mixture.

Examples

– Non-solvent process to separate polymer mixtures; particularly, in the case of Automotive Shredder residue, polyolefin mixtures from ABS/PS/PC mixtures, PVC from all other polymeric material, PUR from all other polymeric materials; in the case of carpets, nylon from PP and SBR latex; in the case of MSW tailings, polyolefins from PET and PVC.
– Low cost solution process for separating simple mixtures of unlike polymers (nylon/PP; PVC/PE, etc.) with simultaneous removal of contaminating colors, additives, flame retardants, etc.
– Processes to separate thermoplastics from thermosets (for example, the polymer components of ASR).
– Processes to separate particles (flakes or powders) of one polymer type from those of another.

Need # 2: Polymer/Non-Polymer Separations   Individual polymer species that have been recovered from waste plastic and are targets for recycle frequently contain material that is detrimental to one or more of their properties and can reduce their marketability. Separation processes to remove these materials would be of great value in plastics recycling, although not as valuable as processes to isolate the individual polymers themselves, since purified single polymers systems would in general be of higher value than purified mixtures.

Examples

– Processes to remove colors from polymers or polymer mixtures (for example, dyes or pigments from nylon or polypropylene carpet fiber);
– Processes to remove trace odorants from polymer (for example, butyric acid from HDPE);
– Processes to remove additives from polymers (for example, lead stabilizers from PVC, flame retardants from PS);
– Processes to remove small (micron/sub-micron) particles from polymer solutions or melts (for example, PET particles from polyolefin melts, fillers from polymers, etc.)

Need # 3: Disassembly Processes   This covers technology to facilitate breaking a complex product into simpler components where the polymers can be more easily isolated and purified.

Disassembly processes, while important steps in plastics recycling, are usually not limiting and are included here for completeness. However, a good disassembly process is often a prerequisite for a good plastics recycling process.

Examples

– For carpets, a process to separate the fibers from the latex and fillers, and also the fibers of different polymers from each other;
– For bottles, cheap and easy ways to remove labels, caps, etc;
– For automotive, a disassembly process to use for complex, multiple-polymer parts such as a dashboard.

Research Area (B): Analytical Methods and Devices

The analytical methods for polymers that have evolved over the years were not designed to deal with the problems encountered in recycling plastics; that is, dealing with polymer systems in which a number of polymer types and a variety of additives and contaminants are present. Also, even if the methods were fully adequate, a need exists for devices that enable them to be adapted to on-line, real time use in field and plant applications where cost, ruggedness and speed of results are important. A few panelists questioned this high a ranking for polymer analysis, but most did not.

This Research Area is of high priority because it impacts on almost all of the Research Areas and Needs studied. There is a high probability improvements can be made in analytical methods; the costs should be moderate and results should be expected in 2–3 years. Improved methods should have pay-off in making decisions on the disposition of waste streams, in controlling production operations and in specifications on final products. Individual research needs and examples are given below:

Need # 1: Analytical Techniques for Use with Complex Polymer Mixtures (preferably capable being adapted to on-line use and able to give both qualitative and quantitative information)   This research need is the most important of the analytical problems because it impacts the most important overall research need: polymer/polymer separations.

This technology would be useful if it could accommodate up to 20 of the most common industrially used polymers; it does not have to deal with an infinite number of polymer species. It would be particularly helpful in dealing with complex mixtures of uncertain history, such as Auto Shredder Residue and plastics recovered from MSW operations. It would facilitate decisions on how to use a particular stream or batch of polymer waste, as well as in process control in any production operation.

Need # 2: Analytical Techniques for Specific Non-Polymer Components and Contaminants   For any given waste polymer stream, there are a finite number of chemicals, fillers and contaminants whose presence and concentration are important to know in order to make decisions on the use of a stream and to control any process involving it.

Need # 3:   Markers   A need exists for a marker and identification (analytical) technology that could signal the presence of a particular polymer type. This marker could be chemically incorporated in the polymer molecule when it is made, or it could be a species which could be bound to the polymer (similar to a dye) at some later date. The signal from this marker could be used to determine the nature of the polymer present in a mixture as well as its concentration. This information in turn could be used to decide the best subsequent treatment or utilization of the stream containing the polymer. As per a panelist's suggestion, the marker might also be used in a polymer/polymer separation process; for example, as a means of selectively putting energy into one polymer in a mixture and not another and thereby facilitate separation.

Need # 4:   A Device for Determining Polymer Type in Field Applications   A need exists for a simple, inexpensive and rugged device to be used in such facilities as auto dismantlers to permit identification of the polymers present in a part.

Research Area (C): Compatibilization

"Compatibilization" means taking a polymer mixture that is not broadly useful because of gross phase separation, and making it more useful through physical processing, the use of additives, or through chemistry carried out on the mixture. It is a process to be used if separation of the polymers is not practical and if the energy savings and economics favor retaining the polymer structures rather than breaking them down into lower molecular weight species or incinerating them in a WTE operation.

  Compared to the polymer/polymer separations research needs discussed above, chances for success are lower, due to the market issues that need to be addressed, assuming that the compatibilization steps were technically successful. All of the products from the research described below would require significant market development efforts.

Need # 1:   Compatibilization Using Additives   Mixtures of two or more polymers may be compatibilized through the use of added components.

Examples

- Graft or block copolymer systems could be tailor-made to compatibilize given types of polymer mixtures. For example, a polyamide graft onto a polypropylene backbone might be a compatibilizer for a nylon/PP system; or a styrene/butadiene/styrene system might be used to compatibilize a polar/non-polar polymer mixture. A systematic study would probably be in order to identify the optimum compatibilizer for a given type of polymer mixture.
- Functionalized Polymers as Compatibilizers.
  - A polymer may be modified to make it an effective compatibilizer by reacting it with various small-molecule reagents (as opposed to grafting another

polymer onto it). For example, EPDM reacted with maleic anhydride might be used to compatibilize mixtures of hydrocarbon and polar polymers.
    – Multifunctional compatibilizers may be needed for multicomponent mixtures.
• Fillers and Reinforcing Agents as Aids to Compatibilization.
    – Fillers such as silica or reinforcing agents such as glass fibers can help make an incompatible system useful, particularly when used with compatibilizing additives.
    – Surface treatments might be developed to make fillers more effective compatibilizers.

Need # 2: Compatibilization Through Processing   The objective is to make an incompatible system (such as a nylon/PP mixture) more useful by producing a micro-dispersion of one polymer phase in the other in particles so small that they have no detrimental effect, or put it into a form (such as fibrils) where it might possibly have a beneficial effect. This would be accomplished through mixing, extruding, drawing or some other specialized process. An example is pulverization of polymers through techniques such as solid state shear extrusion.

Need # 3: In Situ Compatibilization   One or more components of a polymer mixture may contain reactive sites for functionalizing chemicals. Reactions might be carried out on those sites (for example, in an extruder) and produce a product with properties improved over that of the starting mixture. In a sense, co-vulcanization and dynamic vulcanization are commercial examples of this type of technology.

Research Area (D): New Uses/Applications

If research in this area could meet its objective of finding new markets for large quantities of polymer at satisfactory economics, a very valuable result would have been achieved. However, the relatively low chances of technical and commercial success for programs in this area prevent it from having a higher priority ranking. Despite this, several reviewers ranked this their top priority item.
    To be of interest, a new application for recycled polymers must (1) be able to absorb a large volume of material at acceptable economics and (2) effect a significant saving in energy in terms of reduced crude oil imports. The latter could come about by direct replacement of virgin resin, reduced use of energy-intensive materials or extensions in the useful life of petroleum based products. Examples are:

Need # 1: Asphalt Additives   There are many uses for asphalt: roofing, paving, coating and other specialty applications. Polymers can modify asphalt by raising its softening point, improving its ductility, reducing its tendency to crack, improving its elasticity, etc. Asphalt can also tolerate color and odor problems that other applications cannot. Extending the useful life of asphalt or giving the refiner another tool with which to meet asphalt quality targets should be directly translatable into reduced crude imports. A well-structured scoping study to determine the effect of various waste polymers (perhaps with some modest treatment) as additives for different asphalt markets might yield applications that could absorb large amounts of polymer.

Need # 2: Cement and Concrete Additives   Plastics, perhaps as filaments, binders or aggregates might improve the strength or other properties of cement or concrete. Since the manufacture of cement is an energy-intensive process, making the material last longer or enabling less of it to be used should produce energy savings.

Need # 3: Plastic Products as Marine or Other Specialty Wood Replacements   It is not as clear whether there would be significant energy savings; however, enabling the wood used in pilings to be displaced with more durable plastic materials that do not need creosote or other treatment should result in energy savings from the reduced use of petroleum-based products and possibly environmental benefits.

14.2.2   Second Priority

The next three Research Areas, (E) Reprocessing, (F) Design for Recycling, and (G) Sortation of Parts, while important in their own right on an absolute basis, are well below the first four discussed previously in the context of energy conservation.
   They have in common the fact that they still try to retain the polymeric structure of the recycled plastic and so still recover much of the embodied energy of the original material. Although important, these Research Areas are not as significant as those in the First Priority group because:

(1) For the most part, the individual research needs are more narrow; that is, they focus on specific problems rather than on a broad spectrum of problems;
(2) The technologies involved are being advanced fairly well with industrial funding;
(3) To be most useful, they require significant advances in the First Priority programs.

Research Area (E): Reprocessing

This area involves the conversion of recovered waste polymers after reclamation and processing them into pellets or powder for sale or further use. The primary issues are the material specifications that guarantee the user a reasonably uniform product suitable for the intended applications particularly in the future when steady-state recycling is achieved at levels much higher than those encountered today. If Research Area (A) Separation/Reclamation yields positive results, the effort in (E) becomes more valuable.

Need # 1: Generic Thermoplastics   "Generic Thermoplastics" are defined as products essentially of one polymer type, such as HDPE, PP, PS, PVC etc. (or well-defined blends) that have been recovered and reclaimed from waste polymers. Examples of important research needs are:

- Develop information on the effect of multiple recycling on individual polymers and polymer mixtures.
- Develop information on the fate of various plastic additives after multiple recycles.
- Develop stabilizers to meet specific needs of generic single component and blends.
- Develop specifications for generic resins useful for product definition, product quality control and ensuring suitability for specific applications where special grades may be needed.
- Develop a "marker", some type of tag that would be polymer-specific, and would degrade or change in some easily identifiable way each time the polymer was recycled. This would be useful in determining recycle content and in preventing problems from polymers that deteriorate after multiple recycles.
- Develop polymer processing equipment designed to handle the process problems that are associated with handling generic resins whose properties, particularly rheology, have a wider distribution of values than virgin resin.

Need # 2: Generic Thermosets   The same basic problems that exist with the generic thermoplastics discussed above also exist with generic thermosets (cured polyurethanes, unsaturated polyesters, epoxies, etc.); there are some additional problems/opportunities:

- Developing surface treatments that enable ground thermosets to have better adhesion to the matrix in which they may be embedded.
- Develop a practical method to produce ultra-fine ground thermosets.

Because the sales of thermosets are much smaller than thermoplastics, this has a lower priority than need (E)-1 above.

Research Area (F): Design for Recycle

This area covers the problem of designing products so that they are easy to recycle and can readily use recycled plastic. A product that is properly designed from a recycling point of view should be designed in the light of a full life-cycle analysis, with particular attention to the energy implications; that is, following the polymer from its origins in oil or natural gas through its manufacture, conversion into a product, multiple recycle and ultimate disposition into incineration, landfilling or dissipation into the environment and loss. This topic is discussed in more detail in Chapter 3.

This may well be the most important long term technology area for recycle, but for a number of reasons, it is not of first priority when judged against the criteria established:

- For durable and semi-durable goods (autos, appliance, carpets, etc.), products designed for recycle will not be entering the waste stream in significant quantities for at least 10–15 years.
- For non-durable goods (packaging, etc.), industry is already getting geared up to meet the challenges and the problems could be well along to solution before the results of any government sponsored research could have an impact.
- For both durables and non-durables, the problems may not be lack of technology, but fall more in the area of design practices, legislation and standards.

Nevertheless, there are topics in this Research Area worthy of consideration:

Need # 1: Material Specifications   All of the research needs discussed above for Reprocessing also apply here, but there are others as well:

- What should be the specifications for virgin resin compounds when they are to be used in products designed for recycle? How, if at all, should they differ from current specifications and from the specifications for generic resins discussed in Research Need (E)-1 above? For example, replacements for lead stabilizers may be needed for grades of PVC intended for recycle.

Need # 2: Product Disassembly

- Develop a family of adhesives designed to replace mechanical fasteners and other adhesives and to be more adaptable to products where the polymer is intended to be recycled.

Need # 3: Product Reuse   From an energy conservation point of view, where possible, the reuse of a plastic item may well be the best option. There are obvious design and market issues here and some technical issues:

- What are the articles worth considering for multiple reuse; what are the polymers involved; what are the useful lives of the compounds currently used in those applications, and what would be the formulations that should be used if multiple use is intended?

Research Area (G): Sortation of Parts

This Research Area covers the technology used to recover a plastic item or item containing plastic from a larger assembly (such as a car) or from a mixture of plastic and non-plastic items (such as a truckload of household waste). Sortation of particles, as opposed to parts, is part of Research Area A.

Need # 1: Sortation of Film   A need exists for technology to separate plastic film from other waste and to identify the composition of the film. While film is a major use of plastic, little of it is recovered and recycled, particularly from household waste. Experience has shown that sortation at the home will be difficult to achieve; to make an impact on this 10 billion lb/yr application for plastic, new collection and sortation concepts are needed.

Need # 2: Sortation of Automobile Parts   A need exists for a rapid and inexpensive method to identify the plastic in an auto or appliance part to facilitate recycling it. [See also (B)-4, (A)-3.]

Need # 3: An Improved Process for Bottle Sortation   When recycling of plastic bottles began, sortation was mainly done by hand, which is expensive and subject to error. Automatic sortation has since become increasingly popular, but still has problems in missing some containers and misidentifying others. Small amounts of PVC or PET contamination can be major problems in streams that are not supposed to contain them.

14.2.3   Third Priority

This group of Research Areas could be ranked much higher if judged against a different set of criteria; they are grouped here because: (a) they may be more appropriate for industry rather than government funding; (b) they do not have as large a potential for impact on energy savings as those discussed above; or (c) they did not elicit much enthusiasm from the panelists as having much impact on the plastics recycling problem. Nevertheless, there were some worthwhile needs in this Research Area.

Research Area (H): Pyrolysis

Pyrolysis involves heating the polymer in the absence of significant amounts of oxygen and cracking it to smaller molecules or monomers. Some polymers revert to monomers with high selectivity (PMMA to MMA, nylon 6 to caprolactam) and processes using this technology have been practiced industrially for many years. Low selectivity processes (ethylene from polyethylene, propylene from polypropylene, etc.) are not used. However, processes to produce hydrocarbon liquids from waste plastic which may be then used as feedstock for refinery/petrochemical plants are getting considerable attention. Pyrolysis, particularly for producing hydrocarbon liquids for use as refinery or petrochemical feedstock, does not recover a significant fraction of the embodied energy relative to WTE, as discussed in Chapter 3.

Need # 1: Feed and Product Clean-Up   Many elements, particularly chlorine and heavy metals, can be harmful in refinery and petrochemical units. Efficient processes to remove them before the pyrolysis liquids are introduced into these units are needed.

Need # 2:   Low Cost Gasification Technology   In some cases, converting waste plastic to synthesis gas or low BTU gas may be desirable, particularly for residual waste plastic streams that remain after the more valuable and processable materials have been removed. The processes are apt to be feed-specific; that is, technology suitable for auto shredder waste may not be readily adapted to wire and cable waste.

Need # 3:   Small Efficient Pyrolysis Units   One proposal is to install pyrolysis units at Materials Recovery Facilities (MRF). Novel pyrolysis reactors, such as extruders, should be explored for this application.

Research Area (I): Chemical Modification

In some cases, specific chemical treatments might turn a low valued recycled polymer into a higher valued product, for example, making elastomer-like products by chlorination or chlorosulfonation of mixed polyethylenes. This kind of research would be relatively inexpensive to conduct in an exploratory program, but the chances of success must be considered low, especially in view of the significant marketing and market development problems to be faced. It would be best done when there is a specific target market and where the costs of chemical treatment and product properties can be readily projected from work on virgin polymers.

An example of this approach is the use of sulfonated mixed polyolefin waste as concrete additives for improved adhesion.

Research Area (J): Solvolysis

Solvolysis (methanolysis, hydrolysis, glycolysis, etc.) is currently widely practiced on several polymers, most notably PET. It has proven to be of limited value on mixed plastics because of separations problems with the resulting products, among other things. It may find a place for special applications such as certain thermosets where the only alternative is pyrolysis or incineration, and where high valued chemicals might result; for example, as a way of recovering chemicals from rigid polyurethane foam.

14.3   Some Additional Recommendations

14.3.1   Special Studies on Collection

The problem of collecting plastic waste or waste containing plastic is universally considered one of the most important steps in plastics recycling, both of industrial and consumer waste. It determines the quality of material available for recycle, profoundly influences the cost, and the nature of the collection system influences the subsequent steps of sortation, reclamation and so forth. However, specific Research Needs in this area were hard to identify. Rather than attempt to rank "Collection" with the other Research Areas we elected to treat it separately, and we recommend that a separate study on Plastic Waste Collection be undertaken by an appropriate government agency. The issues are probably not primarily technical, but will have important economic, regulatory, and societal components.

For example, one of our panelists pointed out that a system of "whole trash collection", that is, having no sortation at the household or other primary source but having all sortation done in highly automated systems at large and efficient MRFs might capture three or four times the amount of plastic as alternative systems at half to one-third the cost. But he and the rest of the panel passed up this possibility as too visionary. Nevertheless, the long range implications of such a concept are so profound that it and similar options should be analyzed further.

Another related need in "Collection" that should be explored is the possibility of developing an improved information system to gather, analyze and disseminate information on the wide variety of collection systems being used, tried, and studied worldwide. Information on composition of the waste streams was cited as one particular need.

14.3.2   Joint Activities with Industry Groups

There are a great many companies involved in one aspect or another of plastics recycling, and they have formed numerous trade organizations and associations to help coordinate their efforts wherever feasible. It was evident from comments made by several of the Peer Reviewers who are active in these associations that government agencies could be a welcome partner in their programs. The Study Team suggests that in order to take advantage of on-going research and to assure relevance of any planned research, interested government agencies should work closely with these industry associations. Cooperative programs with companies or associations can be effective ways to move government funded research forward quickly to commercialization.

14.3.3   Basic Science

Among the areas of polymer science that are involved in polymer recycling are thermodynamics, polymer interfacial properties, rheology, diffusion and polymer chemistry. While the Study Team did not identify a Research Need in an area of polymer science as such, it does recommend that any program to address a specific need should include activities to utilize and if necessary extend the required basic science.

14.3.4   Research Programs

The Study Team did not identify and rank order Research *Programs* as opposed to Research *Needs*. Accordingly, the needs were collected and prioritized as discussed in previous Sections. However, there are several targets of opportunity in waste plastics recycling where addressing and meeting Research Needs could result in attractive commercial operations. These are outlined below:

14.3.4.1   Recycling of Plastics from Waste Carpets

3.1 billion lb/yr of plastic (mostly nylon and polypropylene) are made into carpet. After 7–12 years, most of this will go to some type of landfill. Of this 3.1 billion lb, 2.5 billion is face yarn, and most of this is nylon, which is an energy-intensive polymer. The excess embodied energy over WTE conversion in carpets is over 10^{14} BTU and well over the 10^{12} BTU minimum target.

A program to capture all of this energy would involve addressing the following Research Needs:

Most Important: Disassembly [Research Need (A)-3].

The most important technical issue in utilizing waste carpet is to develop an efficient process to separate the fibers from the dirt, latex and fillers.

Additional Needs: Polymer/Polymer Separation [(A)-1].
Compatibilization [(C)-1,2,3].
Analysis of Polymer Mixtures [(B)-1].
Polymer/Non-Polymer Separations
[(A)-2].

If the carpet can be efficiently broken down into its components, a number of possibilities then exist for further processing:

a. Separate the nylon and polypropylene fibers and use them;
b. Use a non-solvent process to separate polymers, produce pellets;
c. Use a solvent process to separate and purify polymers for sale as pellets;
d. Compatibilize the mixture;
e. Depolymerize the nylon and reuse the monomers.

The potential energy savings in this and the succeeding examples is the gross amount available, and would have to be debited by any energy consumed in recycling to arrive at a net energy saving figure.

The preferred route will depend on local situations and the results of the research.

This program should have a high probability of success and should yield commercial results in 5–10 years. R&D expenditures should be modest; the chances for industry participation are good.

14.3.4.2   Recycling Tailings from Municipal Solid Waste

The tailings that remain from plastic waste after the PET and HDPE bottles and other desirable materials have been removed could reach over 8 billion lb/yr by 2010. Unless some use is found for this fraction, it will be landfilled or burned. If it can be utilized as plastic, savings of more than 1014 BTU over WTE could be realized. A program to capture this energy would involve the following Research Needs:

Most Important: Compatibilization [(C)-1,2,3].

The probability of success of separating the polymers in this mixture is very low, so to be useful in polymer form it must be compatibilized.

Additional Needs: Reprocessing [(E)-1].
New Markets [(D)-1,2,3].
Pyrolysis [(H)-1,2].

If the mixture can be compatibilized, work needs to be done on processing it and finding markets for the products. If it cannot be compatibilized, work needs to be done on pyrolyzing it.

The chances for success are medium-low for compatibilization approaches, fair to good for pyrolysis. While the R&D phase may be relatively low cost and could be done within 5–6 years, the market development phase could take considerable time and money. Chances for industry participation are fair.

14.3.4.3   Recycling Automotive Shredder Residue

Currently, about 2 billion lb/yr of plastics in auto shredder residue are produced and sent to landfills. If it were possible to recycle this material, a saving of 4×10^{13} BTU/year over WTE would result. A program to capture this would include the following Research Needs:

Most Important: Polymer/Polymer Separation [(A)-1].

A non-solvent process to separate the thermoplastics from thermosets, and then the polyolefins from the more polar polymers would be most desired. Further separation of the nylon, styrenics and polycarbonates would be also desired.

Additional Needs: Reprocessing [(E)-1].
Compatibilization [(C)-1,2,3]
Pyrolysis [(H)-1,2].

The optimum use of the separated polymers would depend on how efficient the separation was.

The chances for success for this program are medium. Among the factors favoring success are the fact that there are some high valued products in the ASR that provide an incentive to recycle it; among the factors that make it difficult is the complexity of the material. This program might take 5–10 years to commercialize; chances for industry participation are good.

14.3.4.4   Recycling Wire and Cable Waste Plastic

Currently, about 500 million lb/yr of waste plastic from metal recovery operations on wire and cable are produced and sent to landfills. Up to 50% of this is PVC, with the rest mostly cross-linked HDPE. This material is not very practical to incinerate, but assuming it were possible, savings of just under 1013 BTU/yr over WTE would be realized. To recover this energy, the following Research Needs should be addressed:

Most Important: Polymer/Polymer Separation [(A)-1].
                            Disassembly [(A)-3].

The first step in dealing with this source of plastic waste is to separate the PVC from other materials.

Additional Needs: Polymer/Non-Polymer Separations
                            [(A)-2].
                            Reprocessing [(E)-1].
                            Pyrolysis [(H)-1,2].

It would be desirable to remove all plasticizers and stabilizers from the PVC and to reformulate it as a generic resin. The cross-linked polyethylene might be used as a generic thermoset or failing that, be pyrolyzed.

The chances for technical success are medium; this is a fairly complex polymer mixture to deal with, but the polymers are quite different from each other. Commercializable results should be available in 5–10 years; chances for industry participation are good.

A significant problem with this waste is the presence of stabilizers based on heavy metals, which can lead to its being classified as a hazardous waste. Technology is needed to remove these materials, and also to find a substitute for them in new formulations.

The rapid growth of fiber optics in communications wire could lead to a large volume of metal-containing wire to be discarded over the next 5–10 years since, in the long term, as glass replaces metal, there will be reduced use of plastics in communication wire. There are no prospects for reduced use of plastics in power cable.

14.3.4.5   New Markets

The Study Team also recommended that a thorough study be undertaken of the potential for recycled plastics as asphalt additives, perhaps with some treatment to impart a degree of elasticity [see (D)-1].

Chapter 15

Market and Business Opportunities and Economic Issues

15.1 General

The recovery/reuse of plastics in waste streams involves both large and small companies with no dominant firms as yet. These companies are involved in conducting operations such as collecting, transporting, grinding, separating, cleaning, and recovering the plastics. There are currently (1993) an excess of 200 post-consumer plastic recyclers and plastic lumber manufacturers in the U.S. The industry is still evolving, particularly since many of the companies are both young and small, with limited capitalizations.

Many changes in concepts, technologies, and "players" can be expected in the years ahead. Moreover, the "rules" that govern the attractiveness of recovery/reuse of plastics will change as local, state, and U.S. federal government agencies continue their efforts to protect the environment. For example, regulations that mandate a specified level of recycled plastics content would distort both acceptability of the product and other market forces such as price, i.e. the level of discounts relative to virgin resins.

Over the next 10–20 years, we can expect a steady growth in the recovery/reuse of plastics from waste streams. Major producers of virgin plastics, many of whom have not been particularly active in recycling, will increase their activity in response to public, regulatory, and market forces. In many cases, they will probably want to work in partnership or even joint ventures with entrepreneurial firms.

In this chapter, we shall examine some of the critical economic issues that can impact the attractiveness of recovery/recycling of polymers. Then we will consider some examples of potential market opportunities that exist in recovery/recycling from:

- Automobile, light trucks, and large appliances-shredded residues (ASR);
- Carpets;
- Wire and cable coverings;
- "Tailings" from plastic-containing streams recovered from MSWs.

Processing some of these wastes for recovery/recycling may offer only transitory opportunities. Others, such as "tailings", may require the development of new technology.

The business opportunities discussed in this chapter do not include developments already well underway that focus primarily on recycled packaging plastics: mostly soft drink, milk, and detergent bottles made from HDPE and PET. The major markets being exploited are plastic lumber, insulation, incorporation with virgin resins into containers, etc. A good review of current commercial practices can be found in Ref. [788].

15.2   Critical Economic Issues

Economic issues are of critical importance in determining the rate of diffusion of new technologies for plastics recovery/recycling. Unfortunately, it is dangerous to even mention investment and cost factors without presenting a long series of reservations. Published cost factors tend to be unreliable and are almost never comparable since they have been developed on different bases, e.g. depreciation policies, rate of interest, and distribution of general costs. These problems are common for cost data in all industries, but they are believed to be particularly important for plastics recovery/recycling endeavors.

However, some limited issues that illustrate the impact of costs on plastics recycling can be addressed using rules of thumb and generally accepted industry wisdom.

15.2.1   Relative Price of Recycled Plastics and Virgin Plastics

There is a general belief in the industry that a plastic fabricator will consider significant use of recycled resin if the price of the recycled resin is at least 20% lower than the price of a comparable virgin resin. The lower price has been required to compensate a fabricator for the *perceived* difficulties in using them. (This perception may change in the future.) When the price for recycled resins is over 30% lower than that for virgin resin, as is the case today (First Quarter 1993) with PET resins, widespread use will occur, and a firm demand develops for the recycled resin.

The prices, at which discarded plastic parts and objects are available, and the costs required to upgrade them (sortation and reclamation) to generic resins that can compete with virgin resins vary widely. However, the following prices may be taken as typical for HDPE and PET bottles (sorted from waste streams) in the northeastern U.S. (First Quarter 1993).

Product	¢/lb of plastic
Mixed bottles	0–4
Sorted bottles	8–12
Ground bottles	10–14
Well-sorted, natural PET bottles	15–18

For both HDPE and PET, processing through reclamation into a flake/pellet that can be used by a plastic fabricator costs an additional 15–25¢/lb.

Putting aside consideration of subsidies or legislation that require a minimum content of recycled plastics, a plastics reclaimer is faced with total 1993 costs of approximately 20–30¢/lb for HDPE and 30–40¢/lb for PET. Therefore, it is possible to sell PET in the range of 40–45¢/lb and "earn" a profit. Moreover, this offers significant advantage to fabricators as compared to the use of virgin resin, selling for 60–65¢/lb. However, HDPE is currently selling for 30–40¢/lb. Even if HDPE is offered at only 20% discount to virgin prices, the reclaimer of HDPE resin will be operating very close to or below his facility's break-even point.

When faced with the situation that currently exists for HDPE (a weak market for the plastic, regardless of its origin), one can only increase the use of recycled resin by:

- Offering subsidies, direct or indirect, to recyclers;
- Mandating recycled plastic contents for certain objects;
- Reducing reclamation costs.

Therefore, not surprisingly, all HDPE reclaimers have programs underway to attempt to reduce their reclamation and transportation costs by approximately 5–10¢/lb.

15.2.2 Trends in the Economics of Recovery/Recycling

Recovery of plastics from waste streams economically presents a number of challenges. For example, reclaiming of industrial plastics waste streams, e.g. scrap film from converters is a relatively simple operation, typically involving grinding, blending, and reextrusion into pellets. However, recovery of plastics from post-consumer products is more complicated; several additional processing steps involving washing, separation, and drying are required to produce resins for recycling.

Historically, capital requirements have generally been rather modest, and, as a result, capital-related charges, e.g. depreciation and maintenance, have been rather low. In general, the most significant costs have been those of the waste plastic (sorted to some degree) at the plant gate and the cost of labor; significant labor costs have been incurred for both inspection and manual handling/sorting of the feed.

Processes for the separation of plastics in the future will be increasingly automated, reducing to some degree labor charges. However, automation and utilization of recovery technologies, such as microsortation (Chapter 6) and solvent separation (Chapter 7), will significantly increase the unit capital investment. As a result, plants will have to be larger. This, in some instances, will result in higher transportation costs since the feed will have to be transported over a greater (average) distance.

15.2.3   Relative Prices of Recycled Plastics and Crude Oil

When recycled plastics are considered as feedstock to fuel processes or low selectivity monomer processes, e.g. ethylene production, then it is important to consider the price of the recycled plastics relative to the price of crude oil. Recycled plastics are just another feedstock; they do not offer any advantages over crude oil, except when the high valued monomers can be produced by pyrolytic processes, e.g. caprolactam and adipic acid.

There are a number of 1993 forecasts available from the DOE that project world crude oil prices through 2010. The outside range of these forecasts is that in 2010 the price will be between $23 and 40/barrel. Because the price of crude oil is subject to periodic shocks, each forecast assumes price levels that are deemed to be most sustainable in light of the amount of oil available worldwide. However, there is general agreement between all the forecasts that, beyond the mid-1990s, world oil prices in real terms will rise. The degree to which the prices may rise or fall in the future appears to depend largely on OPEC decisions.

The Canadian National Energy Board "sees" a price of $27/barrel for West Texas Intermediate (WTI) in 2010 with a possible range of $20–35. This price of $27 should probably be recognized as a high approximation for the world oil price because the WTI price has been more than $1.50 higher than the average cost of crude oil imported into the U.S. for the past three years. Adjusting these projections for the differential leaves the base price lower than that of the WEFA Group projection of $26/barrel in 2010. The high boundary is just slightly above that of DOE's mid-price case but lower than either the DRI/McGraw-Hill Energy Review or the Gas Research Institute forecast. ENRON Corp. has suggested a $30/barrel world oil price in 2005; this is comparable to the DOE forecast for that year.

The price of crude oil impacts recycling in at least two important ways. First, high crude oil prices drive up the costs of virgin resins more than they drive up the cost of recycling, thereby making the use of recycled resins more attractive relative to virgin resins. Second, recycled plastics can be converted by pyrolysis into "synthetic" crude oil, and this process also becomes more attractive as crude oil prices rise.

In the period 1973–1993, crude oil prices were as low as $10/barrel and as high as $40/barrel. At $10/barrel, the most that plastics could be worth as synthetic crude oil would be 4¢/lb, which could never cover the costs of collecting and processing the waste plastic. At $40/barrel, it could be worth 16¢/lb, at which point synthetic crude oil from plastics might be attractive.

Other things being equal, there is a direct relationship between the price of crude oil and the cost of virgin plastics. For example, a doubling of the price of crude oil from $10/barrel to $20/barrel could produce a 20–40% increase in the cost of ethylene and a 10–15% increase in the cost of manufacturing polyethylene depending on the specific circumstances; these cost increases should ultimately be reflected in virgin resin prices. Markets for recycled plastics as replacements for virgin resins that are marginally unattractive at today's (late 1993) crude oil price of $15/barrel might become marginally attractive at crude oil prices of $20–$25/barrel.

Projecting prices of crude oil, even on a year-to-year basis, is very risky, much less projecting them 10–15 years into the future. It should be recognized that, in the recent past, crude oil prices have varied between $10 and $40/barrel, and during that period price projections of $100/barrel for the early 1990s had a high level of credibility.

For what it is worth, most forecasts for crude oil prices in the period 2000–2010 range between $25 and $35/barrel. At these prices, plastics recycling becomes somewhat more attractive than it is today at $15/barrel for crude oil.

15.2.4   Subsidies and Tipping Fees

All methods of solid waste reduction are costly in the sense that they require diversion of resources that have alternative use. Source reduction is costly because it requires modification of production and consumption behavior that firms and households may prefer. Changing behavior implies a higher cost to firms and/or lower levels of satisfaction to household.

Recovery/recycling of plastics is costly—a fundamental fact that is perhaps all too often ignored. Many of the costs of recycling are obvious: transportation, storage, sortation, reclamation, and the other processes incurred by the recovery/recycling organizations and the users of recycling materials. The fact that some of these operations are at times performed by volunteer organizations does not alter the fact that they are costly in terms of the use of society's resources, i.e. what other good works might have been performed or leisure enjoyed had the volunteer effort not been directed to recycling.

Aside from the hidden cost of the time of households and firms and other household and firm inputs that are not priced in the markets, some of the costs (in a life-cycle sense) and especially those for landfilling and incineration are not well established. These costs may in practice be estimated incorrectly or, worse, ignored entirely.

There is some reason to believe that many local government agencies have not priced solid waste collection and disposal services at their full real cost (including the cost of environmental protection). Underpricing of waste disposal in itself encourages overuse of the service. Reducing the incentive to consider disposal costs when acquiring materials that will require disposal stimulates the use and production of these materials. In addition, lowering the disposal costs to a waste producer, in effect, reduces the incentive to recycle the materials from waste streams.

Obviously, even if the cost of solid waste collection and disposal were priced at their full value, there still remains the question: To what extent, if any, should any disposal (tipping) fees, which can be as much as 10¢/lb of waste, that are collected be "captured" with the recycler and the user of recycled materials? This is not an unimportant issue in determining whether a technology is going to be used broadly since the fees (or some portion of them) could be a significant income stream to the companies involved in recovery/reprocessing.

15.3   Policies to Encourage Recycling

Four policies to encourage recycling have been advanced by different groups interested in the recovery/recycling of materials produced from natural resources:

- Taxes on the use of virgin material;
- Deposit/refund programs;
- Subsidies to encourage production of recycled material;
- Recycled content standards.

Unfortunately, there are few analyses of either the structure of these policies or how one would rank them in terms of the private costs necessary to achieve a given reduction in waste generation.

The available studies seem to suggest that a virgin materials tax and deposit/refund programs may be better policies since they encourage recovery/recycling and discourage consumption. By contrast, there is some agreement that a subsidy for recycling may be the worst policy because, by decreasing the price of the recycled plastic, the consumption of all plastics may be encouraged.

Whether or not price-based recycling policies can effectively increase plastic recycling is not clear based upon the available studies on recycling of wastepaper and lead from batteries. However, there can be substantial differences in the costs to our society in accomplishing the same reduction in the production of virgin plastics. For example, a recycling subsidy could end up costing roughly twice that of the most efficient tax deposit approach.

The support by governmental agencies of research and development (R&D), directed at improving the economics of the recovery and recycle of plastics from waste streams, might also be considered by some. However, if the results of the R&D are successful, then the recycling of plastics will increase. Therefore, it is possible to have a large payout for some R&D activities.

15.4   Market Opportunities

Four streams that are collectable or already assembled at a number of specific locations have been identified in Chapter 2:

- Automotive, light truck, and large appliance-shredded residues (ASRs);
- Carpets;
- Wire and cable coatings;
- "Tailings" from plastic-containing streams recoverable from MSWs.

The availability of these streams present a number of markets and business opportunities.

15.4.1 Automobile Shredder Waste

Over 90% of all passenger cars taken out of service are shredded through an established infrastructure for recovery of the contained materials and their disposal. The average shredded automobile generates several hundred pounds of fluff or automobile shredder residue; 15–30% of this is plastic.

The automotive, materials, and recycling industries will be affected in different ways by the regulatory and policy initiatives that will occur during the next four years. Already, many initiatives have been undertaken in the form of joint study groups (e.g. vehicle recycling partnership) and several joint ventures. These may change the nature of the current infrastructure over the next few years.

Participation in this industry may require a "partnership" of some nature with existing dismantlers and shredders. Currently, there are over 12,000 dismantlers and wrecking yards in the U.S. and about 200 shredders that produce more than 50,000 metric tons of ASR a year. Studies conducted by the American Plastics Council show that only 30–40% of a limited number of plastic parts, e.g. bumpers, are separated and reused.

There is *no* doubt that large quantities of selected plastic (scrap) can be removed at dismantlers' yards. Whenever the recovered part can be reused, it will have an average value (include a credit for weight reduction, the CAFE credit) of $2–3/lb. However, there *currently* is no usage or even policy at the original equipment manufacturer (OEM), e.g. Ford, GM, etc., level for reuse.

Reuse of plastic parts may be feasible at the semi-OEM level, initially at a small scale. For example, golf cart bodies and frames for major household appliances would appear to be particularly suitable for recovery/recycling. In automotive, factory remanufacture of vintage automobiles, e.g. the VW Beetle, will also offer potential studies.

Many pilot studies have shown that salvaged plastics parts can be reprocessed into new parts. For example, plastics from salvaged bumpers have been used to mold new tail light housings. However, for this market to grow substantially requires that "wide specifications" for product materials be accepted at the OEM level. Development of specifications, such as those listed below, would permit reasonable levels of mixing with virgin resin (15–30%) or total recycling:

- Recycled reinforced thermoplastics with properties *similar* to virgin glass-reinforced polypropylene;
- Recycled "Xenoy"™ alloy for bumper beam applications;
- Recycled "Noryl"™ GTX resin for fender applications.

Obtaining acceptance of these specifications will require close interaction and test programs at the OEM level. Development of wide specification for reinforced thermoplastics, e.g. recycled nylon/polyester "compatibilized" blends with added glass fibers, is perhaps the most promising area for the smaller companies.

Recovery of plastics from ASRs economically cannot occur without additional developments in technology (Chapter 14). Most likely, the technology that will be developed will be quite different from that currently practiced by shredders. There will be future opportunities for those companies familiar with plastics recovery/ recycling who have built business relationships with dismantlers and shredders.

15.4.2   Carpets

Today, discarded carpets are found primarily in MSW. While a small fraction of carpets are left at the curb for collection, most are picked up by new carpet installers and commercial collectors and then sent to a landfill. Therefore, development of a supply of discarded carpets for recovery/recycle appears to be quite feasible, particularly in urban areas, through the existing infrastructure.

Solvent separation may prove to be quite fruitful since the major components in carpets such as polypropylene, nylon 6, nylon 66, polyethylene terephthalate (PET) all have vastly different solubilities. The recovered nylons and PET could then be converted into molding resins. As an alternative, since the mixture of polymers is rather simple and fairly consistent, the preparation of a compatibilized resin for molding would appear to be feasible.

Nylon producers, e.g. BASF and Du Pont, are conducting development programs directed at monomer recovery. This would not appear to be a promising area for independent companies.

15.4.3   Wire and Cable

Scrap wire and cable coverings are the by-products of metal recovery by specialized reclaimers. The plastic content (roughly 70%) has *not* in the past been recovered; the coverings have either been landfilled or kept in scrap heaps. Landfilling is no longer a permissible option because of the metal content in the coverings from both the wire in the cable and the stabilizer packages.

Upgrading of the U.S. communication system (as currently being discussed) will significantly increase the quantity of scrapped wire and cable and, therefore, coverings. Partnerships with reclaimers are essential since stand-alone plastics recovery units may not be attractive.

Simple solvent separations may be capable of producing acceptable resins for recycling. Moreover, since multicomponent polymer coatings for wire and cable are relatively consistent systems, it should be possible to develop "compatibilized" or blended resins for molding.

15.4.4   Tailings from MSW

This is the most difficult area to develop market opportunities. Conversion of an incompatible mixture of polymers that is highly contaminated into a usable form requires the development of technology (Chapter 14). Development of this technology will be neither rapid nor inexpensive. In the interim, one might consider expanding the recovery of plastics from MSW. At present, only bottles and containers are recovered on a wide-scale basis. However, programs to recover and recycle plastic film from MSW have been shown to be feasible. Expansion of these programs on a commercial basis should be relatively straightforward.

15.5   Summary

With certain exceptions, most notably PET beverage bottles, large-scale recycling of plastic waste is not very attractive economically today. Events that could and probably will change that over the next 10 years are:

1. Lower recycling costs due to larger scale of operations and increased use of automation;
2. Marginally improved prices for recycled products due to higher costs for crude oil;
3. Somewhat improved margins if recycling "captures" a portion of ever-increasing tipping fees;
4. Increasing activity of major corporations (resin producers, automotive firms, etc.) in investing in recycling operations;
5. New technology that reduces the cost and increases the value of recycled products;
6. Public pressure and governmental actions.

The keys to success for companies wishing to participate in the recycling business will not only lie in taking advantage of these trends but in identifying their own particular places in the market and forming linkages with other firms that they need to work with.

Companies that have been successful in the recovery/recycling of plastics from waste streams have typically developed their own proprietary processes for well-defined niche markets. Success in the future will require that they continue this approach. However, they will in the future have to develop partnerships along the lines outlined in this chapter to obtain access to feedstocks and in automotive markets. Control of their labor costs, both through organizational changes and limited automation, is going to be critical.

Some of the technology needed to recover/recycle plastics from the four streams identified in our studies will be developed by research institutes and partnerships, e.g. American Plastics Council. Establishing relationships with these sources of future technology is going to be absolutely critical.

Appendix

Polymer Waste Streams: Statistics and Projections

Estimates of the quantity of plastics in waste streams can be derived from data generated by the Society of the Plastics Industry's (SPI) Committee on Resin Statistics. SPI accumulates statistics on the total non-fiber resin sales in the U.S. monthly from multiple sources. The data are summarized and published on both a monthly and an annual basis; the latter in the SPI annual report, "Facts & Figures of the U.S. Plastics Industry". The annual data are also published each year in the January issue of *Modern Plastics* magazine.

SPI reports for 1990 show that U.S. plastics resin sales were approximately 61 billion pounds (Table 1)[1]. The sales data for the 24 major resin groups in Table 1 have been organized in order of decreasing sales. Historical sales data for 1988 and 1989 are also presented in Table 1.

Data from the SPI reports for 1990, grouped by major resin type and subdivided by market segments, are shown in Tables 2 through 10. Similar data from earlier years have been the primary source for studies on plastics in waste streams done by Franklin Associates[2, 3].

The top five resins in sales volume, LDPE, PVC, HDPE, PP, and PS, account for about 43 billion pounds of resin sales in 1990, or about 70% of the total sales. In the aggregate they were sold into some 268 market application segments, as shown in Tables 2 through 10. A large fraction by weight (LDPE, 49 segments; HDPE, 45 segments; PP, 25 segments; PS, 55 segments; and PVC, 94 segments) within each resin group were sold for packaging applications. These resins represent both a majority of the plastics sold and a majority of the plastics in MSW; therefore, they are the most readily available plastics in waste streams.

The next three resin groups, polyurethanes, phenolics, and thermoplastic polyesters, constituted an additional 8.4 billion pounds in sales volume in 1990 (an additional 14% of total sales). Their use is divided among 52 market applications. They are generally fabricated into a large variety of more durable articles than the top five plastics, or they are used as a part of some complex object. Therefore, they do not show up in the solid waste stream in the same years as produced, and perhaps not for many years later. The nature of the products produced from these resins also makes them less readily collectible as feedstocks for reclamation.

Plastic applications of thermoplastic polyesters consume over 2 billion pounds per year primarily as PET polyester resin. Textile fibers made from PET resins consume an additional 3 billion pounds. PET plastics are used in large volume for soft drink and other food bottles, or rigid containers, and for photographic film base. The recycling of post-consumer PET bottles has been proven to be economically viable.

---

[1]"Resin Statistics Report", *Modern Plastics*, pp. 71–122, January 1991.
[2]Franklin Associates, Prairie Village, KA, "Characterization of Municipal Solid Waste in the United States: 1990 Update", U.S. EPA, EPA/530/SW-90-042A, June 1990.
[3]Franklin Associates, Prairie Village, KA, "Characterization of Plastic Products in Municipal Solid Waste", Final Report, February 1990.

Table 1 U.S. Plastics Resins Sales (Billions of Pounds Per Year)

Resin Group	Historical data[a]		
	1988	1989	1990
Low density PE	10.95	10.80	11.88
Polyvinyl chloride	8.29	8.40	9.30
High density PE	8.08	8.17	8.51
Polypropylene	7.09	7.30	8.13
Polystyrene	5.03	5.13	5.14
Polyurethanes	3.23	3.22	3.27
Phenolics	3.05	2.83	2.83
Thermoplastic polyesters	2.04	2.10	2.34
Urea, Melamine	1.52	1.38	1.44
Unsaturated polyesters	1.37	1.32	1.23
ABS polymers	1.28	1.24	1.21
Styrenics—Miscellaneous	1.10	1.18	1.12
Vinyls—Miscellaneous	0.95	0.90	0.92
Acrylics	0.70	0.74	0.75
Polycarbonates	0.59	0.62	0.62
Thermoplastic elastomers	0.49	0.55	0.58
Nylons	0.57	0.58	0.57
Epoxies	0.47	0.48	0.46
Alkyds	0.32	0.33	0.32
Polyphenylene oxide alloys	0.17	0.20	0.20
Polyacetals	0.14	0.14	0.14
SAN polymers	0.15	0.11	0.13
Cellulosics	0.09	0.09	0.08
(Others)	0.29	0.31	0.33
Totals	57.96	58.25	61.50

[a]Source: *Modern Plastics*, January issue (1989, 1990, 1991).

The remaining sixteen resin groups in Table 1 amount to about 10 billion pounds total, or about 16% of 1990 U.S. resin sales. They are sold in the 0.1 to 1.5 billion pounds per year range per group, and are used in a large number of market application segments. These resins tend to be utilized in more durable applications or as a part of some complex composite object than resins previously discussed; they will be very difficult to accumulate in sufficient quantity to be economic feedstocks for reclamation. However, to the extent that they are included in the municipal solid wastes stream sent to waste-to-energy power plants, their combustion energy will be recoverable.

The split shown between disposal as MSW (recycling/incineration/landfill) and non-MSW for the different resin groups in Tables 2 through 10 is derived from estimates prepared by Franklin Associates. The term "disposal" is meant to represent the location in which the particular products are expected to be found, or

Table 2 LDPE Non-film—1990

	Total production	Fabrication losses	Non-MSW disposal	Recycle	Incinerate	Landfill
	(Millions of pounds)					
Food packaging:						
Baked goods	336	3	0		50	283
Candy	54	1	0		8	45
Dairy	78	1	0		12	66
Frozen foods	116	2	0		33	184
Produce	170	2	0		25	143
Carry-out bags:						
Tee-shirt	186	2	0	0 (a)	28	157
Other merchandise	148	1	0	0 (a)	22	125
Grocery wetpack	98	1	0		15	82
Self-service bags	105	1	0		16	88
Garment bags	149	1	0		22	125
Packaging-other:						
Heavy sacks	171	2	0	2 (b)	25	142
Industrial liners	216	2	0	2 (b)	32	180
Rack and counter bags	248	2	0	2 (b)	37	207
Multi-wall sack liners	52	1	0		8	44
Pallet shrink wrap	35	0	0	1 (c)	5	29
Other shrink wrap	127	1	0		19	107
Stretch wrap	390	4	0	8 (c)	57	321
Textile	205	2	0	2 (b)	30	171
Packaging-miscellaneous	629	6	0		93	529
Non-packaging:						
Agriculture	234	2	0	2 (b)	34	195
Diaper backing	260	3	0		39	219
Household	196	2	0		29	165
Industrial sheeting	256	3	0		38	215
Nonwoven disposables	53	1	0		8	45
Trash & recycle bags	1408	14	0		209	1185
Total	6507	65	0	19	963	5460

Notes: a = 0.05%; Pilot recycling program, 0.05% production recovered/recycled.
  b = 1%; Limited recycling program, 1% production recovered/recycled.
  c = 2%; Limited recycling program, 2% production recovered/recycled.

from which they are thrown away into waste streams. Determination of expected disposal route and rates was made on the basis of production statistics and the nature of the products made. There are no waste analyses substantiating these estimates.

Except for packaging materials, disposal of plastic objects occurs some years after the date of their sale. Disposal in the Franklin Associates studies (Table 11) is divided between MSW, destined for municipal landfills or incinerators, and non-MSW materials, which have a semi-permanent life for many years or decades in homes, commercial and industrial buildings, or buried, etc.; therefore, they do not appear for many years in MSW.

Table 3 LDPE Film—1990

| | (Millions of pounds) | | | | | |
	Total production	Fabrication losses	Non-MSW disposal	Recycle	Incinerate	Landfill
Blow molding:						
Containers	90	0.90	0	0.89 (a)	13	75
Extrusion:						
Pipe and conduit	162	1.52	150	0.00	0	0
Wire and cable	412	4.12	408	0.00	0	0
Coatings	809	8.09	0	0.00	120	681
Sheet	82	0.82	0	0.00	12	69
Other extrusion	571	5.71	362	0.00	13	173
Injection molding:						
Toys	24	0.24	0	0.00	4	20
Housewares	210	2.10	0	0.00	31	177
Closures	268	2.68	0	0.00	40	226
Other injection molding	378	3.78	0	0.00	56	318
Rotomolding:						
Toys	320	3.20	0	0.00	48	269
Other:	973	9.73			144	819
Total	4289	43	920	1	499	2826

Notes: a: Collected as a by-product of bottle recycling.

The columns labeled "Non-MSW Disposal" in Table 11 were obtained by multiplying the production figures after a deduction for fabrication loss and exports by the factors determined in the Franklin Associates studies.

Companies experiencing larger fabrication losses than 1% have either learned how to recycle fabrication wastes internally, sell the wastes on the industrial regrind market, or reduce these wastes in order to avoid crippling financial losses. There is no significant disposal of fabrication wastes in the MSW stream.

Tables 2 through 10 show the distribution by disposal alternative for wastes that do enter the MSW stream. Estimates of "disposal by recycling" were provided by CPRR and are based on the quantities that should be collected from the MSW stream in future years by community recycling collection programs.

Automotive products and heavy appliances are not generally collected as part of MSW. Since these materials are, by definition, not MSW, they are shown as zero in the tables.

The rate of post-consumer waste materials collections is expected to grow rapidly as the infrastructure for such collections grows significantly in future years. The recycling rate estimates used in our studies assume that recycling collection programs will expand using existing technology (primarily expanded multi-material curbside collection programs), or with the aid of technology currently under development, such as automated sortation of mixed recyclable materials. A major factor in the expected increase in collections is the rapidly

Table 4 PVC–1990

	Total production	Fabrication losses	Non-MSW disposal	Recycle	Incinerate	Landfill
			(Millions of pounds)			
Calendering:						
Building & Construction						
Flooring	31	0.31	31		0	0
Paneling	50	0.50	50		0	0
Pond & Pool liners	30	0.30	30		0	0
Roof Membranes	13	0.13	13		0	0
Transporatation						
Auto Upholstery & Trim	58	0.58	57		0	0
Other Upholstery & Trim	20	0.20	20		0	0
Auto Tops	12	0.12	12		0	0
Packaging sheet	115	1.15	114		0	0
Electrical tapes	13	0.13	13		0	0
Consumer & Institutional						
Sporting & Recreational	20	0.20			3	17
Toys	31	0.31			5	26
Baby pants	5	0.05			1	4
Footwear	20	0.20			3	17
Handbags & Cases	18	0.18			3	15
Luggage	19	0.19			3	16
Bookbinding	4	0.04			1	3
Tablecloths & Mats	17	0.17			3	14
Hospitals & Health care	44	0.44			7	37
Credit cards	28	0.28			4	24
Decorative trim	13	0.13			2	11
Stationary & Novelties	6	0.06			1	5
Tapes, labels, etc.	32	0.32			5	27
Floppy disk jackets	30	0.30			4	25
Furniture & Furnishings						
Upholstery	79	0.79			12	66
Shower curtains	20	0.20			3	17
Window shades, blinds	17	0.17			3	14
Water bed sheet	10	0.10			1	8
Wallcoverings	54	0.54			8	45
Other calendering	20	0.20			3	17
Extrusion:						
Pipe and Conduit	3610	36.10	3574		0	0
Siding & Accessories	860	8.60	809	0.43 (a)	6	36
Window profiles	401	4.01	397		0	0
Transportation						
Vehicle floor mats	15	0.15	8		1	6
Bumper strips	5	0.05	5		0	0
Packaging						0
Film	315	3.15			47	265
Sheet	50	0.50			7	42
Wire & Cable	410	4.10	406		0	0
Consumer & Institutional						
Garden hose	60	0.60			9	50
Medical tubing	76	0.76			11	64
Blood/solution bags	75	0.75			11	64
Stationery & Novelties	24	0.24			4	20
Appliances	30	0.30			4	25
Other extrusion	42	0.42			6	35

Table 4 (Continued)

	Total production	Fabrication losses	Non-MSW disposal	Recycle	Incinerate	Landfill
			(Millions of pounds)			
Injection molding:						
Building & Construction						
Pipe fittings	167	1.67	165		0	0
Other building	15	0.15	15		0	0
Bumper parts	10	0.10	10		0	0
Electrical & Electronics						
Plugs & Connectors	60	0.60			9	50
Appliances, Bus. machines	75	0.75			11	63
Footwear	33	0.33			5	28
Hospital & Health care	40	0.40			6	34
Other injection	20	0.20			3	17
Blow molded bottles	223	2.23		4.42 (b)	32	184
						0
Compression molded records	20	0.20			3	17
Dispersion molding:						
Transportation	40	0.40	40		0	0
Packaging closures	40	0.40			6	34
Toys	6	0.06			1	5
Sporting & Recreational	20	0.20			3	17
Footwear	6	0.06			1	5
Handles	15	0.15			2	13
Appliances	14	0.14			2	12
Traffic cones	12	0.12			2	10
Adhesives & Sealants	59	0.59	58		0	0
Other dispersion molding	13	0.13			2	11
Dispersion coating:						
Building flooring	165	1.65	163		0	0
Auto upholstery & Trim	15	0.15	15		0	0
Other upholstery & Trim	8	0.08	8		0	0
Anticorrosion coatings	15	0.15	15		0	0
Apparel & Outerwear	16	0.16			2	13
Luggage	10	0.10			1	8
Tablecloths & Mats	15	0.15			2	13
Hospital & Healthcare	20	0.20			3	17
Furniture upholstery	15	0.15			2	13
Windows shades & Blinds	28	0.28			4	24
Wall coverings	24	0.24			4	20
Carpet backing	25	0.25			4	21
Other	25	0.25			4	21
Vinyl latex adhesives, etc.	65	0.65	64		0	0
Total domestic PVC	8136	81	6091	5	294	1665

Notes: Percent of production that was recovered/recycled:
   a = 1% as scrap returns from original installations.
   b = 2%; collected as a by-product from residential program.

Table 5 HDPE–1990

	Total production	Fabrication losses	Non-MSW disposal	Recycle	Incinerate	Landfill
		(Millions of pounds)				
Blow molding:						
Milk bottles	736	7.36		58 (a)	101	570
Other food bottles	340	3.40		7 (b)	49	280
HH chemical bottles	926	9.26		37 (c)	132	748
Drugs/Cosmetics	202	2.02			30	170
Drums (over 15 gal)	134	1.34	30	13 (d)	13	76
Fuel tanks	103	1.03	102		0	0
Tight head pails	80	0.80			12	67
Toys	72	0.72			11	61
Housewares	53	0.53			8	45
Other blow molding	264	2.64			39	222
Extrustion–coatings/films:						
Coatings	53	0.53			8	45
Merchandise bags	206	2.06			31	173
"Tee-shirt" bags	255	2.55			38	215
Trash bags	168	1.68			25	141
Food packaging	131	1.31			19	110
Deli-paper	18	0.18			3	15
Multiwall sack linears	56	0.56			8	47
Other films	85	0.85			13	72
Extrusion–miscl:						
Corrugated pipe	114	1.14	113		0	0
Water pipe	67	0.67	66		0	0
Industrial pipe	277	2.77	274		0	0
Irrigation pipe	44	0.44	44		0	0
Other pipe	45	0.45	45		0	0
Heavy sheet	332	3.32	178		23	128
Wire and cable	164	1.64	162		0	0
Other extrusion	39	0.39			6	33
Injection molding:						
Dairy crates	67	0.67		7 (e)	9	51
Other crates and pallets	136	1.36			20	114
Pails	414	4.14			61	348
Bottle caps	84	0.84			12	71
Dairy tubs	155	1.55			23	130
Ice cream containers	96	0.96		0 (f)	14	81
Beverage bottle base cup	125	1.25		12 (g)	17	95
Other food containers	55	0.55			8	46
Paint cans	33	0.33			5	28
Housewares	180	1.80			27	151
Toys	82	0.82			12	69
Other injection molding	153	1.53			23	129
Rotomolding	75	0.75			11	63
Other	1174	11.74			174	988
Total Domestic HDPE	7793	78	1014	134	985	5582

Notes: Percent of production that was recovered/recycled:
    a = 8%; curbside collection program.
    b = 2%; curbside collection program.
    c = 4%; curbside collection program.
    d = 10%; reuse programs.
    e = 10%; well established recycling program.
    f = .07%; pilot program.
    g = 30%

Table 6 Polypropylene–1990

	(Millions of pounds)					
	Total production	Fabrication losses	Non-MSW disposal	Recycle	Incinerate	Landfill
Blow molding:						
Medical containers	55	0.55		0 (a)	8	46
Consumer packaging	93	0.93		1 (b)	14	77
Extrusion:						
Coatings	35	0.35			5	29
Fibers and filaments	2130	21.30	706		210	1192
Film—oriented	470	4.70			70	396
Film—unoriented	118	1.18			18	99
Pipe and Conduit	32	0.32	32		0	0
Sheet (over 10 mil)	138	1.38	137		0	0
Straws	56	0.56			8	47
Wire and Cable	47	0.47	47		0	0
Other extrusion	8	0.08	4		1	3
Injection molding:						
Major Appliances	126	1.26			19	106
Small Appliances	59	0.59			9	50
Furniture	105	1.05			16	88
Housewares	272	2.72			40	229
Luggage and cases	12	0.12			2	10
Medical	168	1.68			25	141
Packaging—Closures	412	4.12			61	347
Packaging—Containers	202	2.02			30	170
Toys and Novelties	48	0.48			7	40
Battery cases	96	0.96		67 (c)	4	24
Transportation—other	250	2.50	248		0	0
Other injection molding	190	1.90			28	160
Other uses	1470	14.70			218	1237
Total	6592	66	1173	67	793	4493

Notes: Percent of production that was recovered/recycled:
    a = 0.05%; Pilot program in bottles for medical use.
    b = 1%; curbsid program.
    c = 70%; strong recycling program in battery cases.

growing number of communities across the country establishing multi-material recycling collection programs that include plastics wastes. This growth in collection capability needs to be matched by the growth of reclamation processing capacity.

The limiting factor in the growth of plastics recycling (as with other types of materials) is likely to be the ability to market reclaimed materials. At present, collections and PET processing are somewhat out-pacing marketability. Collection programs are not started unless a reclamation market exists, and reclamation facilities cannot get funding unless feedstocks and downstream markets are identified. Studies by Bennett[1] indicate that the future markets of recovered/recycled

Table 7 Polystyrene–1990

	Total production	Fabrication losses	Non-MSW disposal	Recycle	Incinerate	Landfill
			(Millions of pounds)			
Molding (solid PS only):						
Appliances/consumer electronics						
Air conditioners	35	0.35			5	29
Refrigerators/freezers	65	0.65			10	55
Small appliances	35	0.35			5	29
Cassettes, reels	280	2.80			42	236
Radio/TV/stereo cabinets	160	1.60			24	135
Other	15	0.15			2	13
Furniture and furnishings						
Furniture	36	0.36			5	30
Toilet seats	15	0.15			2	13
Other	16	0.16			2	13
Toys and recreational						
Toys	134	1.34			20	113
Novelties	45	0.45			7	38
Photographic	60	0.60			9	50
Other	20	0.20			3	17
Housewares						
Personal care	75	0.75			11	63
Other	115	1.15			17	97
Building and construction	59	0.59	58	1 (a)	0	0
Footwear	6	0.60			1	5
Medical	90	0.90			13	76
Misc. consumer/industrial	25	0.25			4	21
Packaging and disposables						
Closures	96	0.96			14	81
Rigid packaging	85	0.85		1 (a)	12	71
Produce baskets	24	0.24		0 (a)	4	20
Tumblers/glasses	90	0.90			13	76
Flatwear/cutlery	100	1.00		1 (a)	15	83
Dishes/cups/bowls	58	0.58		1 (a)	9	48
Blow molded items	10	0.10			1	8
Other injection molded	130	1.30			19	109
Extrusion:						
Refrigerators and freezers	85	0.85			13	72
Other appliances	38	0.38			6	32
Furniture and furnishings	25	0.25			4	21
Toys and recreational	35	0.35			5	29
Housewares	58	0.58			9	49
Building and construction	54	0.54	53		0	0
Misc. consumer/industrial	80	0.80	43		5	31
Packaging and disposables						
Oriented sheet and film	245	2.45			36	206
Dairy containers	150	1.50		1 (a)	22	125
Vending and portion cups	260	2.60			39	219
Lids	110	1.10			16	93
Plates and bowls	45	0.45		0 (a)	7	37
Other solid PS extrusions	230	2.30			34	194

Table 7 (Continued)

	(Millions of pounds)					
	Total production	Fabrication losses	Non-MSW disposal	Recycle	Incinerate	Landfill
Extrusion—Foam PS:						
Board	150	1.50	149		0	0
Stock food trays	191	1.91		2 (a)	28	159
Egg cartons	60	0.60			9	50
Single service plates	140	1.40		1 (a)	21	117
Hinged containers	125	1.25		1 (a)	18	104
Cups	40	0.40		0 (a)	6	33
Other foamed sheet	31	0.31	31		0	0
Expandable bead (EPS):						
Billets						
Building and construction	232	2.32	230		0	0
Other	44	0.44	44		0	0
Shapes						
Packaging	103	1.03		1 (a)	15	86
Other	52	0.52			8	44
Cups and containers	153	1.53		2 (a)	22	127
Loose fill	75	0.75		1 (a)	11	62
Other	251	2.51			37	211
Total domestic PS	4941	49	607	13	641	3631

Notes: Percent of production that was recovered/recycled:
    a = 1%; plans of the National Polystyrene Recycle Corp.

plastics are in excess of the waste plastics collection rates used in this study. Bennett's projections are the result of a continuing study that started in the late 1980s. His projections for the year 1996 are generally slightly higher than the estimated collection rates in this study for 1995 (Table 12).

There are numerous market application segments for which little, if any, collections are carried out. These are segments where the nature of the products or its general end-use are such that significant collection from the municipal solid waste stream, by either existing or future technology, is not expected. Unfortunately, these segments in their aggregate represent the majority of plastic products that are produced. Therefore, they are targets of opportunity for new collection initiatives or technologies.

In Tables 2 through 10, "disposal by incineration" refers to the destruction by incineration of MSW, of the residual plastic content after removal of plastics, and other materials by recycling programs. We believe that 15% of the residual plastics in MSW were incinerated in 1990 and that 20% will be incinerated in 1995.

Disposal of the plastics in MSW that are not collected or combusted have been sub-divided by the source of the waste streams: residential, commercial, or institu-

---

[1]R.A. Bennett, "New Product Applications, Evaluations and Markets for Products Manufactured from Recycled Plastics", Technical Report # 53, Center for Plastics Recycling Research (CPRR), 1991.

Table 8 Polyurethane—1990

	(Millions of pounds)					
	Total production	Fabrication losses	Non-MSW disposal	Recycle	Incinerate	Landfill
Flexible foam:						
Bedding	150	1.50	80	1 (a)	10	57
Furniture	685	6.85		3 (a)	101	574
Rug underlay	350	3.50	173	2 (a)	26	146
Transportation	400	4.00	396		0	0
Other	147	1.47			22	124
Rigid foam:						
Building insulation	480	4.80	475		0	0
Refrigeration	154	1.54			23	130
Industrial insulation	83	0.83	82		0	0
Packaging	66	0.66			10	56
Transportation	47	0.47	47		0	0
Other	45	0.45	22		3	19
RIM Elastomers:						
Transportation	174	1.74	172		0	0
Other	38	0.38			6	32
Cast elastomers	118	1.18	117		0	0
Other	328	3.28			49	276
Total	3265	33	1565	6	249	1413

Notes: Percent of production that was recovered/recycled:
a = 0.5%; collection of factory scrap.

tional. The distribution is based on ratios developed by Franklin Associates from the distribution of the different plastic products as manufactured.

Availability of Resins for Recovery/Recycle

In Table 12, the totals are the sums of the "Disposal by Recycling" subtotals given in Tables 2 through 10. The fraction that is recycled of a given plastic application segment was estimated by considering separately residential, commercial, institutional, and industrial wastes.

The total quantity of plastics wastes recycled in 1990 is estimated to be approximately 500 million pounds, or 0.8% of resin sales in that year, as shown in Table 12. Our projections for 1995, 2000, and 2010 assume a 3% per year growth in resin sales. A 3% annual growth rate is in agreement with several published studies and many private opinions[1]. However, individual growth rates for a specific resin can

---

[1]C.A. Lippincott, Director of Statistics, Society of the Plastics Industry, private communication, 1992.

Table 9 Thermoplastic Polyester – 1990

	(Millions of pounds)					
	Total production	Fabrication losses	Non-MSW disposal	Recycle	Incinerate	Landfill
Appliances	8	0.08			1	7
Consumer/recreation	12	0.12			2	10
Electrical/electronics	43	0.43	43		0	0
Industrial	30	0.30			4	25
Transportation	48	0.48	48		0	0
Blow molding						
Soft drink bottles	754	7.54		224 (a)	78	444
Custom bottles	335	3.35		3 (b)	49	279
Extrusion						0
Film	545	5.45		5 (c)	80	454
Magnetic recording film	85	0.85			13	72
Coating, ovenable board	11	0.11			2	9
Ovenable trays	45	0.45			7	38
Sheeting	80	0.80			12	67
Strapping	34	0.34			5	29
Other	39	0.39	22		2	14
Total	2069	21	113	233	255	1448

Notes: Percent of production that was recovered/recycled:
a = 30%; present major collection effort.
b = 1%; present in curbside collection.
c = 1%; recycled X-ray film.

vary significantly from this average. Unfortunately, individual growth rates cannot be developed except retrospectively. By the year 2000, increased collection activities and general sales growth should increase the quantity of waste plastics recycled to 4 billion pounds, or 4.8% of sales. By 2010, the total recycled is expected to increase to 8+ billion pounds, or 7.3% of resin sales.

Our estimates of recycling of plastics recovered from MSW are a small but significant portion of the total resin sales in any year. Collections are estimated to grow to about 20% of the quantity of plastics discarded in MSW. Therefore, a significant amount of waste plastics will not be collected.

Collection of waste plastics from MSW can possibly be increased by the employment of more rigorous collection/sorting methods, such as whole garbage sorting. This system is utilized in a few communities in the country to maximize recycling collections, although not expressly for the purpose of increasing waste plastics collection. In some cases, whole garbage sorting is combined with other waste reduction technologies, such as composting and/or the manufacture of refuse-derived fuels.

Table 10 ABS–1990

	Total production	Fabrication losses	Non-MSW disposal	Recycle	Incinerate	Landfill
		(Millions of pounds)				
Extrusion:						
Appliances	143	1.43			21	120
Pipe	120	1.20	119		0	0
Leisure products	17	0.17			3	14
Luggage	9	0.09			1	8
Packaging	5	0.05			1	4
Rectreational vehicles	25	0.25	25		0	0
Other	103	1.03			15	87
Injection molding:						
Appliances	70	0.70			10	59
Business machines	58	0.58		1 (a)	9	48
Pipe fittings	20	0.20	20		0	0
Other construction	8	0.08	8		8	0
Consumer electronics	19	0.19			3	16
Furniture	6	0.06			1	5
Luggage	3	0.03			0	3
Recreational	38	0.38			6	32
Telephone handsets	19	0.19		4 (b)	2	13
Other telecommunicator	11	0.11			2	9
Transportation	201	2.01	199		0	0
Other injection molding	74	0.74			11	62
Modifiers	39	0.39			6	33
Other uses	26	0.26			4	22
Total	1014	10	370	4	94	535

Notes: Percent of production that was recovered/recycled:
  a = 1%; computer returns based on pilot programs.
  b = 20%; long term program by ATT.

Commercial and Institutional Waste Streams

Many businesses have large quantities of plastic packaging films that can be source separated and collected for recycling. Stretch wrap (film, garment shipping bags, dry cleaner bags, grocery carry-out bags and box liner film are being collected). Low density polyethylene film and bags dominate in the film area. PET film base from the silver recovery from obsolete X-ray pictures contribute to the PET totals listed in Table 12.

The estimates for the recycling of polystyrene are based on the National Polystyrene Recycling Corporation plans for the collection of PS foam food service items from commercial and institutional sources, and the collection of post-use commercial foam PS packaging materials. Rigid PS containers, form and food service items will also appear to some degree in the residential collection stream.

Table 11 Summary 1990 U.S. Resin Sales and Disposal (Billions of Pounds, % of Sales)

Resin group	Sales	Disposal			
		in MSW[a]		not in MSW	
	lb	%	lb	%	lb
Low density PE	11.9	92.5	11.0	7.5	0.9
Polyvinyl chloride	9.3	23.3	2.2	76.7	7.1
High density PE	8.5	85.1	7.2	14.9	1.3
Polypropylene	8.1	80.7	6.6	19.3	1.6
Polystyrene	5.1	88.9	4.6	11.1	0.6
Polyurethanes	3.3	45.9	1.5	54.1	1.8
Phenolics	2.8	3.6	0.1	96.4	2.7
Thermoplastic polyesters	2.3	88.1	2.1	11.9	0.3
Urea, Melamine	1.4	7.7	0.1	92.3	1.3
Unsaturated polyesters	1.2	10.3	0.1	89.7	1.1
ABS polymers	1.2	65.0	0.8	35.0	0.4

Source: Franklin Associates
[a]Municipal solid waste (MSW) is defined in Franklin Associates studies as solid waste generated at residences, commercial establishments, and institutions. Construction and demolition debris or automotive scrap are not included in MSW.

Table 12 Recycling Plastics in Waste Streams[a] (Millions of Pounds, % of Sales)

Resin group	1990		1995		2000		2010	
	lb	%(b)	lb	%(b)	lb	%(b)	lb	%[b]
LDPE—film	19	0.3	197	2.6	400	4.6	1332	11.3
LDPE—non-film	1	0.2	65	1.0	168	2.3	629	6.5
Polyvinyl chloride	13	0.1	57	0.5	88	2.0	296	5.0
High density polyethylene	146	1.7	783	8.0	1353	11.9	2629	17.3
Polypropylene	72	0.9	188	2.0	428	4.1	599	4.5
Polystyrene	13	0.3	139	2.3	430	6.2	980	10.6
Polyethylene terephthalate	224	9.6	541	20.0	944	26.0	1260	29.9
Polyurethane	5	0.2	17	0.5	59	1.8	213	6.3
ABS	5	0.4	16	1.1	66	4.1	207	9.5
Totals	498	0.88(c)	2003	2.8(c)	3936	4.8(c)	8145	7.3[c]

[a]Collection of plastics in waste streams will be substantially larger than the quantity recycled. The difference is known as "tailings" from reprocessing.
[b]"%" is percent of resin group sales.
[c]"Total" is percent of total resin sales.
Source: CPRR Estimates

Table 13 1990 U.S. Synthetic Fiber Production

Polymer type		Million pounds
Yarn		
	– Industrial	334.5
	– Carpet	980.0
	– Textile	357.4
Polyester	– Industrial	360.6
	– Textile	744.6
Polyolefin		1416.6
Total yarn		4193.7
Staple, tow, fiberfill:		
Nylon		989.6
Acrylic, modacrylic		505.8
Polyester		2089.9
Olefin		405.5
Total staple		3990.8
Total synthetic Noncellulosic fiber		8184.4

Source: Fiber Economics Bureau

Industrial Waste Streams

Approximately 70–80% of discarded polypropylene storage battery cases are recycled as a result of the existing reverse distribution system when replacement batteries are sold, and the laws requiring the recycling of lead/acid storage batteries from scrapped automobiles.

For many years, ABS telephone bodies have been recycled through the ATT Co. service when telephones were telephone company property. While telephones are now primarily privately owned, communication industry competition will drive replacement exchange collection at the retail level. Several large computer manufacturers have instituted a reverse distribution system for outmoded computers, with the recycling of the large plastic cabinets. Small hand tools and small appliances will be recycled to some extent in a similar fashion.

Synthetic Fiber Wastes

Eight billion pounds per year of synthetic textile fibers were produced in 1990, as reported by the Fiber Economics Bureau (Table 13)[1].

---

[1]"Manufactured Fiber Review", Fiber Economics Bureau, Roseland, NJ, January 1992.

Textile fiber wastes are composed of post-consumer wastes (fabrics) and industrial wastes from fiber producers, textile mills, and end-product manufacturers. Synthetic polymer fibers also enter the municipal solid waste stream in a highly commingled and non-retrievable form. Except for consumer carpet wastes, which are potentially collectible because they are accumulated in specific locations, only a small portion of these wastes are targets of opportunity for reprocessing/recycling.

Current data on the magnitude of fiber waste streams are not available. However, Lehner[1] has estimated that 1.6 to 2.0 billion pounds of fiber and fabric waste are produced and that 75 to 85% of these wastes are already recycled. In addition, he also estimated that there are some 2.5 billion pounds of post-consumer textile wastes (not all synthetic polymers) collected annually and that 90% of these wastes are already recycled.

Lehner estimates that the 1.6 to 2.0 billion pounds of textile fiber wastes from industrial production processes can be broken down as follows:

Fiber Producer:

– 160 to 230 MM lb of cotton gin motes;
– 180 to 260 MM lb of synthetic fiber wastes.

Fiber Users:

– 360 to 490 MM lb of textile mill waste;
– 120 to 160 MM lb of carpet mill waste;
– 45 to 80 MM lb of manufacturer and user wasters.

Fiber Product Manufacturers:

– 630 to 720 MM lb of apparel cuttings;
– 55 to 90 MM lb of sheeting, towel, and blanket waste.

Textile wastes are collected and sorted for sale as used clothing (generally sold overseas), fiber for reprocessing, and wiping cloths. The Council for Textile Recycling, an association of some 350 firms doing this work, reports the collection and processing of some 2.5 billion pounds of textile wastes annually[2].

The 2.5 billion pounds of recycled textile wastes are about 29% of the 8.8 billion pounds of textiles produced in the U.S. each year. Of the 2.5 billion pounds recycled, approximately 500 million pounds are collected by collecting agencies, typically as used clothing. The balance is sold to used clothing dealers, exporters, and rag graders.

Companies collecting textile waste recycle 93% (Table 14) of the waste processed. The balance about 200 million pounds is returned to the MSW stream because it is too contaminated or commingled to be useful.

---

[1]C. P. Lehner, paper presented at the May 1991 Spring Seminar, Council for Textile Recycling, Gatlinburg, TN.
[2]"Textile Recycling Fact Sheet", Council for Textile Recycling, Bethesda, MD.

Table 14 Disposition of Collected Post-Consumer Textile Waste

Disposition	Percent		
	Domestic	Export	Total
Used clothing	< 1	35	35
Reprocessed fiber	7	26	33
Wipers, rags	25	0	25
Landfill	7	0	7
Total	39	61	100

Source: Council for Textile Recycling

Post-consumer carpet wastes, in contrast to textile wastes, are a large, untapped opportunity for reclamation of useful materials. According to the Carpet and Rug Institute[1], the U.S. carpet industry in 1990 produced over 1.3 billion square yards of carpet material. About 70% of this production was used for replacement of old carpets, which were largely discarded into the MSW stream. Using an estimated average of 4.0 pounds per square yard for waste carpets, about 4 billion pounds of carpet wastes enter the MSW stream.

Compared to other types of textile wastes, post-consumer carpet wastes represent a significant target of opportunity for recovery/recycling. Carpet wastes are often accumulated in relatively large amounts before being sent to the MSW disposal system. Therefore, they can readily be made available for sorting at material recovery facilities or MSW transfer stations.

Clean carpet scrap is available from the carpet industry and from manufacturers, e.g. the automobile industry, that cut carpets to fit specific shapes. This waste amounts to about 1000 million pounds; unfortunately, it is widely dispersed.

Waste from Scrapped Automobiles and White Goods

Recycling of plastics containing wastes from scrapped vehicles presents a set of more complex issues arising from the complexity of the products and white goods and the wide range of materials used. At present, materials recycling[2] and energy recovery from such wastes are almost nonexistent. However, the potential for significant materials or energy recovery is substantial, since large quantities of materials are involved, and they can be readily collected in a commingled form.

---

[1] R. Carroll Turner, The Rug and Carpet Institute, Dalton, GA, private communication, 1992.
[2] Some undefined quantity of used auto parts are reclaimed from junked autos (mainly late models) for use as repair parts.

SPI statistics indicate that the U.S. plastics industry currently sells approximately 2 billion pounds of plastics each year for use in cars, vans, and light trucks. These plastics enter the waste stream when the vehicles are disposed of after an average 10–12 year lifetime. An additional quantity of plastics wastes come from the scrapping of imported vehicles. About 1.2 billion pounds of plastics are sold to the appliance (white goods) industry. Approximately 10–20 years after manufacture, this material also enters waste streams as appliances are discarded.

Current materials-recycling efforts for scrapped vehicles and appliances are for the recovery of the metal components, primarily steel, from scrapped vehicles and appliances.

Vehicles and large appliances are usually processed together in large shredding units. The residues from the shredding operations are highly commingled and contaminated material known as "Auto Shredder Residue" (ASR). ASR is a complex mixture of plastics, paper, wood, tar, road dirt, glass, metals, other inert materials, and water and various automotive oils and fluids. ASR also includes polymeric and other residues from the large appliances, which have been processed together with scrapped vehicles.

There is no significant infrastructure or technology for the recycling of plastics wastes as objects (parts) from scrapped motor vehicles. The Environmental Forum Panel at the Society of Plastics Engineers '92 Annual Technical Conference in Detroit, MI (May 7, 1992), indicated that the industry plans to establish such an infrastructure in the future.

Current practices send discarded vehicles (those "totaled" in accidents or discarded due to old age) to a local scrap dealer. The scrap dealer "dismantles" or removes those parts of the vehicle considered saleable as repair parts or which have high intrinsic materials value, e.g. precious metals in the exhaust converter.

The hulks and vehicles from which repair parts have not been removed are then flattened to reduce handling and shipping costs, and sent to large shredding units. The shredded chunks are processed in to recover primarily steel. When received at the shredders, the scrapped vehicles are highly distorted; they can no longer be capable of being dismantled into individual parts.

There are approximately 10,000 to 12,000 scrap dealers in the U.S. who in total handle 10–12 million scrapped vehicles each year, or an average of 1000 vehicles per year, or 4 vehicles per scrap dealer each working day. Plastic parts generally do not have sufficient value to make their removal economically worthwhile. An infrastructure to accommodate recycling is not available, although it is possible to create one.

We estimate that shredding produces about 6 billion pounds per year of ASR.

Wire and Cable

There is a constant flow of scrap electrical wire and cable into the waste stream. This can be old wire, such as scrapped power and/or telephone transmission lines, or new wire, such as short pieces remaining after manufacture of wire-containing devices and off-specification wires.

Typically, scrap wire is sent to a metals recovery facility where the wire is chopped into short lengths, the valuable metal cores (usually copper or aluminum) removed for metals recovery. Scrap wire was in the past incinerated to liberate the contained metal.

The metal recovery operations generate a large organic residue known as "fluff". There is little use for this fluff; it has been landfilled or accumulated in large piles, awaiting acceptable recovery/recycling technologies.

Wire and cable fluff contains plastics, such as polyvinyl chloride and polyethylene (some of the PE is cross-linked), rubber, fibers, paper, metals (both copper and aluminum) and dirt. The wire and cable fluff typically contains approximately 70 to 80% plastic insulation residues. Some old telephone cable also contains oils and greases, which were used to exclude air from the cable. The plastics include plasticizers, stabilizers, and fillers.

Metal recovery from scrapped wire and cable is carried out on a significant scale. On the order of 1 billion pounds per year of fluff are generated.

There are a number of commercial plants world wide that reclaim polyethylene and/or polyvinyl chloride from wire and cable fluff. Recovery typically involves a combination of various air and water classification and flotation steps, followed by repelletization of the reclaimed plastic resins. The recovery processes are not as effective with aged, weathered wires removed from transmission lines as they are with "newer" wires.

Bibliography

1. Barham, V.F., Recyclingplas VI Conf. Proc., P.I.A., Washington, D.C., 55 (1991).
2. Meszaros, M.W., Recyclingplas VI Conf. Proc., P.I.A., Washington, D.C., 85 (1991).
3. Kowalczyk, J.E., Report to Mich. State Legisl., APV/Entropic Techn. Corp., (1989).
4. Fagan, F.N., and T. Hirota, Recyclingplas VI Conf. Proc., P.I.A., Washington, D.C., 72 (1991).
5. DeMaio, A.J., Recyclingplas VI Conf. Proc., P.I.A., Washington, D.C., 58 (1991).
6. Farrisay, W.J., Recyclingplas VI Conf. Proc., P.I.A., Washington, D.C., 15 (1991).
7. Stanley, A., Recyclingplas VI Conf. Proc., P.I.A., Washington, D.C., 2 (1991).
8. Wladyslaw, K.Z., U. Muszynka, and P. Kusztal, PL 151,021, Osrodek Badawczo-Rozwojowy (1990).
9. Paul, D.R., and S. Newman (Eds), Polymer Blends, vol. 1, Academic Press, New York, pp. 90,95,96 (1978).
10. Guettes, B., R. Marquardt, S. Pohl, G. Tischer, and H.J. Grossmann, DD 226,575, VEB Synthesewerk Schwarzheide (1985).
11. Nierderdellmann, G., and E. Grigat, DE 3,232,461, Bayer, A.G. (1984).
12. Ahn, T.O., Y.J. Lee, S.M. Lee, and H.M. Jeong, J. Macromol. Sci., Phys., B29 (1), 91 (1990).
13. Grigat, E., Recycling, (Int. Recycling Congr.), Verlag Umwelttechnik, Berlin (1979).
14. Muller, A.J., J.L. Feijoo, M.E. Alvarez, and A.C. Febles, Polym. Eng. Sci., 27 (11), 796 (1987).
15. Schalles, H., Kunstst. Ger. Plast., 77 (11), 3 (1987).
16. Vaidya, U.R., and V.M. Nadkarni, J. Appl. Polym. Sci., 34, 235 (1987).
17. Vaidya, U.R., and V.M. Nadkarni, J. Appl. Polym. Sci., 35, 775 (1988).
18. Hartung, P., and G. Menning, Kunstst. Ger. Plast., 75 (5), 19 (1985).
19. Yang, H.W.H., R. Farris, and J.C.W. Chien, J. Appl. Polym. Sci., 23, 3375 (1979).
20. Seymour, R.B., Polym. Eng. Sci., 16 (12), 817 (1976).
21. Menges, G., Kunstst. Ger. Plast., 75 (10), 2 (1985).
22. Abbas, K.B., Polym. Eng. Sci., 20 (5), 376 (1980).
23. Ionescu, M., V.T. Dumitriu, I. Mihalache, F. Stoenescu, and S. Mihail, RO 89,944, Combinatul Petrochimic Midia (1986).
24. Throne, J.L., Polym. Eng. Sci., 17 (9), 682 (1977).
25. Holmstrom, A., and E.M. Sorvik, Polym. Eng. Sci., 17 (9), 700 (1977).
26. Abbas, K.B., Polym. Eng. Sci., 20 (10), 703 (1980).
27. Garcia-Rejon, A., and C. Alvarez, Polym. Eng. Sci., 27 (9), 640 (1987).
28. Schick, J., Kunstst. Ger. Plast., 77 (11), 7 (1987).
29. Sikora, R., and M. Bielinski, Kunstst. Ger. Plast., 78 (4), 27 (1988).
30. Menges, G., B.V. Eysmondt, A. Feldhaus, and H. Offergeld, Kunstst. Ger. Plast., 78 (7), 3 (1988).
31. Herbold, K., Kunstst. Ger. Plast., 79 (4), 3 (1989).
32. Gehing, T., Kunstst. Ger. Plast., 79 (4), 4 (1989).
33. Christensen, A., Kunstst. Ger. Plast., 79 (4), 5 (1989).
34. Brandt, S., and B. Landers, Kunstst. Ger. Plast., 79 (4), 10 (1989).
35. Hesselbach, J., A. Franck, G. Wendling, and P. Eyerer, Kunstst. Ger. Plast., 79 (4), 11 (1989).
36. Kaufen, H., Kunstst. Ger. Plast., 79 (4), 23 (1989).
37. Linhof, W.L., and H.G. Olbrich, Kunstst. Ger. Past., 79 (4), 26 (1989).
38. Benoit, F., Kunstst. Ger. Plast., 79 (4), 28 (1989).
39. Matthes, G., Kunstst. Ger. Plast., 79 (5), 14 (1989).
40. Hess, V., Kunstst. Ger. Plast., 79 (5), 11 (1979).
41. Starke, L., Kunstst. Ger. Plast., 79 (4), 7 (1989).
42. Deanin, R.D., and C.S. Nadkarni, Adv. Polym. Technol., 4 (2), 173 (1984).
43. Throne, J.L., Adv. Polym. Technol., 7 (4), 347 (1987).
44. Deanin, R.D., and A.R. Yniguez, Adv. Polym. Technol., 4 (3,4), 277 (1984).
45. Leaversuch, R.D., Mod. Plast., 66 (3), 69 (1989).
46. Leaversuch, R., Mod. Plast., 66 (8) , 44 (1988).
47. Sneller, J., Mod. Plast., 57 (2) , 46 (1980).
48. Munk, G., R.P. Hegler, and G. Mennig, Kunstst. Ger. Plast., 79 (4), 31 (1989).
49. Staff writer, Mod. Plast., 55 (1), 61 (1978).

50. Calendine, R., M. Palmer, and P. Von Bramer, Mod. Plast., 57 (5), 64 (1980).
51. Smoluk, G., Mod. Plast., 57 (3), 62 (1980).
52. Staff writer, Mod. Plast., 57 (4), 82 (1980).
53. Murphy, W.R., M.S. Otterburn, and J.A. Ward, Polymer, 20, 333 (1979).
54. Sawaguchi, T., K. Suzuki, T. Kuroki, and T. Ikemura, J. Appl. Polym. Sci., 26, 1267 (1981).
55. Bufe, F., and H. Schalles, Kunstst. Ger. Plast., 75 (5), 6 (1985).
56. Pottfoff, P., Kunstst. Ger. Plast., 75 (8), 13 (1985).
57. Broock, T.R.T., D.W. Peabody, US 2,937,151, The Goodyear Tire & Rubber Co. (1960).
58. Reinbold, H., Kunstst. Ger. Plast., 75 (5), 8 (1985).
59. Wilms, H., Kunstst. Ger. Plast., 75 (9), 2 (1985).
60. Reinhard, M., Kunstst. Ger. Plast., 75 (9), 18 (1985).
61. Schumacher, F., Kunstst. Ger. Plast., 75 (9), 31 (1985).
62. Schnause, R., Kunstst. Ger. Plast., 74 (12), 5 (1984).
63. Schick, J., Kunstst. Ger. Plast., 71 (2), 5 (1981).
64. Oertel, G., Kunstst. Ger. Plast., 71 (1), 2 (1981).
65. Hartmann, W., Kunstst. Ger. Plast., 71 (1), 15 (1981).
66. Stoeckhert, K., Kunstst. Ger. Plast., 71 (1), 15 (1981).
67. Lietz, G., Kunstst. Ger. Plast., 73 (8), 12 (1983).
68. Carlstrom, W.L. , R.T. Stoehr, and G.R. Svoboda, Mod. Plast., 62 (5), 100 (1985).
69. Staff writer, Mod. Plast., 65 (5), 48 (1988).
70. Staff writer, Plast. Technol., 30 (3), 12 (1984).
71. Staff writer, Plast. Eng., 43 (12), 11 (1987).
72. Staff writer, Plast. Eng., 43 (12), 54 (1987).
73. Staff writer, Plast. Eng., 42 (2), 5 (1986).
74. Bollard, A.E., Plast. Rubber Intern., 7 (6), 227 (1982).
75. Basta, N., W. Stadig, and H. Short, Chem. Eng., 91 (6), 22 (1984).
76. O'Sullivan, D., C&EN, October 21, 25 (1985).
77. Thayer, A.M., C&EN , January 30, 7 (1989).
78. Farrissey, W.J., R.E. Morgan, and J.D. Weaver, 37th ANTEC Tech. Pap., Soc. Plast. Eng., 1522 (1991).
79. Staff writer, Plast. Technol., 33 (10), 7 (1987).
80. Avery, S., Mod. Plast., 66 (7), 41 (1986).
81. Steiner, K.W., Kunstst. Ger. Plast., 74 (4), 2 (1984).
82. Kente, R., Kunstst. Ger. Plast., 74 (4), 8 (1984).
83. Fakirov, S., Kunstst. Ger. Plast., 74 (4), 17 (1984).
84. Birnkraut, H.W., Kunstst. Ger. Plast., 72 (7), 15 (1982).
85. Curlee, T.R., Recyclingplas V Conf. Proc., P.I.A., Washington, D.C., 21 (1990).
86. Mack, W.A., Recyclingplas V Conf. Proc., P.I.A., Washington, D.C., 80 (1990).
87. Considine, W.J., Recyclingplas V Conf. Proc., P.I.A., Washington, D.C., 100 (1990).
88. Chretien, G., Recyclingplas V Conf. Proc., P.I.A., Washington, D.C., 123 (1990).
89. Seneri, E., Recyclingplas V Conf. Proc., P.I.A., Washington, D.C., 142 (1990).
90. Tomaszek, T., Recyclingplas V Conf. Proc., P.I.A., Washington, D.C., 153 (1990).
91. Coran, A.Y., and R. Patel, Rubber Chem. Technol., 56, 1045 (1983).
92. Segume, T., M. Oosawa, S. Sato, Y. Haraguchi, T. Mikami, T. Nishio, T. Yokoi, T. Nomura, and N. Kawamura, EP 364,304, Tonen Co., Ltd. (1990).
93. Jody, B.J., E.J. Daniels, Recyclingplas VI Conf. Proc., P.I.A., Washington, D.C., 38 (1991).
94. Forman, M., Recyclingplas VI Conf. Proc., P.I.A., Washington, D.C., 28 (1991).
95. Suwanda, D., R. Lew , and S.T. Balke, J. Appl. Polym. Sci., 35, 1019 (1988).
96. Flynn, M.S., Recyclingplas VI Conf. Proc., P.I.A., Washington, D.C., 47 (1991).
97. Engelmann, P.V., M.D. Monfore, E.W. Dawkins, and J.A. McInerney, Plast. Eng., 48 (2), 27 (1992).
98. Suwanda, D., R. Lew, and S.T. Balke, J. Appl. Polym. Sci., 35, 1033 (1988).
99. Choudhury, N.R., and A.K. Bhowmick, J. Appl. Polym. Sci., 38, 1091 (1989).
100. Jones, J., Chem. Eng., January 2, 87 (1978).
101. Ram, A., and S. Getz, J. Appl. Polym. Sci., 29, 2501 (1984).

102. Traugott, T.D., J.W. Barlow, and D.R. Paul, J. Appl. Polym. Sci., 28, 2947 (1983).
103. Vaidya, U.R., and V.M. Nadkarni, Proc. of ACS Div. of PMSE, ACS, Washington, D.C., 1029 (1990).
104. Tormala, P., E. Paakkonen, and K. Luoto, J. Appl. Polym. Sci., 30, 423 (1985).
105. Tindall, G.W., and R.L. Perry, US 5,045,122, Eastman Kodak Co. (1991).
106. Foster, R.H., Polym. Prepr., ACS Div. Polym. Chem., 32 (2), 154 (1991).
107. Blatz, P.S., Polym. Prepr., ACS Div. Polym. Chem., 32 (2), 152 (1991).
108. Dagli, S.S., M. Xanthos, and J.A. Biesenberger, Polym. Prepr., ACS Div. Polym. Chem., 32 (2), 150 (1991).
109. Stein, R.S., Polym. Prepr., ACS Div. Polym. Chem., 32 (2), 146 (1991).
110. Simpson, R., and S. Selke, Polym. Prepr., ACS Div. Polym. Chem., 32 (2), 148 (1991).
111. Richard, R.E., W.H. Boon, M.L. Martin-Shultz, and E.A. Sisson, Polym. Prepr., ACS Div. Polym. Chem., 32 (2), 144 (1991).
112. Rebeiz, K.S., D.W. Fowler, and D.R. Paul, Polym. Prepr., ACS Div. Polym. Chem., 32 (2), 142 (1991).
113. Wu, Y., G. Tesoro, and P.I. Engelberg, Polym. Prepr., ACS Div. Polym. Chem., 32 (2), 140 (1991).
114. Vane, L.M., and F. Rodriguez, Polym. Prepr., ACS Div. Polym. Chem., 32 (2), 138 (1991).
115. Wielgolinski, L.J., Polym. Prepr., ACS Div. Polym. Chem., 32 (2), 135 (1991).
116. Super, M.S., R.M. Enick, and E.J. Beckman, Polym. Prepr., ACS Div. Polym. Chem., 32 (2), 133 (1991).
117. Liedermooy, I., S. Fitzgerald, and C.L. Beatty, Polym. Prepr., ACS Div. Polym. Chem., 32 (2), 131 (1991).
118. Cao, L., S.G. Byun, D.W. Baugh, C.L. Beatty, and R. Ramer, Polym. Prepr., ACS Div. Polym. Chem., 32 (2), 129 (1991).
119. Loomis, G.L., J.M. Romesser, and W.J. Jewell, Polym. Prepr., ACS Div. Polym. Chem., 32 (2), 127 (1991).
120. Brecker, L.R., Polym. Prepr., ACS Div. Polym. Chem., 32 (2), 125 (1991).
121. Klemchuk, P.P., Polym. Prepr., ACS Div. Polym. Chem., 32 (2), 123 (1991).
122. Boettcher, F.P., Polym. Prepr., ACS Div. Polym. Chem., 32 (2), 114 (1991).
123. Labana, S.S., Polym. Prepr., ACS Div. Polym. Chem., 32 (2), 116 (1991).
124. Narayan, R., and S. Bloembergen, Polym. Prepr., ACS Div. Polym. Chem., 32 (2), 119 (1991).
125. Bennett, R.A., Polym. Prepr., ACS Div. Polym. Chem., 32 (2), 121 (1991).
126. Kinstle, J.F., L.D. Forshey, R. Valle, and R.R. Cambell, Polym. Prepr., ACS Div. Polym. Chem., 32 (2), 446 (1983).
127. Michaeli, W., L. Wolters, and M. Bittner, Kunstst. Ger. Plast., 81 (7), 3 (1991).
128. Wagner, J.P., M.A. El-Ayyoubi, and R.B. Konzen, Polym.-Plast. Technol. Eng., 30 (8), 827 (1991).
129. Bauer, G., Kunstst. Ger. Plast., 81 (4), 15 (1991).
130. Kampouris, E.M., C.D. Papaspyrides, and C.N. Lekakou, Polym. Eng. Sci., 28 (8), 534 (1988).
131. Ishihara, Y., H. Nambu, T. Ikemura, and T. Takesue, J. Appl. Polym. Sci., 38, 1491 (1989).
132. Fettes, E.M. (Ed), Chemical Reactions of Polymers, Interscience, New York, 70 (1964).
133. Cambell, G.A., and W.C. Meluch, J. Appl. Polym. Sci., 21, 581 (1977).
134. Ulrich, H., A. Odinak, B. Tucker, and A.A.R. Sayigh, Polym. Eng. Sci., 18 (11), 844 (1978).
135. Vaidya, U.R., and V.M. Nadkarni, J. Appl. Polym. Sci., 38, 1179 (1989).
136. Bradslaw, J., and J.L. Gerlock, Ind. Eng. Chem. Proc. Des. Div., 23, 552 (1984).
137. Uemichi, Y., Y. Makino, and T. Kanazuka, J. Analyt. Appl. Pyrol., 14, 331 (1989).
138. Bartlett, D.W., D.R. Paul, and J.W. Barlow, Mod. Plast., 58 (12), 60 (1981).
139. Lindsey, C.R., J.W. Barlow, and D.R. Paul, J. Appl. Polym. Sci., 26, 9 (1981).
140. Laguna, O., E.P. Collar, and J. Taranco, J. Appl. Polym. Sci., 38, 667 (1989).
141. Baliga, S., and W.T. Wong, J. Polym. Sci., 27, 2071 (1989).
142. Short, H.C., Chem. Eng., January 29, 64 (1987).
143. Fisher, F.T., M.L. Kasbohm, and J.R. Rivero, Chem. Eng. Progr., (10), 75 (1976).
144. Staff writer, Plast. Technol., 34 (11), 27 (1988).
145. Staff writer, Plast. Eng., 42 (2), 14 (1986).

146. Tomaszek, T.R., E. Makris, and S.J. Chen, Plast. Eng., 40 (8), 29 (1984).
147. Burdick, T.E., and B.D. Bauman, Mod. Plast., 61 (10), 76 (1984).
148. Staff writer, Mod. Plast., 58 (11), 66 (1981).
149. Wendt, C.H., Plast. Eng., 38 (2), 29 (1982).
150. Kadykowski, R., Plast. Eng., 40 (6), 47 (1984).
151. Mali, D.T.J., Plast. Technol., 28 (10), 69 (1982).
152. Staff writer, Plast. World, (12), 66 (1982).
153. Staff writer, Plast. World, (3), 8 (1983).
154. Lodge, C., Plast. World, (5), 14 (1989).
155. Staff writer, Plast. World, (7), 10 (1989).
156. Staff writer, Plast. World, (4), 11 (1984).
157. Staff writer, Plast. World, (5), 23 (1983).
158. Sieger, R.B., Civil Eng., (5), 88 (1978).
159. Snyder, N.W., Chem. Eng./Deskbook Edition, October 21, 65 (1974).
160. Staff writer, Chem. Eng., May 26, 72 (1975).
161. Bruckner, H., U. Frank, H. Fransen, W. Rasshofer, H. Schaper, and H.U. Schmidt, Kunstst. Ger. Plast., 81 (9), 3 (1991).
162. von Hassell, A., Plast. World, September, 88 (1991).
163. Hallden-Abberton, M., ACS Div. of PMSE Prepr., 65, 361 (1991).
164. Lambla, M., C. Maier, R. Kowalski, and B. Jones, ACS Div. of PMSE Prepr., 65, 356 (1991).
165. Williams, D., and M. Bevis, J. Mat. Sci., 15, 2834 (1980).
166. Williams, D., and M. Bevis, J. Mat. Sci., 15, 2843 (1980).
167. Spaak, A., Recyclingplas I Conf. Proc., P.I.A., Washington, D.C., 20 (1986).
168. Maczko, J., Recyclingplas II Conf. Proc., P.I.A., Washington, D.C., 59 (1987).
169. Iijima, R., Recyclingplas II Conf. Proc., P.I.A., Washington, D.C., 70 (1987).
170. Milgrom, J., Recyclingplas II Conf. Proc., P.I.A., Washington, D.C., 97 (1987).
171. Alexander, R.L., US 3,406,127, Gulf Oil Corp. (1968).
172. Sabourin, D., Recyclingplas III Conf. Proc., P.I.A., Washington, D.C., 83 (1988).
173. Morey, B.K., US 4,362,276, Occidental Res. Corp. (1982).
174. Frulla, F.F., A. Ordinac, and A.A.R. Saying, US 3,708,440, Upjohn Co. (1973).
175. Wolf, H.O., US 3,225,094, E.I. du Pont de Nemours & Co. (1965).
176. Saunders, J.H., J.A. Burroughs, L.P. Williams, D.H. Martin, J.H. Southern, R.L. Ballman, and K.R. Lea, J. Appl. Polym. Sci., 19, 1387 (1975).
177. Hendewerk, M.L., US 5,001,197, Exxon Chem. Pat., Inc. (1991).
178. Datta, S., and D.J. Lohse, US 4,999,403, Exxon Chem. Pat., Inc. (1991).
179. McAlpin, J.J., and W.Y. Chow, US 4,710,540, Exxon Chem. Pat., Inc. (1987).
180. Chow, W.Y., and J.J. McAlpin, US 4,801,630, Exxon Chem. Pat., Inc. (1989).
181. Fry, S.E., D.W. Magouyrk, and A.J. Blankenship, US 4,966,947, Eastman Kodak Co. (1990).
182. Woodhams, R.T., US 4,978,698, The Univ. of Toronto Innov. Found. (1990).
183. Walters, S., Plast. News, November 9, 12 (1992).
184. McAlpin, J.J., and W.Y. Chow, US 4,952,631, Exxon Chem. Pat., Inc. (1990).
185. Grigsby, R.A., Jr., G.P. Speranza, M.E. Brennan, and E.L. Yeakey, US 4,536,522, Texaco, Inc. (1985).
186. Swint, S.A., K.D. Webber, and C.I. Chung, RETEC Tech. Pap., Soc. Plast. Eng., White Haven, PA (1990).
187. Willey, L.J., RETEC Tech. Pap., Soc. Plast. Eng., White Haven, PA (1990).
188. Nurse, R.H., and S. Fuzessery, RETEC Tech. Pap., Soc. Plast. Eng., White Haven, PA (1990).
189. Mack, W.A., RETEC Tech. Pap., Soc. Plast. Eng., White Haven, PA, (1990).
190. Kamath, V.R., and L.H. Palys, RETEC Tech. Pap., Soc. Plast. Eng., White Haven, PA (1990).
191. Narayan, R., RETEC Tech. Pap., Soc. Plast. Eng., White Haven, PA (1990).
192. Allenza, P., J. Schollmeyer, H. Oltmann, and R.P. Rohrbach, RETEC Tech. Pap., Soc. Plast. Eng., White Haven, PA (1990).

193. Rebeiz, K.S., D.W. Fowler, and D.R. Paul, RETEC Tech. Pap., Soc. Plast. Eng., White Haven, PA, (1990).
194. Maczko, J., RETEC Tech. Pap., Soc. Plast. Eng., White Haven, PA (1990).
195. Fleming, R.A., RETEC Tech. Pap., Soc.Plast. Eng., White Haven, PA (1990).
196. Simioni, F., S. Bisello, and M. Tavan, Cell. Polym., 2, 281 (1983).
197. Simioni, F., M. Modesti, and C.A. Brambilla, Cell. Chem., 8, 387 (1989).
198. Buekens, A.G., Conserv. Recycl., 1, 247 (1977).
199. Bockhorn, H., M. Burckschat, and H. Deusser, J. Analyt. Appl. Pyrol., 8, 427 (1985).
200. Cudmore, W.J.G., US 4,578,502, Cudmore, W.J.G. (1986).
201. Tesoro, G., H. Chum, and A. Power, Comp. Instit., 47th Ann.Conf., Soc. Plast. Ind., Session 4C, 1–8 (1992).
202. Rodrigues-Fernandez, O., and M. Sanchez-Adame, 37th ANTEC Tech. Pap., Soc. Plast. Eng., 1176 (1991).
203. Pellegria, R., and A. Ghisotti, US 4,596,603, Texaco S.p.A. (1986).
204. Mandoki, J.W., US 4,605,762, Celanese, Mexicana S.A. (1986).
205. McDaniel, K.G., US 4,644,019, Texaco Inc. (1987).
206. Ashcraft, C.R., and M.L. Kerr, US 4,650,721, Mobil Oil Corp. (1987).
207. Fukuda, T., K. Saito, S. Suzuki, H. Sato, and T. Hirota, US 4,851,601, Mobil Oil Corp. (1989).
208. Kennedy, R.B., US 4,521,544, Assignees (Crehan, P.J., R.J. Fricke) (1985).
209. Brennan, M.E., US 4,444,920, Texaco, Inc. (1984).
210. Kobayashi, T., UK 2,136,437, Kabushiki Kaisha Rinne K.T.I. (1985).
211. McDonald, W.J., US 4,413,969, James Mackie & Sons Ltd. (1983).
212. Xanthos, M., AIChE Spr. Nat. Meeting, AIChE, New Orleans, LA, 24a (1992).
213. Xanthos, M., T.J. Nosker, and K.E. Van Ness, Proc. 4th Int. Cong. Compalloy '92, Short Hills, NJ, 59 (1992).
214. Gerlock, J.L., J. Braslaw, and J. Albright, US 4,317,939, Ford Motor Co. (1982).
215. Gerlock, J.L., J. Braslaw, and J. Albright, US 4,316,992, Ford Motor Co. (1982).
216. Jacono, C., and S. Tribastone, US 4,987,166, Enichem Anic S.p.A. (1991).
217. Van Der Groep, L.A., US 4,997,880, High Tech Plast. B.V. (1991).
218. King, V.E., Recyclingplas VII Conf. Proc., P.I.A, Arlington, VA, (1992).
219. Rees, R.W., US 3,050,507, Shawinigan Chemicals, Ltd. (1962).
220. Hallmark, R.K., M.J. Skowronski, and W.D. Stephens, EP 152,915, Jim Walter Resourses, Inc (1985).
221. Liu, Y.C., and R. Edwards, EP 408,470, Eastman Kodak Co. (1991).
222. Bertolino, G., EP 334,420, Tecnocolor S.a.s di Celebrano A. & C. (1989).
223. Coughlin, M.C., and T.T. Schenck, EP 113,916 , E.I. du Pont de Nemours & Co. (1984).
224. Armer, T.A., EP 203,630, Shell Int. Res. Maayschappij B.V. (1986).
225. Anonymous, IN 81-BO64, Nirlon Synth. Fibers & Chem., Ltd (1982).
226. Leaversuch, R.D., Mod. Plast., 68 (7), 39 (1991).
227. Rebeiz, K.S., D.W. Fowler, and D.R. Paul, Polym-Plast. Technol. Eng, 30 (8), 809 (1991).
228. Fillman, W., Plast. Rubber: Process., (9), 104 (1978).
229. Lever, M.D.A., and R.S.P. Parker, Plast. Rubber: Process., (6), 63 (1978).
230. Staff writer, Plast. News, November 2, (1992).
231. Mallan, G.M., Chem Eng., 83 (7), 90(1976).
232. Poller, R.C., J. Chem. Tech. Biotechnol., 30, 152 (1980).
233. Castellanos, O.L., and E.P. Collar, Resources, Conserv. Recycl., 2, 37 (1988).
234. Technical Information Center, "Stain Blockers for Nylon Fibers", Report No. 31, TRI, Princeton NJ, (1989).
235. Frederix, H., Kunstst. Ger. Plast., 68 (5), 19 (1975).
236. Ranby, B., Kunstst. Ger. Plast., 68 (5), 10 (1978).
237. Wiesenkamper, W., Kunstst. Ger. Plast., 68 (5), 23 (1978).
238. Staab, G.A., C.L. Beatty, and A.L. Fricke, Proc., 13 Meeting, Seminar VI, CPRR/Rutgers U., Sept. 24–25, (1991).

239. Wadsworth, L.C., M. Dever, and G. Bhat, Proc., 13th Meeting, Seminar VI, CPRR/Rutgers U., Sept. 24–25, (1991).
240. Bennett, R.A., Proc. 13th Meeting, Seminar VI, CPRR/ Rutgers U., Sept. 24–25, (1991).
241. Stapp, P.R., Proc. 13th Meeting, Seminar VI, CPRR/ Rutgers U., Sept. 24–25, (1991).
242. Oblinger, F.G., US 4,281,197, Ford Motor Co. (1981).
243. Marvel, C.S., G.D. Jones, T.W. Mastin, and G.L. Schertz, J. Am. Chem. Soc., 64, 2356 (1942).
244. Fisa, B., A. Bouti, B.D. Favis, and F. Lalande, 37th ANTEC Tech. Pap., Soc. Plast. Eng., 1135 (1991).
245. Yu, R.X., P. Zhu, and M. Lambla, 37th ANTEC Tech. Pap., Soc. Plast. Eng., 1051 (1991).
246. Staff writer, Plast. Technol., 38 (2), 65 (1992).
247. Ulrich, H., Adv. Urethane Sci. Technol., 5, 49 (1978).
248. Xanthos, M., and S.S. Dagli, Polym. Eng. Sci., 31 (13), 929 (1991).
249. Clements, J.S., 26th ANTEC Tech. Pap., Soc. Plast. Eng., 551 (1980).
250. Ulrich, H., A. Odinak, B. Tucher, and A.A.R. Sayingh, 25th ANTEC Tech. Pap., Soc. Plast. Eng., 41 (1979).
251. Dawans, F., EP 443,932, Institut Francais du Petrole (1991).
252. Bauer, G., DE 4,024,601, Aalen Fachhochschule (1991).
253. Clavier, P., EP 322,310, (1989).
254. Polowinski, S., H. Struszczyk, and S. Koch, PL 143,526, Politechnika Lodz (1988).
255. Bauer, G., DE 3,702,495, Aalen Fachhochschule (1988).
256. Bentley, J.M., J.P. Brown, and G. Frijns, EP 248,570, ICI PLC (1987).
257. Morozov, Yu. L., Yu. M. Alter, R.I. Sharapov, and A.P. Tkachuk, Kauch. Rezina, 1, 25 (1988).
258. Michalski, A., Wlokna Chem., 13 (2), 144 (1987).
259. Uliyanov, V.P., Yu. L. Morozov, Yu. M. Alter, V.I. Gudimenko, A.P. Tkachuk, and R.I. Sharapov, Kozh.-Obuvn. Prom-st., 10, 20 (1987).
260. Ivanova, N., Ya. T'svetkova, V. Vulchev, and D. Rozalinov, God. Vissh. Khim., 28 (3), 13 (1987).
261. Zaikov, G.E., and P.P. Nechaev, Vysokomol. Soedin., 27 (5), 983 (1985).
262. Akhmedov, U.K., S.G. Kamaryan, V.E. Ivanov, K.S. Akhmedov, M.G. Pleshkov, A.G. Sidyakin, T.I. Iskandarov, SU 1,199,760, (1985).
263. Simioni, F., A. Scipioni, G. Navazio, and S. Bisello, Lett. Arti, Cl. Sci. Fis., Mat. Nat., 141, 21 (1983).
264. Zvironaite, B., P. Zukas, E. Dicmoniene, R. Urinciene, A. Kaminskas, and A. Lasis, SU 1,106,819, All-Union Sci.-Res. Inst. Insl. Acoust. Constr. Mat. (1984).
265. Petru, V., L. Bartok, N.I. Lucaciu, E.D. Borbely, and R.F. Pape, RO 82,464, Combinatul Petrochimic "Solventul" (1983).
266. Niederdellmann, G., N. Roemer, J. Schenk, H. Hetzel, and E. Grigat, EP 47,913, Bayer A-G (1982).
267. Koeble, L., J. Apprich, and L. Loeble, DE 2,902,509, (1980).
268. Gerlock, J.L., EP 11,662, Ford-Werke A.G. (1980).
269. Hara, K., and H. Higaki, JP 54,117,580, Asahi Chem. Ind. Co. Ltd. (1979).
270. Anonymous, JP 54,070,377, Ford Motor Co. (1979).
271. Mahoney, L.R., BE 869,046, Ford Motor Co. (1978).
272. Azman, J., Koza Obuca, 27 (8), 226 (1978).
273. Grigat, E., Mater. Tech., 4, 141 (1978).
274. Penfold, J., and J. Kuypers, Urethanes Envron., Conf., Plast. Rubber Inst., London, England, H1 (1976).
275. Cobiancu, N., B. Marculescu, M. Vasiliu, F. Marculescu, and V. Posea, Ind. Usoara: Text., Tricotaje, Confectii Text., 28 (9), 385 (1977).
276. Petrov, A.A., E.M. Alzenshtein, and N.N. Velikanov, Khim. Volokna, 6, 56 (1977).
277. Anonymous, BE 833,013, Bayer A.G. (1976).
278. Gilbert, G.S., K.J. Giacin, T. Van Gordon, A. Vahidi, and J.R. Giacin, ACS, Div. Org. Coat. Plast. Chem., Pap., 34 (2), 462 (1974).
279. Braslaw, J., and L.R. Mahoney, DE 2,362,921, Ford-Werke A.G. (1974).

280. Johnson, O.B., DE 2,362,920, Ford-Werke A.G. (1974).
281. Johnson, O.B., DE 2,362,919, Ford-Werke A.G. (1974).
282. Latypov, Kh., B.R. Shukurov, U. Rakhimov, S.A. Zainutdinov, and K.S. Akhmedov, Dolk. Akad. Nauk Uzb. USSR, 30 (12), 18 (1973).
283. Mahoney, L.R., S.A. Weiner, and F.C. Ferris, Environ. Sci. Technol., 8 (2), 135 (1974).
284. Dmitrieva, L.A., Yu. N. Bychkov, V.M. Kharitonov, V.B. Kvasha, A.A. Dubynin, and B.I. Goguadze, Tovarnye Zkaki, 50 (15), 49 (1973).
285. Kharitonova, V.P., S.P. Dorofeev, M.S. Pustil'nik, and S.S. Frolov, Khim. khim. Tekhnol., 15 (2), 311 (1972).
286. Leidner, J., 25th ANTEC Tech. Pap., Soc. Plast. Eng., 539 (1979).
287. Yen, Y.C., 25th ANTEC Tech. Pap., Soc. Plast. Eng., 109 (1979).
288. Bataille, P., C. Jolicoeur, and H.P. Schreiber, 26th ANTEC Tech. Pap., Soc. Plast. Eng., 475 (1980).
289. Laguna, O., E.P. Collar, and J. Taranco, J. Polym. Eng., 7 (3), 169 (1987).
290. Akkapeddi, M.K., and J. Gervasi, ACS Polym. Prep., 29 (1), 567 (1988).
291. Todd, D.B., Polym.-Plast. Technol. Eng., 28 (2), 123 (1989).
292. Hyun, M.E., and S.C. Kim, Polym. Eng. Sci., 28 (11), 743 (1988).
293. Willis, J.M., and B.D. Favis, Polym. Eng. Sci., 28 (21), 1416 (1988).
294. Van Ballegooie, P., and A. Rudin, Polym. Eng. Sci., 28 (21), 1434 (1988).
295. Pabedinskas, A., W.R. Cluett, and S.T. Balke, Polym. Eng. Sci., 29 (15), 993 (1989).
296. Campbell, J.R., S.Y. Hobbs, T.J. Shea, and V.H. Watkins, Polym. Eng. Sci., 30 (17), 1056 (1990).
297. Cheung, P., D. Suwanda, and S.T. Balke, Polym. Eng. Sci., 30 (17), 1063 (1990).
298. Tang, Y., C. Tzoganakis, A.E. Hamielec, and J. Vlachopoulos, Adv. Polym. Technol., 9 (3), 217 (1989).
299. Tzoganakis, C., Adv. Polym. Technol., 9 (4), 321 (1989).
300. Dorne, Von W.G., Kunstst.-Plast. 33 (2), 20 (1986).
301. Timmann, H., and A. Dreyer, Kunstst. Ger. Plast., 39 (7), 637 (1986).
302. Lichtenstein, N., Staub-Reinhalt. Luft, 42 (3), 115 (1982).
303. Bockhorn, H., M. Burckschat, and H. Deusser, Erdöl, Kohle, Erdgas, Petrochem, 38 (12), 549 (1985).
304. Albright, L.F., B.L. Crynes, and W.H. Harrison (Eds), Pyrolysis: Theory Ind. Pract., Academic Press, New York, 177 (1983).
305. Domke, B., Prax. Naturwiss., Chem., 35 (8), 2 (1986).
306. Diebold, J.P., Therm. Convers. Solid Wastes Biomass (130), ACS, Symp. Ser, 209 (1980).
307. Herne, B., WLB, Wasser, Luft Betr., 25 (4), 46 (1981).
308. Kaminsky, W., Resource Recov. Conserv., 5 (3), 205 (1980).
309. Kaminsky, W., H. Sinn, Therm. Convers. Solid Waste Biomass (130), ACS Symp. Ser., 423 (1980).
310. Chambers, C., J.W. Larsen, W. Li, and B. Wiesen, Ind. Eng. Chem. Process Des. Dev., 23, 648 (1984).
311. Hilado, C.J., and P.A. Huttlinger, J. Fire & Flammability, 12 (1), 65 (1981).
312. Kagayama, M., M. Igarashi, M. Hasegawa, and J. Fukuda, Therm. Convers. Solid Wastes Biomass (130), ACS Symp. Ser., 525 (1980).
313. Frommelt, H., Wiss. Fortschr., 30 (1), 5 (1980).
314. Kaminsky, W., J. Merkel, C. Stiller, and L. Wieprecht, Proc.-Recycling World Congr., 3rd (1), 1/10/1 (1980).
315. Igarashi, M., Y. Hayafune, R. Sugamiya, and Y. Nakagawa, Proc. Nat. Waste Process. Conf., 11th, 271 (1984).
316. Bracker, G., and U. Liss, Recycl. Int.: Recovery Energy Mater. Residues Waste, [Contrib.-Int. Recycl. Congr. (IRC)], Int. Recycl. Congr., 502 (1982).
317. Connor, M.A., Chemeca 80, Conf. Proc, Inst. Eng. Aust., Barton, Australia, (1980).
318. Kaminsky, W., Chem. Rundsch., 34 (9), 1 (1981).
319. Bracker, G.P., G. Collin, G. Grigoleit, E. Michel, and M. Zander, Chem-Ing.-Tech., 53 (10), 820 (1981).

320. Kaminsky, W., Kompostierung Brennstoffgewinnung, E. Freitag Verlag Umwelttech, 563 (1983).
321. Scott, D.S., S.R. Czernik, and D. Radlein, Energy Biomass Wastes, 14, 1009 (1991).
322. Ottiger, R.S., M.E. Banks, and W.D. Lusk, ACS, Div. Water, Air Waste Chem., Gen. Pap, 10 (2), 223 (1970).
323. Takesue, T., Petrol. Petrochem. Intern., 12 (4), 36 (1972).
324. Lechert, H., V. Woebs, Q. Sung, W. Kaminsky, and H. Sinn, EP 321,807, ASEA Brown Boveri A.G. (1989).
325. Schueneman, G.T., and C.L. Beatty, 38th ANTEC Tech. Pap., Soc. Plast. Eng., 2155 (1992).
326. Brown, C.L., and E.G. Soto, 38th ANTEC Tech. Pap., Soc. Plast. Eng., 2150 (1992).
327. Birt, W.O., 38th ANTEC Tech. Pap., Soc. Plast. Eng., 2142 (1992).
328. Pavlock, M.A., 38th ANTEC Tech. Pap., Soc. Plast. Eng., 2146 (1992).
329. Seidl, K.S., 38th ANTEC Tech. Pap., Soc. Plast. Eng., 1550 (1992).
330. Day, S.L.D., 38th ANTEC Tech. Pap., Soc. Plast. Eng., 1542 (1992).
331. Tayebi, A., and A.K. Mithal, 38th ANTEC Tech. Pap., Soc. Plast. Eng., 1196 (1992).
332. Patel, H.N., and F.S. Lai, 38th ANTEC Tech. Pap., Soc. Plast. Eng., 1192 (1992).
333. Engelmann, P.V., J.A. McInerney, and M.D. Monfore, 38th ANTEC Tech. Pap., Soc. Plast. Eng., 1189 (1992).
334. Zahavich, A.T.P., E. Takacs, B. Latto, and J. Vlachopoulos, 38th ANTEC Tech. Pap., Soc. Plast. Eng., 1186 (1992).
335. Jin, H., J. Phelps, and A. Grugnola, 38th ANTEC Tech. Pap., Soc. Plast. Eng., 228 (1992).
336. Jin, H., J. Phelps, and A. Grugnola, 38th ANTEC Tech. Pap., Soc. Plast. Eng., 224 (1992).
337. Paul, D.R., C.E. Locke, and C.E. Vinson, Polym. Eng. Sci., 13 (3), 202 (1973).
338. Locke, C.E., and D.R. Paul, Polym. Eng. Sci., 13 (4), 308 (1973).
339. Levie, B., J.P. Diebold, and R. West, Res. Thermochem. Bio. Conver. (Int. Conf.), Eds. A.V. Bridgwater, J.L. Kuester, Elsevier, London, England, 312 (1988).
340. Bellman, U., and W. Kaminsky, Umwelt, 19 (6), 336 (1989).
341. Bockhorn, H., and M. Burckschat, Chem.-Ing.-Tech., 61 (10), 813 (1989).
342. Mosbacher, R., Kunststoffe-Plast. 36 (8), 16 (1989).
343. Lin, C.P., EP 344,376, Lin, C.P. (1989).
344. Scott, D.S., S.R. Czernik, J. Piskorz, and D. St. A.G. Radlein, Energy and Fuels, 4 (4), 407 (1990).
345. Dummersdorf, H.U., W. Jahn, W. Noack, and W. Heidel, DD 285,506, VEB Chemieanlagen-baukombinat Leipzig-Grimma (1990).
346. Hoffmockel, M., W. Kaminsky, K. Pohlmann, S. Schaedel, and H. Sinn, DE 3,932,927, Inst. Anorg. Angew. Chem., Univ. Hamburg (1991).
347. Lai, W.C., and B. Krieger-Brockett, ACS Div. Fuel Chem. Preprint 36 (2), 683 (1991).
348. Metzemacher, H.D., and R. Seeling, EP 121,055, Lonza A.-G. (1991).
349. Sezume, T., A. Kobayashi, and K. Inamori, WO 90/12054, Tonen Co. (1990).
350. Kitakoa, Y., and H. Sueyoshi, Convers. Refuse Energy, Int. Conf. Tech. Exhib., 1st, IEEE, 555 (1975).
351. Schoeters, J.G., A.G. Buekens, and H. Masson, Int. Conf. Future Energy Concepts, 3d, Conf. Publ., IEE, 184 (1981).
352. Menges, G., and R. Fischer, Kunstst. Ger. Plast., 81 (1), 3 (1991).
353. Weber, A., XXIII Congresso FISITA 1990 "Materiali nel ciclo vitale del'auto", v.43,n.8–9, 603 (1990).
354. Stewart, M.E., A.J. Cox, S.E. George, and D.R. Paul, Adv. High Perf. Polym. Alloys, 5th Int. Conf. Proc., ECM, Plymouth, MI, (1992).
355. Krak, H., person. comm. with Attilio Bisio, June, (1991).
356. Curlee, T.R., "Recycling of Plastics", in "Concise Encycl. Mat. Econ., Policy, and Manage-ment", Ed., M. Beaver, Pergamon Press, New York, (1991).
357. Curlee, T.R., and S. Das, Mat. Soc., 15 (1), 41 (1991).
358. Curlee, T.R., and S. Das, Resources, Conservation and Recycling, 5, 343 (1991).
359. Loomans, B.A., and J.E. Kowalczyk, US 4,908,104, APV Chem. Mach. Inc. (1990).
360. Loomans, B.A., and J.E. Kowalczyk, US 5,017,269, APV Chem. Mach. Inc. (1991).

361. Curlee, T.R., J. Environ. Systems, 18 (3), 193 (1989).
362. Yu, T.C., H.C. Wang, K.W. Powers, and A.F. Yee, 38th ANTEC Tech. Pap., Soc. Plast. Eng., 2385 (1992).
363. Curlee, T.R., and S. Das, Report for U.S.D.O.E, Oak Ridge Nat. Lab., (1989).
364. Renfree, R.W., T.J. Nosker, D.R. Morrow, L.W. Suttner, K.E. Van Ness, and E.D. Wyatt, 38th ANTEC Tech. Pap., Soc. Plast. Eng., 2396 (1992).
365. Waller, D.L., and C.J. Kibert, 38th ANTEC Tech. Pap., Soc. Plast. Eng., 2350 (1992).
366. Summers, J.W., B.K. Mikofalvy, H.K. Boo, J.M. Krogstie, W.A. Seli, and J.C. Rodriguez, 38th ANTEC Tech. Pap., Soc. Plast. Eng., 2365 (1992).
367. Menges, G., R. Fischer, and V. Lackner, Intl. Polymer Processing, 7 (4), 291 (1992).
368. Li, T., M. Roha, A. Hiltner, and E. Baer, 38th ANTEC Tech. Pap., Soc. Plast. Eng., 2635 (1992).
369. Duvall, J., C. Sellitti, A. Hiltner, and E. Baer, 38th ANTEC Tech. Pap., Soc. Plast. Eng., 2639 (1992).
370. Bank, D.H., S. Seibel, and A. Moet, 38th ANTEC Tech. Pap., Soc. Plast. Eng., 2644 (1992).
371. Maldas, D., and B.V. Kotka, 38th ANTEC Tech. Pap., Soc. Plast. Eng., 1073 (1992).
372. Champagne, M., P. Perrin, and R.E. Prud'homme, 37th ANTEC Tech. Pap., Soc. Plast. Eng., 1037 (1991).
373. Dzeskiewicz, K., C. Klahr, and R.E. Farrell, 38th ANTEC Tech. Pap., Soc. Plast. Eng., 809 (1992).
374. Rebeiz, K.S., D.W. Fowler, and D.R. Paul, 38th ANTEC Tech. Pap., Soc. Plast. Eng., 805 (1992).
375. Rajalingam, P., and W.E. Baker, 38th ANTEC Tech. Pap., Soc. Plast. Eng., 799 (1992).
376. Campanelli, J.R., M.R. Kamal, and D.G. Cooper, 38th ANTEC Tech. Pap., Soc. Plast. Eng., 270 (1992).
377. Ritzmann, H., DAVOS Recycle '92, Maack Business Services, 5/5–1 (1992).
378. Kleine-Kleffmann, U., A. Hollstein, and I. Stahl, DAVOS Recycle'92, Maack Business Services, 5/6–1 (1992).
379. Super, M.S., R.M. Enick, and E. Beckman, DAVOS Recycle '92, Maack Business Services, 5/7–1 (1992).
380. Frankenhaeuser, M., DAVOS Recycle '92, Maack Business Services, 3/4–1 (1992).
381. Ernst, H., DAVOS Recycle '92, Maack Business Services, 5/4–1 (1992).
382. Feuerherd, K.H., DAVOS Recycle '92, Maack Business Services, 3/5–1 (1992).
383. Hammer, F., DAVOS Recycle '92, Maack Business Services, 10/3–1 (1992) .
384. Rebeiz, K.S., and D.W. Fowler, DAVOS Recycle '92, Maack Business Services, 10/5–1 (1992).
385. Stannard, D.C., DAVOS Recycle '92, Maack Business Services, 3/1–1 (1992).
386. Meszaros, M., DAVOS Recycle '92, Maack Business Services, 3/2–1 (1992).
387. Huybrechts, S., DAVOS Recycle '92, Maack Business Services, 3/3–1 (1992).
388. Hallden-Abberton, M., Polym. Mat. Sci. Eng., 65, 361 (1991).
389. Bellahcene, M., and N. Bounafa, 37th ANTEC Tech. Pap., Soc. Plast. Eng., 721 (1991).
390. Ogando, J.J., Plast. Technol., 36 (6), 43 (1992).
391. Vanderhider, J.A., and H.R. Fransen, DAVOS Recycle '92, Maack Business Services, 6/6–1 (1992).
392. Norwalk, S., Recyclingplas VII, P.I.A., Washington, D.C., (1992).
393. Sitek, F.A., R.V. Todesco, and K. Hoffmann, DAVOS Recycle '92, Maack Business Services, 11/4–1 (1992).
394. Burkle, D., DAVOS Recycle '92, Maack Business Services, 11/1–1 (1992).
395. Thakkar, A.N., and S.J. Grossman, 37th ANTEC Tech. Pap., , Soc. Plast. Eng., 647 (1991).
396. Burlet, R., DAVOS Recycle '92, Maack Business Services, 8/4–4 (1992).
397. Beyer, S., DAVOS Recycle '92, Maack Business Services, 8/3–1 (1992).
398. Fisher, M., DAVOS Recycle '92, Maack Business Services, 6/4–1 (1992).
399. Higuchi, S., DAVOS Recycle '92, Maack Business Services, 6/2–1 (1992).
400. Wolf, R., DAVOS Recycle '92, Maack Business Services, 12/2–1 (1992).
401. Meister, B., and H. Schaper, DAVOS Recycle '92, Maack Business Services, 12/5–1 (1992).

402. Martin, R., R. Reis, and B. Vosteen, DAVOS Recycle '92, Maack Business Services, 12/6–1 (1992).
403. Frankel, H., DAVOS Recycle '92, Maack Business Services, 14/1–1 (1992).
404. Kenny, G., and R.S. Bruner, DAVOS Recycle '92, Maack Business Services, 14/2–1 (1992).
405. Gottesman, R.T., DAVOS Recycle '92, Maack Business Services, 15/2–1 (1992).
406. Dupont, L.A., and V. Gupta, DAVOS Recycle '92, Maack Business Services, 15/3–1 (1992).
407. Blessing, J.M., DAVOS Recycle '92, Maack Business Services, 16/2–1 (1992).
408. White, F.S., Recyclingplas VII Conf. Proc, P.I.A., Arlington, VA, (1992).
409. Bauman, G.F., Recyclingplas VII Conf. Proc., P.I.A., Arlington, VA, (1992).
410. Daniels, L., Recyclingplas VII Conf. Proc., P.I.A., Arlington, VA, (1992).
411. Gunderson, G.W., Recyclingplas VII Conf. Proc., P.I.A., Arlington, VA, (1992).
412. Winn, K., Recyclingplas VII Conf. Proc., P.I.A., Arlington, VA, (1992).
413. Evans, R., K. Tatsumoto, S. Czernik, and L. Chun, Recyclingplas VII Conf. Proc., P.I.A., Arlington, VA, 175 (1992).
414. Oblath, R.M., and E.N. Nowak, Recyclingplas VII Conf. Proc., P.I.A., Arlington, VA, (1992).
415. Roy C., and M.M. Dubuc, Recyclingplas VII Conf. Proc., P.I.A., Arlington, VA, (1992).
416. Ramer, R.M., AIChE Spring Nat. Meeting, AIChE, New Orleans, LA, 24b (1992).
417. Malloy, R.A., AIChe Spring Nat. Meeting, AIChE, New Orleans, LA, 24e (1992).
418. Reed, J., AIChE Spring Nat. Meeting, AIChE, New Orleans, LA, 24d (1992).
419. Rowell, R.M., AIChE Spring Nat. Meeting, AIChE, New Orleans, LA, 25a (1992).
420. Rials, T., AIChE Spring Nat. Meeting, AIChE, New Orleans, LA, 25b (1992).
421. Narayan, R., AIChE Spring Nat. Meeting, AIChE, New Orleans, LA, 25c (1992).
422. Koch, P., AIChE Spring Nat. Meeting, AIChE, New Orleans, LA, 25d (1992).
423. Park, S.C., AIChE Spring Nat. Meeting, AIChE, New Orleans, LA, 25e (1992).
424. Muhs, P., A. Plage, and H.D. Shuman, Kunstst. Ger. Plast., 82 (4), 8 (1992).
425. Starke, L., Z. Funke, and N. Kolzsch, Kunstst. Ger. Plast., 82 (1), 12 (1992).
426. Gruzner, R.E., and A. Koine, Kunstst. Ger. Plast., 82 (4), 5 (1992).
427. Starke, L., Z. Funke, and N. Kolzsch, Kunstst. Ger. Plast., 82 (4), 37 (1992).
428. Gebauer, M., and K. Buhler, Kunstst. Ger. Plast., 82 (1), 7 (1992).
429. Fuzessery, S., DAVOS Recycle '92, Maack Business Services, 10/6–1 (1992).
430. Pizzini, L.C., and J.T. Patton, US 3,441,616, Wyandotte Chem. Corp. (1969).
431. Saito, K., US 3,843,339, Ind. Sci. Tech. (1974).
432. Himes, G.R., US 4,868,057, Shell Oil Co. (1989).
433. Liu, N.C., and E. Baker, Adv. Polym. Technol., 11 (4), 249 (1992).
434. Akhtar, S., and J.L. White, Polym. Eng. Sci., 32 (10), 690 (1992).
435. Brown, S.B., and D.J. McFay, ACS Polym. Preprints, 27 (1), 333 (1986).
436. Schut, J.H., Plast. Technol., 38 (7), 99 (1992).
437. The Society of the Plastics Industry, Inc., "Facts and Fig. of the U.S. Plastics Industry", Washington, D.C., (1991).
438. Franklin Assoc., "Comparative Energy Evaluation of Plastic Products and their Alternatives for the Building and Construction and Transportation Industries", Soc. Plast. Ind., Washington, D.C., (1991).
439. Franklin Assoc., "A Comparison of Energy Consumption by the Plastics Ind. to Total Energy Consumption in the U.S.", Soc. Plast. Ind., Washington, D.C., (1990).
440. Niederdellmann, G., and H. Petersen, "Hydrolysis of Plastic Wastes with the Aim of Recovering and Reprocessing the Starting Components", Bayer A.G., (1984).
441. Niederdellmann, G., H. Hetzel, and H. Petersen, "Hydrolysis of Plastic Wastes with the Aim of Recovering and Reprocessiing the Starting Components", Bayer A.G, (1983).
442. Zhang, J., CN 1,033,067, (1987).
443. Fleming, R.A., "Design for recycling: A Plastic Bottle Recycler's Perspective", Soc. Plast. Ind., Washington, D.C., (1992).
444. Gates, D., "Report on Conversion of Polyester/Cotton Industrial Wastes to Higher Value Products", DOE, Washington, D.C., (1986).
445. Benerjie, A.K., US 5,030,662, Polymerix, Inc (1991).
446. Negi, T., JP 3,115,447, Kuraray Co., Ltd. (1991).

447. Michaeli, W., U. Berghaus, and G. Speuser, Chem.-Ing.-Tech., 63 (3), 221 (1991).
448. Anonymous, Purasuchikkusu, 41 (9), 80 (1990).
449. Li, T., W. Sun, and X. Yang, CN 1,051,880, China Petrochem. Corp. (1991).
450. Sorbet, B., and L. Jose, WO 9,111,305, Maderas Navarra S.A. (1991).
451. Stracke, M., AT 392,962, (1991).
452. Fujita, Y., D. Schulz, Y.W. Chow, R. Austin, J. Horrion, A. Montagna, K.O. McElrath Jr., A. Trozollah, and D. Jay, WO 9,114,248, Exxon Chem. Pat. (1991).
453. Chow, W.Y., G.R. Smith, and W.K. Wong, WO 9,108,257, Exxon Chem. Pat., Inc. (1991).
454. Abe, H., Y. Suzuki, M. Tsuji, K. Nagaoka, and T. Sanada, EP 407,224, Sumitomo Chem. Co., Ltd. (1991).
455. Freed, W.T., and M.T. Frantz , EP 427,388, Rohm and Haas Co. (1991).
456. Fasulo, G.C., D. Ghidoni, G. Cigna, A.G. Rossi, and I. Borghi, EP 427,268, Montedipe S.r.l. (1991).
457. Sezume, T., S. Sato, M. Oosawa, and K. Inamori, WO 9,012,837, Tonen Co., Ltd. (1990).
458. Patton, T.L., WO 9,015,101, Exxon Chem. Pat., Inc. (1990).
459. Chundury, D., A.S. Scheibelhoffer, and J.C. Vaughn, WO 9,005,759, Ferro Corp. (1990).
460. Orikasa, Y., and S. Sakazume, EP 368,295, Nippon Petrochem. Co. (1990).
461. Riffle, J.S., G.D. Sinai-Zingde, and A.E. Brink, WO 9,014,377, Virginia Tech. Intellect. Props., Inc. (1990).
462. McCord, E.F., US 4,971,864, E.I. du Pont de Nemours & Co. (1990).
463. Burget, B.E., and D.E. Rank, US 4,950,718, Dow Chem. Co. (1990).
464. Mizuno, H., S. Koide, M. Nomura, N. Kawamura, T. Nishio, and T. Nomura, EP 376,081, Idemitsu Petrochem. Co., Ltd. (1990).
465. Lunt, J., S.A.M. May, and P.A. Leivo, US 4,921,910, Polysar, Ltd. (1990).
466. Zabrocki, V.S., EP 347,794, Dow Chem. Co. (1989).
467. Randall, J.C., and T. Huff, EP 351,208, Exxon Chem. Pat., Inc. (1990).
468. Brown, S.B., and R.C. Lowry, EP 347,539, GE Co. (1989).
469. Stewart, M.E., Adv. Polym. Tech., in press.
470. Campbell, J.R., EP 340,566, GE Co. (1989).
471. Ilenda, C.S., W.J. Work, R.K. Graham, and N. Bortnick, EP 335,649, Rohm and Haas Co. (1989).
472. Mehra, V., EP 333,471, E.I. du Pont de Nemours & Co (1989).
473. Iwanami, K., K. Kitano, K. Narukawa, M. Sakuma, T. Mikami, M. Esaki, F. Kato, K. Egashira, and H. Wakabayashi, EP 340,040, Tonen Co., Ltd. (1989).
474. Iwanami, K., K. Kitano, K. Narukawa, M. Sakuma, T. Mikami, M. Esaki, F. Kato, K. Egashira, and H. Wakabayashi, EP 333,518, Tonen Co., Ltd. (1989).
475. Wang, C.W., J.R. Campbell, and T.J. Shea, EP 326,895, GE Co. (1989).
476. Moggi, G., G. Cirillo, and M.A.E. Benedetti, EP 295,717, Ausimont S.p.A. (1989).
477. Fasulo, G.C., A. Vezzoli, and G. Vittadini, EP 291,352, Maontedipe S.p.A. (1988).
478. Mason, C.D., W. Sacks, T. Engelmann, and S. Verma, WO 8,802,764, Allied Corp. (1988).
479. Shedd, C.D., and D.J. Anzini, US 4,696,967, BP Perf. Polym., Inc. (1987).
480. Stuart, V.I.W., and D.B. Priddy, US 4,704,431, Dow Chem. Co. (1989).
481. Lee, G.F. Jr., J.M.H. Heuschen, and R. Van der Meer, WO 8,705,311, GE Co. (1987).
482. Burgert, B.E., and D.E. Ranck, EP 215,150, Dow Chem. Co. (1987).
483. Topolski, A.S., EP 210,725, E.I. du Pont de Nemours & Co (1987).
484. Lucas, B.M., US 4,629,639, El Paso Products Co. (1986).
485. Hahnfeld, J.L., EP 195,829, Dow Chem. Co. (1986).
486. Booze, J.D., and P.M. Subramanian, EP 90,554, E.I. du Pont de Nemours & Co (1983).
487. Grancio, M.R., D.F. Stewart, and J.F. Cass, US 4,386,187, Sweetheart Plastics, Inc. (1983).
488. Grancio, M.C., D.F. Stewart, and J.F. Cass, EP 42,153, Sweetheart Plastics, Inc. (1981).
489. Coran, A.Y., and R. Patel, EP 36,279, Monsanto Co. (1981).
490. Subramanian, P.M., EP 15,556, E.I. du Pont de Nemours & Co (1980).
491. Fagerburg, D.R., US 4,180,518, Eastman Kodak Co. (1979).
492. Willis, J.M., V. Caldas, and B.D. Favis, J. Mat. Sci., 26 (17), 4742(1991).

493. Joshi, M., S.N. Maiti, and A. Misra, Polym. Sci. , Symp. Proc. Polym. '91, 2, McGraw-Hill, New Delhi, India, 951 (1991).
494. Ouhadi, T., R. Fayt, R. Jerome, and P. Teyssié, J. Appl. Polym. Sci., 32 (6), 5647 (1986).
495. Subramanian, P.M., Intern. Polym. Proc. III, 1, 33 (1988).
496. Todd, D., W.R. Keeler, and R.C. Balfour, US 3,202,647, Shell Oil Co. (1965).
497. Epstein, B.N., US 4,174,358, E.I. du Pont de Nemours & Co. (1979).
498. Bartlett, D.W., D.R. Paul, and J.W. Barlow, Mod. Plast., 58 (12), 60 (1981).
499. Mizuno, H., Y. Tsubokura, and Y. Suetsugu, JP 3,220,255, Idemitsu Petrochem. Co., Ltd. (1991).
500. Moriyama, T., H. Honda, and H. Takida, EP 444,977, Atochem (1991).
501. Moriya, T., and K. Igari, JP 3,149,238, Kuraray Co., Ltd. (1991).
502. Fujita, Y., and S. Toki, JP 3,081,333, Tonen Co., Ltd. (1991).
503. Moriya, T., and K. Igari, JP 3,149,239, Kuraray Co, Ltd. (1991).
504. Asano, K., T. Uemura, and H. Takida, EP 440,560, Atochem (1991).
505. Tsuda, T., and T. Azuma, JP 3,119,045, Toa Gosei Chem. Ind. Co., Ltd. (1991).
506. Fujita, Y., and S. Toki, JP 3,081,334, Tonen Co., Ltd. (1991).
507. Nishimoto, H., and H. Senda, JP 3,091,547, Sanyo Chem. Ind., Ltd. (1991).
508. Takita, H., H. Kato, and Y. Akamatsu, JP 3,033,137, Nippon Chem. Ind (1991).
509. Umeniwa, N., and Y. Suzuki, JP 3,024,138, Asahi Chem. Ind. Co., Ltd. (1991).
510. Moulies, J.C., P. Borg, and P. Nogues, EP 418,129, Atochem S.A. (1991).
511. Oyanagi, Y., and S. Onishi, JP 2,179,713, Mitsubishi Petro. Co., Ltd. (1990).
512. Higami, K., and N. Ochiai, JP 1,313,665, Asahi Chem. Ind., Ltd. (1989).
513. Mori, M., H. Okamoto, JP 2,145,678, Sunstar Eng. Inc. (1990).
514. Ono, A., M. Inoue, and M. Takagi, JP 2,276,841, Oji-Yuka Synth. Paper Co., Ltd. (1990).
515. Ezaki, Y., and H. Aibe, DE 4,020,603, Arakawa Chem. Ind., Ltd. (1991).
516. Imai, T., and M. Motai, JP 02,2245,009, Japan Synthetic Rubber Co., Ltd. (1990).
517. Simoens, A., FR 2,641,540, Solvay et Cie. (1990).
518. Konishi, S., Y. Shibata, and Y. Takai, JP 02,199,129, Sanyo Chem. Ind., Ltd. (1990).
519. Kucera, M., D. Kimmer, and E. Poloucek, CS 263,262, (1989).
520. Tsuda, T., and T. Azuma, JP 02,020,527, Toa Gosei Chem. Ind., Ltd. (1990).
521. Parsy, R., and N. Rivas, EP 331,554, Atochem S.A. (1989).
522. Glotin, M., R. Parsy, and P. Abadie, DE 3,909,273, Atochem S.A. (1989).
523. Kitagawa, S., and S. Masaki, JP 63,128,021, Mitsubishi Petro. Co., Ltd. (1988).
524. Akazawa, T., and T. Okaya, JP 62,177,047, Kuraray Co., Ltd. (1987).
525. Koehler, K.H., K. Reinking, G. Weber, and R. Prinz, DE 3,610,596, Bayer A.G. (1987).
526. Sakuma, M., Y. Fujita, Y. Kitano, M. Sakaizawa, Y. Yagi, N. Yamamoto, and T. Yokokura, JP 62,158,739, Tonen Sekiyu Kagaku, Inc. (1987).
527. Karger-Kocsis, J., B. Kozma, M. Schober, G. Marton, B. Shulman, G. Murlasits, J. Balazs, and T. Karnitscher, HU 41,427, Taurus Gumiipari Vallalat (1987).
528. Anonymous, JP 61,221,243, Dow Chem. Co. (1986).
529. Anonymous, JP 60,072,943, Dainichi Nippon Cables, Ltd. (1985).
530. Nauman, E.B., and J.C. Lynch, WO 91/03515, Dept. of Chem. Eng. and Environ. Eng., Rensselaer Polytechnic Inst. (1991).
531. Nauman, E.B., US 4,594,371, Dept. of Chem. Eng. and Environ. Eng., Rensselaer Polytechnic Inst. (1986).
532. Gabriele, M.C., Plast. Technol., 38 (6), 58 (1992).
533. Nauman, E.B., S.T. Wang, and N.P. Balsara, Polymer, 27, 1637 (1986).
534. Nauman, E.B., US 4,666,961, Dept. of Chem. Eng. and Environ. Eng., Rensselaer Polytechnic Inst. (1987).
535. Lambla, M., R.X. Yu, and S. Lorek, ACS-Symp. Ser., 395, ACS, 67 (1989).
536. Schut, J.H., Plast. Techol., 38 (8), 50(1992).
537. Sasamoto, T., P. Desai, and A.S. Abhiraman, ACS PMSE Prepr., 67, , 393 (1992).
538. Amin, M.B., S.H. Hamid, A.G. Maadhah, and A.M. Al-Jarallah, ACS PMSE Prepr., 67, 397 (1992).
539. Boudreau, K.A., and R.A. Malloy, ACS PMSE Prepr., 67, 401 (1992).

540. Nir, M.M., A. Ram, and J. Milz, ACS PMSE Prepr., 67, 405 (1992).
541. Vasanthakumar, N., K.S. Ranga, and G.S. Brat, ACS PMSE Prepr., 67, 407 (1992).
542. Bokar, P., and F. Lai, ACS PMSE Prepr., 67, 409 (1992).
543. Butler, S., L. Chao, and C.L. Beatty, ACS PMSE Prepr., 67, 411 (1992).
544. Li, Q., and M.A. Buese, ACS PMSE Prepr., 67, 457 (1992).
545. Tesoro, G., and Y. Wu, ACS PMSE Prepr., 67, 459 (1992).
546. Rowell, R.M., ACS PMSE Prepr., 67, 461 (1992).
547. Meister, J.J., and M.J. Chen, ACS PMSE Prepr., 67, 463 (1992).
548. Katz, H.S., and R. Agarwal, ACS PMSE Prepr., 67, 464 (1992).
549. Koch, P.E., and L. Dzeskiewicz, ACS PMSE Prepr., 67, 466 (1992).
550. Chung, T.C., ACS PMSE Prepr., 67, 98 (1992).
551. DeNicola, A.J., A.F. Galambos, and M.D. Wolkowicz, ACS PMSE Prepr., 67, 106 (1992).
552. Rhubright, D., and T.C. Chung, ACS PMSE Prepr., 67, 112 (1992).
553. Sipinene, A.J., and D.R. Rutherford, ACS PMSE Prepr., 67, 185 (1992).
554. Heidary, S., and B. Gordon III, ACS PMSE Prepr., 67, 190 (1992).
555. Liu, N.C., and W.E. Baker, ACS PMSE Prepr., 67, 305 (1992).
556. Majumdar, B., H. Keskkula and D.R. Paul, ACS PMSE Prepr., 67, 307 (1992).
557. Teh, J.W., and A. Rudin, ACS PMSE Prepr., 67, 309 (1992).
558. Yu, D.W., M. Xanthos, and C.G. Gogos, ACS PMSE Prepr., 67, 313 (1992).
559. Akkapeddi, M.K., and B. VanBuskirk, ACS PMSE Prepr., 67, 317 (1992).
560. Kaskel, R., 38th ANTEC Tech. Pap., , Soc. Plast. Eng., 2369 (1992).
561. Williams, D., and M. Bevis, J. Mat. Sci., 16 (12), 3335 (1981).
562. Williams, D., and M. Bevis, J. Mat. Sci., 17 (7), 1915 (1983).
563. Shelly, S., K. Fouhy, and S. Moore, Chem. Eng., July, 30 (1992).
564. Menges, G., and V. Lackner, Kunstst. Ger. Plast., 82 (2), 11 (1992).
565. Good, E.H., Proceedings, Assoc. Rot. Molding, Chicago, IL, (1992).
566. Pearson, W.E., person. comm. with M. Xanthos, January, (1992).
567. Bonsignore, P.V., B.J. Jody, and E. Daniels, Int. Cong. Expo., Tech. Paper, S.A.E., Detroit, Michigan, 59 (1991).
568. Jody, B.J., and E.J. Daniels, Hazard. Waste & Hazard. Mat., 8 (13), 219 (1991).
569. Jones, F.L., person. comm. with D. Todd, March, (1992).
570. Plochocki, A., V. Notorgiacomo, S. Dagli, and J. Biesenberger, 34th ANTEC Tech. Pap., Soc. Plast. Eng., 1250 (1988).
571. Borggreve, R.J.M., R.J. Gaymans, and J. Schuijer, Polymer, 30, 71 (1989).
572. Han, C.D., and H.K. Chuang, J. Appl. Polym. Sci., 30, 2431 (1985).
573. Chuang, H., and C. Han, J. Appl. Polym. Sci., 30, 2457 (1985).
574. Hobbs, S.Y., R.C. Bopp, and V.H. Watkins, Polym. Eng. Sci., 23, 380 (1983).
575. Kim, B.K., S.Y. Park, and S.J. Park, Eur. Polym. J., 27, 349 (1991).
576. Chen, C.C., E. Fontan, K. Min, and J.L. White, Polym. Eng. Sci., 28, 69 (1988).
577. Subramanian, P.M., and V. Mehra, Polym. Eng. Sci., 27, 1987 (663).
578. Serpe, G., J. Jarrin, and F. Dawans, Polym. Eng. Sci., 30, 553 (1990).
579. Curto, D., A. Valenza, and F.P. Lamantia, J. Appl. Polym. Sci., 39, 865 (1990).
580. Raval, H., S. Devi, Y.P. Singh, and M.H. Mehta, Polymer, 32, 493 (1991).
581. Chen, C.C., and J.L. White, 37th ANTEC Tech. Pap., Soc. Plast. Eng., 969 (1991).
582. Fairley, G., and R.E. Prud'homme, Polym. Eng. Sci., 27, 1495 (1987).
583. Favis, B.D., and J.M. Willis, J. Polym. Sci., Part B: Polym. Phys., 28, 2259 (1990).
584. Akkapeddi, M.K., and B. VanBushirk, ACS Polym. Prepr., 32 (2), 602 (1992).
585. Liu, N.C., W.E. Baker, and K.E. Russell, J. Appl. Polym. Sci., 41, 2285 (1990).
586. Datta, S, and D.J. Lohse, ACS PMSE Prepr., 64, 121 (1991).
587. Dagli, S.S., M. Xanthos, and J.A. Biesenberger, 36th ANTEC Tech. Pap., Soc. Plast. Eng., 1924 (1990).
588. Liu, Q., J.M. Bronk, A. Verma, and J.S. Riffle, ACS PMSE Prepr., 64, 158 (1991).
589. Ide, F., and A. Hasegawa, J. Appl. Polym. Sci., 18, 963 (1974).
590. Borggreve, R.J.M., R.J. Gaymans, Polymer, 29 (8), 1441 (1988).
591. Lavengood, R.E., A.F. Harris, and A.R. Padwa, EP 202,214, Monsanto, Co. (1986).

592. Pillon, L.Z., and L.A. Utracki, Polym. Eng. Sci., 24, 1300 (1984).
593. Higgins, J.S., D.J. Walsh, Polym. Eng. Sci., 24 (8), 555 (1988).
594. Gattiglia, E., A. Turturro, and E. Pedemonte, J. Appl. Polym. Sci., 38, 1807 (1989).
595. Chang, F.C., and Y.C. Hwu, ACS PMSE Prepr., 64, 155 (1991).
596. Oshinski, A.J., H. Keskkula, and D.R. Paul, ACS PMSE Prepr., 64, 153 (1991).
597. Walsh, D.J., and G.L. Cheng, Polymer, 25 (4), 499 (1984).
598. Gelles, R., M. Modic, and J. Kirkpatrick, 34th ANTEC Tech. Pap., Soc. Plast. Eng., 513 (1988).
599. Carrot, C., J. Guillet, and J.F. May, Plast. Rubb. Process, 16, 61 (1991).
600. Triacca, V.J., S. Ziaee, J.W. Barlow, H. Keskkula, and D.R. Paul, Polymer, 32, 1401 (1991).
601. Stevenson, G.M., US 3,501,420, Eastman Kodak Co. (1970).
602. Costin, R., and C. Billet, Proc. 2nd Int. Conf. Comp. React. Polym. Alloying, Compalloy '90, New Orleans, LA, 293 (1990).
603. Sakai, T., DAVOS Recycle '90, Maack Business Services, 109 (1990).
604. Deanin, R.D., S.A. Orroth, and R.I. Bhagat, Polym. Plast. Tech. Eng., 29, 289 (1990).
605. MacKnight, W.J., R.W. Lenz, P.V. Musto, and R.J. Somani, Polym. Eng. Sci., 25, 1124 (1985).
606. Borggreve, R.J.M., R.J. Gaymans, Proc. Int'l. Meet. Polym. Sci. Technol., Eds., P. Lemstra, L.A. Kleintjens, Elsevier, London, 248 (1988).
607. Borggreve, R.J.M., R.J. Gaymans, and A.R. Luttmer, Makromol. Chem., Macromol. Symp., 16, 195 (1988).
608. Borggreve, R.J.M., R.J. Gaymans, J. Schuijer, and J.F.I. Housz, Polymer, 28, 1489 (1987).
609. Chuang, H.K., and C.D. Han, J. Appl. Polym. Sci., 30, 165 (1985).
610. MacDowell, J.T., US 3,222,299, E.I. du Pont de Nemours & Co. (1965).
611. Greco, R., M. Malinconico, E. Martuscelli, G. Ragosta, and G. Scarinzi, Polymer, 28, 1185 (1987).
612. Cimmino, S., L. D'Orazio, R., Greco, G. Maglio, M. Malinconico, C. Mancarella, E. Martuscelli, R. Palumbo, and G. Ragosta, Polym. Eng. Sci., 24, 48 (1984).
613. Weaver, E.P., EP 86,069, Uniroyal, Inc. (1983).
614. Akkapeddi, M.K., J.C. Haylock, and J.A. Gervasi, US 4,847,322, Allied-Signal Inc. (1989).
615. Martuscelli, E., F. Riva, C. Sellitti, and C. Silvestre, Polymer, 26, 270 (1985).
616. Mizuno, S., and T. Sugie, US 4,165,307, Dai Nippon Ink & Chem. Inc. (1979).
617. Lai, Y.C., ACS PMSE Prepr., 64, 161 (1991) .
618. Angola, J.,C., Y. Fujita, T. Sakai, and T. Inoue, J. Polym. Sci., Polym. Phys., 26, 807 (1988).
619. Xanthos, M., A. Patel, S. Day, S.S. Dagli, C. Jacob, T.J. Nosker, and R.W. Renfree, 38th ANTEC Tech. Pap., Soc. Plast. Eng., 596 (1992).
620. Wu, S., Polymer, 26, 1855 (1985).
621. Wu, S., Polym. Eng. Sci., 27, 335 (1987).
622. Kuphal, J.A., L.H. Sperling, and L.M. Robeson, J. Appl. Polym. Sci., 42, 1525 (1991).
623. Hert, M., J.C. Jannell, and P. Robert, Proc. 6th Annual Meeting, PPS, paper 01–10 (1990).
624. Hepp, L.R., EP 149,192, GE Co. (1985).
625. Devaux, J., P. Godard, and J.P. Mercier, Polym. Eng. Sci., 22, 229 (1982).
626. Devaux, J., P. Godard, J.P. Mercier, R. Touillaux, and J.M. Dereppe, J. Polym. Sci., Polym. Phys., 20, 1881 (1982).
627. Han, C.Y., and W.L. Gately, US 4,689,372, GE Co. (1987).
628. Subrananian, P.M., Polym. Eng. Sci., 27, 1574 (1987).
629. Subramanian, P.M., Polym. Eng. Sci., 25, 483 (1987).
630. Hourston, D.J., S. Lane, H.X. Zhang, J.P.C. Bootsma, and D.W. Koetsier, Polymer, 32, 1140 (1991).
631. Hanrahan, B.D., S.R. Angeli, and J. Runt, Polym. Bull., 15, 455 (1986).
632. Lazarus, S.D., I.C. Twilley, and O.E. Snider, US 3,317,519, Allied Chem. Corp. (1967).
633. Golovoy, A., M.F. Cheung, and H. Van Oene, Polym. Eng. Sci., 27, 1642 (1987).
634. Mondragón, I., and J. Nazábal, J. Appl. Polym. Sci., 32, 6191 (1986).
635. Mondragón, I., M. Gaztelumendi, and J. Nazábal, Polym. Eng. Sci., 28, 1126 (1988).
636. Remiro, P.M., and J. Nazábal, J. Appl. Polym. Sci., 42, 1639 (1991).
637. Gaylord, N.G., J. Macromol. Sci., Macromol. Chem., A26, 1211 (1989).

638. Xanthos, M., Polym. Eng. Sci., 28, 1392 (1988).
639. Galli, E., Plast. Compound., 9 (5), 20 (1986).
640. Sakai, T., 34th ANTEC Tech. Pap., Soc. Plast. Eng., 1853 (1988).
641. Chen, B.S.Y., and D.E. Henton, US 4,886,856, Dow Chem. Co. (1989).
642. Simmons, A., and W.E. Baker, Polym. Eng. Sci., 29 (16), 1117 (1989).
643. Brown, S.B., and C.M. Orlando, Reactive Extrusion, in Encycl. Polym. Sci. Eng., Ed., J.I.. Kroschwitz, J. Wiley & Sons, 14, New York, 169 (1988).
644. Golba, J.C. Jr., and G.T. Seeger, Plast. Eng., 43 (3), 57 (1987).
645. Cambell, J., P.M. Conroy, and R.A. Florence, ACS Polym. Prepr., 27 (1), , 331 (1986).
646. Agarwal, P.K., I. Duvdevani, D.G. Peiffer, and R.D. Lundberg, J. Polym. Sci., Polym. Phys., 25, 839 (1987).
647. Joyce, R.P., and A.P. Berzinis, Proc. 4th Int. Cong. Compalloy '91, New Orleans, LA, January, 65 (1991).
648. Butta, E., G. Levita, A. Marchetti, and A. Lazzeri, Polym. Eng. Sci., 26, 63 (1986).
649. Sankaran, S., and M. Chanda, J. Appl. Polym. Sci., 39, 1459 (1990).
650. Sankaran, S., and M. Chanda, J. Appl. Polym. Sci., 39, 1635 (1990).
651. Pearson, R.A., and A.F. Yee, J. Mat. Sci., 21, 2475 (1986).
652. Chen, T.K., and Y.H. Jan, Polym. Eng. Sci., 31, 577 (1991).
653. Fowler, M.W., and W.E. Baker, Polym. Eng. Sci., 28, 1427 (1988).
654. Mongragón, I., P.M. Remiro, and J. Nazábal, Eur. Polym. J., 23, 125 (1987).
655. Abe, K., S. Yamauchi, and A. Ohkubo, DE 3,300,232, Mitsubishi Petrochem. Co., Ltd. (1983).
656. Beniska, J., M.M. Sain, and I. Hudec, ACS, Polym. Prepr., 28 (2), 379 (1987).
657. Siadat, B., R.D. Lundberg, and R.W. Lenz, Polym. Eng. Sci., 20 (8), 530 (1980).
658. Cheung, P., D. Suwanda, and S.T. Balke, The Reactive Extrusion of PE/PP Blends, NRCC, Polyblends '89 Conf., Boucherville, Quebec, November, (1989).
659. Chiu, N. Y, and S.J. Fang, J. Appl. Polym. Sci., 30, 1473 (1985).
660. Yu, D.W., C.G. Gogos, and M. Xanthos , 36th ANTEC Tech. Pap., Soc. Plast. Eng., 1917 (1990).
661. Shih, C.K., and J.M. Torradas, 33rd ANTEC Tech. Pap., Soc. Plast. Eng., 1006 (1987).
662. Coran, A.Y., A.K. Bhowmick, and H.L. Stephens (Eds), "Handbook of Elastomers", ch. 8, Marcel Dekker, New York, 299 (1988).
663. Yonekura, K., A. Uchiyama, and A. Matsuda, US 4,785,045, Mitsui Petrochem. Ind., Ltd. (1988).
664. Roberts, A.D., Ed., "Natural Rubber Science and Technology", ch. 9, Oxford Univ. Press, Oxford, 344 (1988).
665. Xanthos, M., F. Riahi, and N. Bouassida, 31st ANTEC Tech. Pap., Soc. Plast. Eng., 963 (1985).
666. Balint, L.J., and J. Greenburg, US 4,764,607, Allied-Signal, Inc. (1988).
667. Akkapeddi, M.K., B. VanBuskirk, and J. Gervasi, Proc. PPS Summer Meeting, PPS, Amherst, MA, August 16–17, paper 7E (1989).
668. Woodbrey, J.C., and M.V. Moncur, US 4,320,213, Monsanto Co. (1982).
669. Epstein, B.N., US 4,172,859, E.I. du Pont de Nemours & Co. (1979).
670. Owens, F.H., and J.J. Clovis, US 3,668,274, Rohm and Haas Co. (1972).
671. Hammer, C.F., and H.K. Sinclair, US 3,972,961, E.I. du Pont de Nemours & Co. (1976).
672. Watanabe, K., A. Izuka, K. Sumita, and M. Kita, Proc. 2nd Int. Cong. Compalloy '90, New Orleans, LA, March, 271 (1990).
673. Greve, B.N., US 4,983,549, Budd Co. (1991).
674. Rozek, T.S., Proc. 2nd. Int. Cong. Compalloy '90, New Orleans, LA, March, 239 (1990).
675. Ueno, K., and T. Maruyama, US 4,315,086, Sumitomo Chem. Co. (1982).
676. Nishio, T., T. Sanada, and S. Hosoda, JP 62,187,747, Sumitoto Chem. Co., Ltd. (1987).
677. Gallucci, M., R. Robert, and R.W. Avakian, EP 182,163, GE Co. (1986).
678. Tsunetani, M., and T. Tanaka, JP 62,232,455, Asahi Chem. Ind. Co., Ltd. (1987).
679. Sheer, S., and M. Lauma, US 4,317,764, E.I. du Pont de Nemours & Co. (1982).
680. Takahashi, K., and Y. Tajima, JP 61,174,253, Polyplastics Co., Ltd. (1986).

681. Nakamura, Y., K. Mori, and K. Wada, Kobushi Ronbunshu, 41, 539 (1984).
682. Monte, S., and G. Sugerman, Proc. 2nd Int. Cong. Compalloy '90, New Orleans, LA, 327 (March 1990).
683. Willis, J.M., B.D. Favis, and J. Lunt, Polym. Eng. Sci., 30, 1073 (1990).
684. Yoshida, M., J.J. Ma, K. Min, J.L. White, and R.P. Quirk, Polym. Eng. Sci., 30, 30 (1990).
685. Moffett, A.J., and M.E.J. Dekkers, Polym. Eng. Sci., 32, 1 (1992).
686. McKay, I.D., J. Appl. Polym Sci., 43, 1593 (1991).
687. Carlstrom, W.L., R.W. Reineck, and G.R. Svoboda, US 4,223,068, Freeman Chem. Corp. (1980).
688. Neujokas, A.A., and K. Ryan, US 5,051,528, Eastman Kodak Co. (1991).
689. Wu, S., J. Appl. Polym. Sci., 35, 549 (1988).
690. Cimmino, S., F. Coppola, L. D'Orazio, R. Greco, G. Maglio, M. Malinconico, C. Mancarella, E. Martuscelli, and G. Ragosta, Polymer, 27, 1874 (1989).
691. Christensen, R.E., R.G. Austin, and D.M. Clayton, 38th ANTEC Tech. Pap., Soc. Plast. Eng., 794 (1992).
692. Bevington, J.C., and R.G.W. Norrish, J. Chem. Soc., Article #155, 771 (1948).
693. Bevington, J.C., and R.G.W. Norrish, J. Chem. Soc., Article #108, 482 (1949).
694. Gruschke, K., T.W. Hammerschick and H. Medem, US 3,403,115, Hoechst (1968).
695. Tanner, D., US 2,999,056, E.I. du Pont de Nemours & Co. (1962).
696. Dorough, G.L., US 2,432,296, E.I. du Pont de Nemours & Co. (1947).
697. Hardy, V.R., US 2,304,637, E.I. du Pont de Nemours & Co. (1942).
698. Nat. Chem. Lab., Report of the National Chemical Laboratory, Teddington, England, 41 (1958).
699. Staff writer, Plast. Eng., 48 (12), 35 (1992).
700. Scobbo, J.J. Jr., 23 rd Intl. SAMPE Conf., Kiamesha Lake, NY, 995 (1991).
701. Gaylord, N.G., US 4,506,056, Gaylord Res. Inst. (1985).
702. Gaylord, N.G., and R. Mehta, J. Polym. Sci.: Part A: Polym. Chem., 26, 1189 (1988).
703. Xanthos, M. (Ed.), "Reactive Extrusion: Principles and Practice", Hanser, New York, 196 (1992).
704. Stokke, D.D., S.M. Shaler, and R.N. Hawke, SAMPE Quarterly, 23 (4), 58 (1992).
705. Mijangos, C., J.M. Gomez-Elvira, G. Martinez, and J. Michel, Macromol. Chem., Macromol. Symp., 25, 209 (1989).
706. Ostrowski, H.S., US 3,884,850, Fiber Industries, Inc. (1975).
707. Svoboda, G.R., J.T. Suh, W.L. Carlstrom, and G.L. Maechtle, US 4,048,104, Freeman Chem. Corp. (1977).
708. Stack, G.M., PPS Abstracts, PPS, Regional Meeting for the Americas, Knoxville, TN, Oct 19–21, 215 (1992).
709. Aharoni, S.M., and T. Largman, US 4,417,031, Allied-Signal, Inc. (1983).
710. Largman, T., and S.M. Aharoni, US 4,433,116, Allied-Signal, Inc. (1984).
711. Noel, O.F. III., Abstracts, PPS Regional Meeting for the Americas, Knoxville, TN, Oct 19–21, 222 (1992).
712. Hernandez, M.E., and C.W. Macosko, Abstracts, PPS Regional Meeting for the Americas, Knoxville, TN, Oct 19–21, 152 (1992).
713. Collins, R.J., US 2,955,954, E.I. du Pont de Nemours & Co. (1960).
714. Lunt, J., S.A.M. May, and P.A. Leivo, US 5,043,392, Polysar Ltd. (1991).
715. England, R.J., US 3,544,622, E.I. du Pont de Nemours & Co. (1970).
716. Cairns, J.L., H.D. Foster, A.W. Larser, A.K. Schneider, and R.S. Schreiger, J. Am. Chem. Soc., 71, 651 (1949).
717. Floyd, D.E., Polyamide Resins, 2nd Ed., Reinhold, New York, 41 (1966).
718. Malloy, R., personal comm. with S. Patel, December, (1992).
719. Khanna, Y.P., E.A. Turi, S.M. Aharoni, and T. Largman, US 4,417,032, Allied-Signal, Inc. (1983).
720. Priest, D.J., J. Polym. Sci., A-2 (9), 1771 (1977).
721. Fayt, R., R. Jerome, and Ph. Teyssié, Polym. Eng. Sci., 27 (5), 328 (1987).
722. Peterlin, A., and G. Meinel, J. Polym. Sci., B3, 1059 (1965).

723. Kircher, K., "Chemical Reactions in Plastics Processing", Hanser, New York, 174 (1987).

724. Allbee, N., Plast. Compound., 15 (4), 20 (1992).

725. Lenz, R.W., "Organic Chemistry of Synthetic High Polymers", Interscience, New York, 692 (1967).

726. Kennedy, J.P., J. Macromol. Sci., A12 (2), 327 (1978).

727. Kohan, M.I., "Nylon Plastics", Ed., M.I. Kohan, John Wiley & Sons, New York, 457 (1973).

728. Saleem, M., and W.E. Baker, J. Appl. Polym. Sci., 39, 655 (1990).

729. Barlow, J.W., and D.R. Paul, Polym. Eng. Sci., 24 (8), 525 (1984).

730. Bachman, G.B., H. Hellman, K.R. Robinson, R.W. Finholt, E.J. Kahlar, L.J. Filar, L.V. Heisey, L.L. Lewis, and D.D. Micucci, J. Org. Chem., 12, 108 (1947).

731. Zenftman, H., J. Chem. Soc., Article # 202, 982 (1950).

732. Xi, X., Z. Liwu, and L. Huilin, Polym. Eng. Sci., 27 (6), 398 (1987).

733. Hanford, W.E., US 2,396,786, E.I. du Pont de Nemours & Co. (1946).

734. Jones, G.D., "Styrene", Eds. R.H. Boundy and R.F. Boyer, Reinhold, New York, 674 (1954).

735. Xi, X., M. Xiande, and C. Keqiang, Polym. Eng. Sci., 27 (6), 391 (1987).

736. Morton, A.A., and L.D. Taylor, J. Org. Chem, 24, 1167 (1959).

737. Jayabalan, M., and T. Balakrishnan, Polym. Eng. Sci., 25 (9), 553 (1985).

738. Koberstein. J.T., and S. Anastasiadis, ACS PMSE Prepr., 55, 634 (1988).

739. Metz, D.J., and R.B. Mesrobian, J. Polym. Sci., 16, 345 (1955).

740. Chinai, S.N., J.D. Matlack, A.L. Resnick, and R.A. Guzzi, P.B. Report 161,047, U.S. Dept. of Commerce, Washington, (1959).

741. Bourland, L., 34th ANTEC Tech. Pap., Soc. Plast. Eng., 631 (1988).

742. Keyon, W.O., and G.P. Waugh, J. Polym. Sci., 32, 83 (1958).

743. Unruh, C.C., J. Appl. Polym. Sci., 2, 358 (1959).

744. Shiah, C.M., and I.M. Chen, 38th ANTEC Tech. Pap., Soc. Plast. Eng., 1398 (1989).

745. Eichhorn, J., L.C. Rubens, C.E. Fahlgren, and G.J. Pomranky, US 3,009,906, Dow Chem. Co. (1961).

746. Bourland, L., 34th ANTEC Tech. Pap., Soc. Plast. Eng., 638 (1988).

747. Markham, R.L., Proc. 4th Int. Cong. Compalloy '91, New Orleans, LA, January, 3 (1991).

748. Baxter, W.N., US 2,849,431, E.I. du Pont de Nemours & Co. (1958).

749. Herbst, H., K. Hoffman, R. Pfaendner and F. Sitek, Kunstst. Ger. Plast., 82 (9), 34 (1992).

750. La Mantia, F.P., Adv. Polym. Technol., 12 (1), 47 (1993).

751. Fleischer, D., K.F. Muck, and G. Reuschel, Kunstst. Ger. Plast., 82 (9), 21 (1992).

752. Hock, C.W., J. Polym. Sci., Polym. Letters, B3, 573 (1965).

753. Crescentini, L., W.B. Fisher, R.E. Mayer, J.D. DeCaprio, and R.K. Nilson, US 4,582,642, Allied-Signal, Inc. (1986).

754. Dyer, E., and G.C. Wright, J. Am. Chem. Soc., 81, 2138 (1959).

755. Staff writer, Plast. Technol., 35 (2), 67 (1989).

756. Dyer, E., and W. Bartels, Jr., J. Am. Chem. Soc., 76, 591 (1954).

757. Huang, J.C., D.C. Chang, and R.D. Dean, Adv. Polym. Technol., 12 (1), 81 (1993).

758. Lamparter, R.A., B.A. Barna, and D.R. Johnsrud, US 4,542,239, Board of Control of Michigan Technol. Univ. (1985).

759. Glans, J.H., M. Akkapeddi, and K. Murali, US 5,037,897, Allied-Signal, Inc. (1991).

760. Shay, J., RETEC Tech. Pap., Soc. Plast. Eng., Ft. Mitchell, KY, 179 (1991).

761. Jerome, B.A.R., and Ph. Teyssie, J. Polym. Sci., 24, 551–558 (1986).

762. Naitove, M.H., Plast. Technol., 38 (12), 23 (1992).

763. Simmons, A., and W.E. Baker, Polym. Comm., 31, 20 (1990).

764. Malik, A.I., and E.E. Mast, US 4,078,143, E.I. du Pont de Nemours & Co. (1978).

765. Paul, D.R., and S. Newman (Eds), "Polymer Blends", vol. 2, Academic Press, New York, 53 (1978).

766. Crescentini, L., W.B. Blackman Jr., J.D. DeCaprio, W.B. Fisher, R.J. Lilley Jr., and J.W. Wagner, US 4,311,642, Allied-Signal, Inc. (1982).

767. Hammer, C.F., Macromolecules, 4, 69 (1971).

768. Hickman, J.J., and R.M. Ikeda, J. Polym. Sci: Polym. Phys. Ed., 2, 1713 (1973).

769. Koleske, J.V., and R.D. Lundberg, J. Polym. Sci., Part A-2 7, 795 (1969).

770. Lundberg, R.D., F.P. Del Giudice, and R.G. Kelso, US 3,629,374, Union Carbide Corp. (1971).
771. Allen, G., M.J. Bowden, D.J. Blundell, F.G. Hutchinson, G.M. Jeffs, and J. Vyvoda, Polymer, 14, 597 (1973).
772. Matsuo, M., T.K. Kwei, D. Klempner, and H.L. Frisch, Polym. Eng. Sci., 10, 327 (1970).
773. Yenwo, G.W., L.H. Sperling, J. Pulido, J.A. Manson, and A. Conde, Polym. Eng. Sci., 17 (4), 251 (1977).
774. Kim, S.C., D. Klempner, K.C. Frisch, and H.L. Frisch, Macromolecules, 9, 263 (1976).
775. Klempner, D., H.L. Frisch, and K.C. Frisch, J. Polym. Sci., Part A-2 (8), 921 (1970).
776. Bonfield, J.H., R.C. Hecker, and O.E. Snider, US 3,182,055, Allied Chem. Corp. (1965).
777. Grigat, E., and H. Hetzel, US 4,051,212, Bayer (1977).
778. McNeil, I.C., N. Grassie, J.N.R. Samson, A. Jamieson, and T. Straiton, J. Macromol. Sci. Chem., A12, 503 (1978).
779. Guyot, A., M. Bert, A. Michel, and R. Spitz, J. Polym. Sci., A1 (8), 1596 (1970).
780. Raj, R.G., and B.V. Kokta, 37th ANTEC Tech. Pap., Soc. Plast. Eng., 1883 (1991).
781. Janicki, S.L., M.F. Bain Jr., and R.J. Groleau, 38th ANTEC Tech. Pap., Soc. Plast. Eng., 1201 (1992).
782. Hon, D.N.S., W.Y. Cao, and C.J. Buhion, Plast. Eng., 48 (10), 25 (1992).
783. Naitove, M.H., Plast. Technol., 36 (8), 15 (1990).
784. Staff writer, Automot. Eng., (10), 41 (1992).
785. Svoboda, G.R., US 4,417,001, Freeman Chem. Corp. (1983).
786. Utracki, L.A., "Polymer Alloys and Blends", Hanser, New York, 248 (1990).
787. Johnson, R.M., E.M. Melling, US 4,377,415, Nat. Gypsum Co. (1983).
788. Ehrig, R.J. (Ed), "Plastics Recycling: Products and Processes", Hanser, New York, (1989).
789. Hamid, S.H., M.B. Amin, and A.G. Maadhah (Eds), "Handbook of Polymer Degradation", Marcel Dekker, Inc., New York, (1992).
790. Schnabel, W., "Polymer Degradation", Hanser, New York, (1981).
791. Staff writer, Plastic News, October 12, 42 (1992).
792. Staff writer, Plastics News, October 12, 46 (1992).
793. Staff writer, Plastics News, October 12, 46 (1992).
794. Monks, R., Plast. Technol., 38 (11), 27 (1992).
795. Mikofalvy, B.K., H.K. Boo, J.W. Summers, D.H. Mittendorf, and W.A. Sell, 38th ANTEC Tech. Pap., Soc. Plast. Eng., 265 (1992).
796. Rowand, R., Plastics News, April 13, 31 (1992).
797. Technol. Info. Center, "Management of Polymer and Fiber Solid Waste. Part II: Recycling", Textile Research Institute, Princeton, NJ, (1991).
798. Kronman, M., Underwater USA, October, (1992).
799. Bennett, R.A., Technical Report #53, CPRR/ Rutgers U., Piscataway, NJ, (1991).
800. Morrow, D.R., and T.J. Nosker, Technical Report #57, CPRR/ Rutgers Univ., Piscataway, NJ, (1991).
801. Plast. Inst. of America, Inc., "Secondary Reclamation of Plastics Waste" Research Report-Phase I, Technomic Publishing Co., Lancaster, PA, (1987).
802. Plast. Inst. of America, Inc., "Secondary Reclamation of Plastics Waste" Research Report-Phase II, Technomic Publishing Co., Lancaster, PA, (1987).
803. Hafner, E.A., AU 503,398, Hafner Ind., Inc. (1976).
804. Fischer, D., Z. Funke, and L. Starke, Plaste Kautsch., 39 (8), 273 (1992).
805. Jentzsch, J., H. Michael, E. Herscher, and D. Kaune, DE 4,102,237, Tech. Univ. Chemnitz (1992).
806. Jody, B.J., E.J. Daniels, and P.V. Bonsignore, "Treatment and Recycling of Shredder Fluff: Final Report on Phase I, Proof of Concept", A.N.L., Argonne IL, (1992).
807. Neumann, W., H. Holtschmidt, J. Peter, and P. Fischer, US 3,193,522, Farbenfabriken Bayer Aktiengesellschaft (1965).
808. Dagli, S.S., P.G. Kelleher, M. Monroy, A. Patel, and M. Xanthos, Adv. Polym. Technol., 10 (2), 125 (1990).

809. Andrews, G.D., and P.M. Subramanian (Eds), "Emerging Technologies in Plastics Recycling", ACS, Washington, DC, (1992).
810. Naitove, M.H., and M.C. Gabriele, Plast. Technol., 38 (11), 77 (1992).
811. Bledzki, A.K., K. Kurek, and C.H. Barth, 38th ANTEC Tech. Pap., Soc. Plast. Eng., 1558 (1992).
812. Patel, S.H., K.E. Gonsalves, S.S. Stivala, L. Reich, and D.H. Trivedi, Adv. Polym. Techol., 12/1, 35 (1993).
813. Meluch, W.C., US 3,978,128, GM Corp. (1976).
814. Frulla, F.F., A. Ordinak, and A.A.R. Saying, US 3,738,946, The Upjohn Co. (1973).
815. Tucker, B., and H. Ulrich, US 3,983,087, The Upjohn Co. (1976).
816. Faudree, T.L. III, US 4,230,566, Petrozorbent Corp. (1980).
817. Shütz, W., US 4,339,358, (1982).
818. Carroll, W., and T.R. McClellan, US 4,382,108, The Upjohn Co. (1983).
819. Oh, S., G. Ivanov, and F. Shutov, Extend. Abstrs., AIChE, Miami Beach, FL, November, 186c (1992).
820. Shutov, F., G. Ivanov, and H. Arastoopour, ACS PMSE Prepr., 67, 404 (1992).
821. Staff writer, Plast. Technol., 39 (2), 14 (1993).
822. Farrissey, W.J., R.E. Morgan, and J.D. Weaver, ACS Polym. Prepr., 32 (2), 157 (1991).
823. Berengi, E., and R. Gould, "1992–1993 Materials Recovery and Recycling Yearbook Directory & Guide", Governm. Adv. Assoc., New York, NY, (1992).
824. Resource Management Associates, "A Survey of Mixed Plastics Recycling Programs for the Dept. of Sanitation of New York City", Napa, CA, July, (1990).
825. Rankin, S., "Plastics Collection and Sorting", Chap. C, D, E, G, CPRR/ Rutgers U., Piscataway, NJ, Fall, (1990).
826. Pearson, W.E., and S. Rankin, "Plastics Recycling: An Overview", CPRR/ Rutgers U., Piscataway, NJ, Spring, (1989).
827. Merriam, C.N., and M.S. Belanger, "Economic Modeling of New Jersey Recycling Infrastructure", CPRR/ Rutgers U., Piscataway, NJ, (1992).
828. Yeh, M.S., and H. Franklin, "Automatic Sortation of Post Consumer Plastic Rigid Containers", Tech. Report # 62, CPRR/ Rutgers U., Piscataway, NJ, (1991).
829. Hanesian, D., E. Phillips, and J. Wenzel, "Final Report to the N.J. Commission on Science & Technol." for 1990–1991, CPRR/ Rutgers U., Piscataway, NJ, (1991).
830. Anonymous, DAVOS Recycle '92, Maack Business Services, 14/1–8 (1992).
831. Dinger, P., Biocycle, March, 80 (1992).
832. Mapleston, P., Mod. Plast., 69 (13), 34 (1992).
833. Franklin Assoc., Ltd., "Characterization of Plastic Products in Municipal Solid Waste", Prairie Village, KS, February, (1990).
834. Enikolopian, N.S., Proc., Int. Recycling Congress at the Re' 93 Trade Fair, vol. I, Hexagon, Ltd, Geneva, Switzerland, 321 (1993).
835. Shevchenko, V.G., A. Yu. Karmilov, and A.T. Ponomarenko, Proc. Int'l. Recycl. Congr., Re' 93 Trade Fair, v. III, Hexagon Ltd, Geneva, Switzerland, 427 (1993).
836. Krivit, D., 13th Meeting, Seminar VI Proc., CPRR/ Rutgers U., Sept. 24–25, (1991).
837. Center for Plastics Recycling Research, Model Cities Project, Technical Report # 55, CPRR/ Putgers U., Piscataway, NJ, (1992).
838. Center for Plastics Recycling Research, Development and Verification of Pride 1, Technical Report # 43, CPRR/ Rutgers U., Piscataway, NJ, (1989).
839. Benham, J.L., and J.F. Kinstle (Eds), "Chemical Reactions on Polymers", ACS Symp. Series 364, ACS, Washington, DC, (1988).
840. Costanza, R., Science, 210, 1219 (1980).
841. Midwest Research Inst., "Plastics, Resourse and Environmental Profile Analysis Report", Manufacturing Chemists Association, (1974).
842. Fink, P., Das Papier, 35, 86 (1981).
843. Moller, F.J., and W.C. Bauer, Proc. 6th IAPRI Congress, Hamburg, Germany, September, 145 (1989).

844. Gaines, L.L., and S.Y. Shen, "Energy and Material Flows in the Production of Olefins and their derivatives", ANL, Prepared for U.S. DOE, (1980).

845. H.M. Mittlehauser Corp., "Energy/Material Flows Associated with Cyclic Petrochemicals", ANL CNSV-TM-56, sponsored by U.S. DOE, (1979).

846. Klobbie, E., US 4,187,352, (1974).

847. Leidner, J., "Plastic Waste: Recovery of Economic Value", Marcel Dekker, New York, (1981).

848. Staff writer, Polym. Age, 4, 12 (1974).

849. Staff writer, Recource Recycl., 6(3), 16 (1987).

850. Renfree, R.W., T.J. Nosker, S. Rankin, T.M. Kasternakis, and E.M. Phillips, 35th ANTEC Tech. Pap., 1809 (1989).

851. Nosker, T.J., R.W. Renfree, and D.R. Morrow, Plast. Eng., 26 (2), 33 (1990).

852. Morrow, D.R., T.J. Nosker, K.E. Van Ness, and R.W. Renfree, 2nd Annual Plast. Recycl. Fair, Soc. Plast. Eng., Burbank, CA, April 26, (1990).

853. Ramer, R.A., S.G. Byun, and C.L. Beatty, RETEC Tech. Pap., Soc. Plast. Eng., Charlotte, NC, October 20–31, (1989).

854. Inculet, I., G.S. Castel, and J.D. Brown, DAVOS Recycle '92, Maack Business Services, 10/1–1 (1992).

855. Yarar, B., Proc., 13th Meeting, Seminar VI, CPRR/ Rutgers U., Sept. 24–25, (1991).

856. Beckman, E.J., and R.M. Enick, Proc., 13th Meeting, Seminar VI, CPRR/Rutgers U., Sept. 24–25, (1991).

857. Gregory, W.D., Proc., 14th Meeting, Seminar VII, CPRR/Rutgers U., Oct. 21–22, (1992).

858. Maczko, J., Proc., 14th Meeting, Seminar VII, CPRR/Rutgers U., Oct. 21–22, (1992).

859. Nauman, E.B., M.V. Ariyapadi, N.P. Balsara, T.A. Grocela, J.S. Furno, S.H. Liu, and R. Mallikarjun, Chem. Eng. Comm., 66, 29 (1988).

860. Staff writer, Plast. Eng., 49 (5), 8 (1993).

861. Dittman, F.W., S.I. Albin, B.R. Hannigan Jr., and J.R. Fernandes, Technical report # 32, CPRR/ Rutgers U., Sept. 24–25, (1988).

862. Gunwan, L. and J.K. Haken, J. Polymer Sci., Polym. Chem. Ed., 23, 2539 (1985).

863. Montano, G., C. Puglisi, D. Vitalini and Y. Morishima, J. Anal. Appl. Pyrol., 13, 161 (1988).

864. Radhakrishnan, T.S. and M. Rao, J. Anal. Appl. Pyrol., 9, 309 (1986).

865. Chien, J.C.W. and J.K.Y. Kiang, Makromol. Chem., 181, 45 (1980).

866. Chien, J.C.W. and J.K.Y. Kiang, Macromolecules, 13, 280 (1980).

867. Mul, G.J., R.J. Gritter and G.E. Adams, Appl. Polymer Spectrosc., 257 (1987).

868. Milina, R., J. Anal. Appl. Pyrol., 3, 179 (1981).

869. Walker, J.Q., J. Chromatogr. Sci., 15, 267 (1977).

870. Sapre, A.V. and Krambeck, F.J. Ed., "Chemical Reactions in Complex Mixtures", Van Nostrand Reinhold, New York, (1990) .

871. Wei-chuan Lai and B. Krieger-Brockett, ACS Div. Fuel Chem. Prepr., 683 (1991).

872. Serio, M.A. Charpenay, S., Bassilakis, and Solomon, R., ACS Polymer Prepr., 644–675 (1991).

873. Stivala, S.S., J. Kimura, and S.M. Gabay, "Degradation and Stabilization of Polyolefins", Applied Sci. Publishers, 63 (1983).

874. Liebman, S.A., and E.J. Levy, "Pyrolysis and Gas Chromatography in Polymer Analysis", Marcel Dekker, New York (1985).

875. K. Matsumoto, S. Kurizu, and T. Oymato, "Conversion of Refuse to Energy", Montreux, November 3–5, (1975).

876. Kroff, J., and K.H. Keim, Kraftstoff, A6, 223–226 (1989).

877. Data Summary of Muncipal Solid Waste Management Alternatives, Vol. 6: Appendix D, SRI International, (1992).

878. Technical News, NREL Sci. & Technol. in Rev., February, 10 (1992).

879. Anthony, R.G. and Dosch, R.G., Chem. Eng. Progress, January, 14 (1993).

880. G. Scott, Recovery Conserv., 1, 381 (1976).

881. K.J. Thome-Kozmiensky, Recycling International, Pyrolysis of Waste, EF-Press. Berlin, (1985).

882. Hickman, Jr., H.L., W.D. Turner et. al., "Thermal Conversion Systems for Municipal Solid Waste", Noyes Data Corp., Park Ridge, NJ, (1984).
883. Wilson, E. et al., "Engineering and Economic Analysis of Waste to Energy System", Section 9, US-EPA Report 600/7–78–086, (1978).
884. Dyirka, M. and W.M. Harrington, ASME National Waste Processing Conference, Washington, D.C., May, (1980).
885. Stanffer, R.F., Resource Recyling, Jan/Feb., 24–25 & 50–56 (1989).
886. Morris, J. and Conzoneri, D., Resource Recycling, November, 25–31 (1992).
887. Rudd, D.F. et al., "Petrochemical Technology Assessment", John Wiley , New York, 233–234 (1981).
888. Thomas F. Corbin, Edward A. Davis, and Jack A. Dellinger, US 5,169,870, BASF Corporation (1992).
889. A. Golovoy and M. Zinbo, Polym. Eng. Sci., 29 (24), 1733–1737 (1989).

Index